KF
390.5
.D6
R36
1988

NOLO PRESS SELF-HELP LAW

P9-DYJ-476

DOG

LAW

BY MARY RANDOLPH

022613

Shoals Community College
Learning Resource Center

IMPORTANT

Nolo Press is committed to keeping its books up-to-date. Each new printing, whether or not it is called a new edition, has been revised to reflect the latest law changes. This book was printed and updated on the last date indicated below. Before you rely on information in it, you might wish to call Nolo Press (415) 549-1976 to check whether a later printing or edition has been issued.

PRINTING HISTORY

New "**Printing**" means there have been some minor changes, but usually not enough so that people will need to trade in or discard an earlier printing of the same edition. Obviously, this is a judgment call and any change, no matter how minor, might affect you.

New "**Edition**" means one or more major, or a number of minor, law changes since the previous edition.

FIRST EDITION	October 1988
SECOND PRINTING	June 1989
EDITORS	Ralph Warner
	Barbara Kate Repa
TECHNICAL CONSULTANT	Flash
ILLUSTRATIONS	Linda Allison
PRODUCTION	Stephanie Harolde
BOOK DESIGN	Jackie Clark
	Toni Ihara
PRINTING	Delta Lithograph

Library of Congress Catalog Card Number: 88-063101
ISBN 87337-078-3
Copyright © 1988 & 1989 by Mary Randolph
All Rights Reserved

ACKNOWLEDGMENTS

I owe the idea for this book to Steve Elias, who also made many good suggestions on the manuscript.

Editors Jake Warner and Barbara Kate Repa kept me, and the book, going. Without their sharp minds and sharp wits, this book wouldn't be half as good and writing it wouldn't have been half as fun.

I'm very grateful to the people who reviewed the manuscript or provided expertise: my friend Loren Gerstein, a mediator with Community Boards of San Francisco; Terri McGinnis, practicing veterinarian and author of *The Well Dog Book* and *The Well Cat Book*; Mike Mansel of Insurance Associates; Phyllis Wright, Vice President of the Humane Society of the United States; and two of Nolo's dog-lovers, Robin Leonard and Lulu Cornell.

Jackie Clark came up with the wonderful cover and design of this book. Toni Ihara and illustrator Linda Allison also helped make the book look so good.

Finally, my thanks to all the people of Nolo Press, who've kept me supplied with dog cartoons, anecdotes, news stories, and title suggestions (how about "In Pro Pup" or "Dog Do's and Don'ts"?).

RECYCLE YOUR OUT-OF-DATE BOOKS & GET 25% OFF YOUR NEXT PURCHASE!

Using an old edition can be dangerous if information in it is wrong. Unfortunately, laws and legal procedures change often. To help you keep up to date we extend this offer. If you cut out and deliver to us the title portion of the cover of any old Nolo book we'll give you a 25% discount off the retail price of any new Nolo book. For example, if you have a copy of TENANT'S RIGHTS, 4th edition and want to trade it for the latest CALIFORNIA MARRIAGE AND DIVORCE LAW, send us the TENANT'S RIGHTS cover and a check for the current price of MARRIAGE & DIVORCE, less a 25% discount. Information on current prices and editions is listed in the NOLO NEWS. Generally speaking, any book more than two years old is of questionable value. Books more than four or five years old are a menace. This offer is to individuals only.

OUT OF DATE = DANGEROUS

dog 6/89

CONTENTS

INTRODUCTION

This book is for people who own dogs, live next door to dogs, get bitten by dogs or otherwise deal with dogs—which, with the American dog population at an estimated 52 million, includes just about everybody.

Back when most Americans lived on farms or small towns, few legal rules affected dogs and their owners. After all, unless dogs harmed livestock—an offense for which there were universally harsh penalties—most were unlikely to run afoul of the law.

Not so in modern society. Increasing urbanization—97% of Americans now live in cities, towns or villages, according to one estimate—has meant stepped-up animal regulation. In both crowded cities and sprawling suburbia, there is too much traffic and too little open space to allow dogs to run loose. And to protect ourselves from dogs whose owners we no longer know, vaccinations, licenses, and sometimes even liability insurance are required.

Legal questions come up constantly. How many dogs can my neighbor keep? What can I do if the dog down the street barks all night? What can I do if I buy a dog and find out it's not healthy? Am I legally liable if my dog bites a child who's teasing it? Can my landlord, who told me I could have a dog, evict me for violating the no pets clause in the form lease I signed?

The answers to these questions and hundreds like them must be sought in the law books, which most people don't have the time or training to use. This book answers many common questions, or shows how to find the answers as quickly and easily as possible.

HOW TO USE THIS BOOK

Most law that governs animals is local: it is controlled by cities and counties. State law is involved to a lesser, but increasing, degree, and federal law hardly at all. So "dog law" varies every time you cross a city boundary. Obviously, we can't tell you what the law is in every town in the country. But we can tell you what to look for, what to expect, and steer you to the right place or people so you can find it yourself.

In fact, the local nature of dog law is usually an advantage when you're trying to find out the rules in your town. Your legal research may be as simple as going to the public library, opening up the big three-ring binder that contains the city ordinances, and reading the entries under "Dogs." For questions that can't be answered that easily, we offer some legal research tips in the Appendix.

A note on footnotes: The last thing we want to do is interrupt readers constantly with footnotes. But we do want to provide legal citations when discussing statutes, court decisions or interesting articles, so that interested people can look them up for themselves. So we've compromised. Important sources are footnoted throughout the book, but you only need to look at the notes if you want to find a particular law or cross-reference. Footnotes are collected at the end of each chapter.

1

DOGS AND PEOPLE

domestication / dogs as companions /
dogs as therapists / legal history

First as scavengers, later as companions, servants and protectors, dogs have been with us a long, long, time. But the fate of dogs in the crowded modern world is uncertain. Dogs fit easily into past human societies based on hunting and gathering, and later on agriculture, but less room is left for them in today's cities. In 1987, the number of cats in the United States for the first time exceeded the number of dogs (52 million dogs, 56 million cats). Writer Cullen Murphy summed up, only half-facetiously, the broader implications of this watershed event in the *Atlantic Monthly* magazine:

"Consider an America congenial to the dog: it was a place of nuclear or extended families, of someone always home, of children (or pet) looked after during the day by a parent (or owner), of open spaces and family farms, of sticks and leftovers, of expansiveness and looking outward and being outside; it was the America of Willa Cather and Lassie and Leon Leonwood Bean. Consider an America conducive to the cat: it is a place of working men and women with not much time, of crowded cities, of apartment buildings with restrictive clauses, of day-care and take-out food, of self-absorption and modest horizons; it is the America of Tama Janowitz and *Blade Runner* and The Sharper Image catalogue."[1]

Increasing intolerance for dogs is shown in more and more laws, which regulate when dogs must be confined, where their owners may take them, and even how many may live in each house. But before we get into the legal rules, let's take a brief look back at the shared history of people and dogs, to see how they've come to play such a ubiquitous role in our society.

A Little History

Only two animals have entered the human household otherwise than as prisoners and become domesticated by other means than those of enforced servitude: the dog and the cat.
—Konrad Lorenz[2]

Most people think they know how dogs came to be part of the human family: someone living in a cave took in an orphaned wolf puppy, tamed it, and got attached to it. Or wild dogs hung around the caves looking for scraps and gradually got tame. Or jackals started hunting in cooperation with humans and were rewarded with a share of the kill. Probably none of these theories is accurate. But luckily for all of us who like to speculate, we may never know for sure.

Experts differ on just when dogs were domesticated. Some say the evidence indicates domestication as far back as 14,000 to 10,000 years B.C.; others say 8,000 B.C. is more like it. Almost all agree that dogs were the first domesticated animal.

What wild animal metamorphosed into the modern dog—an animal we now know so well that its Latin name is *Canis familiaris*? That's a mystery, too. Based on behavioral patterns, chromosomal evidence, and the fossil record, the leading candidates are the wolf (most likely, a small subspecies such as the Asiatic wolf), the jackal, or a common ancestor of both. The jackal is favored by some scientists because it is smaller and less threatening than the wolf, and so more likely to have been tolerated or welcomed by people. Those who push for the wolf as ancestor point to similarities between wolf and dog behavior. One well-known scientist, Michael Fox, argues that the dog was, essentially, already a dog by the time it became domesticated, and was later cross-bred with wolves to produce some of the more "wolfish" breeds such as the Alaskan malamute and Siberian husky.[3]

It is likely that when people first took dogs in, human society was still in the hunting and gathering stage. Early on, dogs were probably of very little, if any, help with hunting. Their main value in such societies appears to be keeping humans warm at night, alerting them to intruders, and cleaning up garbage. Dogs stayed with humans through the Neolithic revolution (about 10,000 years ago), when agriculture replaced hunting and gathering and permanent settlements replaced the nomadic way of life.

Only after people settled in geographically stable communities did selective breeding of domestic animals begin in earnest. It is that breeding—the human tinkering with canine evolution—that eventually led to the astonishing variety of domestic dogs alive today. Human owners bred dogs to emphasize certain desired characteristics and, over the years, developed breeds with the traits they needed. Thus the coursing hounds—salukis, greyhounds and others—got the long legs, good eyesight, and slender build they needed to chase prey long distances over open terrain. (Believe it or not, the original idea was not to have them chase mechanical rabbits around a track.) Other hounds—bassets, beagles, and bloodhounds, for example—got their extraordinarily keen noses, which enable them to trail prey. Herding dogs such as collies and sheepdogs were bred for intelligence and the herding instinct. Toy poodles, Chihuahuas and other tiny dogs are scaled-down versions of full-sized ancestors. The list goes on.

The Dog's Place Today

Today, in most places dogs are companions first and workers second, if at all. Of course, dogs that herd sheep, sniff out drugs, help their disabled owners, or guard buildings are highly valued, but the main contribution of most dogs these days is as companions. Dogs make people smile and laugh, give them uncomplicated and unconditional love, and stick with them when others have gone. And they must be doing a good job: despite the headaches of keeping a dog in many areas, there are more than 50 million dogs in the United States.

Pets as Companions

Pet owners who responded to a *Psychology Today* magazine survey in 1984 said, not surprisingly, that the main benefit of having a pet was companionship and pleasure.[4] The magazine asked both readers who owned pets and those who didn't to answer questions. Thirteen thousand replied, including enough non-owners (12%), the magazine concluded, to allow some conclusions to be drawn about differences between the two groups. Pet owners were more satisfied with their lives, both past and present. (That result may be partially explained by demographics: the owners were as a group more affluent, though less well-educated, than the non-owners; also, more of them were married.)

WHAT ELSE PET OWNERS TOLD *PSYCHOLOGY TODAY*

Ninety-nine percent talk to their pets.

Three-quarters felt getting a pet made for more fun and laughter in the family.

Half keep pictures of their pet in a wallet or on display.

One quarter have a drawing or portrait of their pet.

One quarter celebrate the pet's birthday.

Perhaps European immigrants brought their love for pets with them. A 1987 Options magazine survey reported that:

One in 10 British people considered their pets more important to their happiness than their spouses.

One in five liked their pets better than their children.

More than half preferred to stay home with their pets rather than socialize with friends.

Many parents get a dog "for the children," because they believe that growing up with a dog gives a child companionship and teaches responsibility, gentleness and compassion. They're right, according to at least one researcher. On a standardized personality test (the Minnesota Multiphasic Personality Inventory), graduate students who had owned dogs as children showed significantly higher self-esteem ("ego strength") than those who had not had pets. The researcher theorizes that having a dog lets a child form attachments without fear, because of the unconditional acceptance the dog gives the child. The dog's trust helps the child trust himself.

And perhaps children should consider getting a dog "for the parents." According to a recent study of 454 new parents, men who are attached to their pet dogs also make better fathers. The dog-owning dads consistently scored higher on tests geared to measure their perceptions of happiness with their relationship with their babies, their marriages and their role as fathers.

Pets as Therapists

A psychotherapist would have much to learn from watching the way a dog listens.

—Dr. Victor Bloom[5]

Four out of five people who responded to the *Psychology Today* survey said that when they were lonely or upset, pets were often their closest companions. One woman in a difficult family situation wrote that without her dog, she "could not tolerate life."

This finding explains why the most visible benefits of an animal's companionship are reaped by people who lack normal human relationships: disturbed children, lonely older people, or prison inmates. Therapists and administrators now routinely use animals to treat or manage such patients.[6]

For the most part, animals entered into the world of psychological therapy serendipitously. One psychiatrist, for example, happened to have his dog in his office when a young patient came early for an appointment; the dog became an integral part of the child's therapy. In the 1970s, an entire course of research was triggered when troubled adolescents in an Ohio State University hospital—many of whom had refused to communicate with the staff—asked to play with dogs used for behavioral research, which they had heard barking in a nearby kennel. Even the most withdrawn patients improved after contact with the dogs.

BUT STOP ME IF I ANTHROPOMORPHIZE

Quotes from three dog owners who formed a Puppy Play Group that meets every day on New York's Upper East Side for the ostensible purpose of fostering "happy, well-socialized dogs who can relate well to other dogs."

"Minnie always goes to group. Group has made a new dog out of her. Now she's really coming out of her shell." (Owner of Minnie, a dog that has been to three animal counselors and treated with a sound-activated collar that administers electric shocks in attempts to curb her chronic barking.)

"'Xander is a very small dog. But he has been in group since puppyhood and is quite unneurotic." (Owner of Alexander, a dog that wears a solid gold medallion.)

"I feel like a terrible mother. I didn't have a birthday party for Moira this year. And the dogs really look forward to seeing each other—although I could be anthropormorphizing." (Owner of Moira, one of the few dogs in the group with a steady dog-boyfriend, Toby.)[7]

It is not an exaggeration to say that pets can give people a reason to live. Often, people institutionalized in prisons or hospitals, for example, have no goals, no responsibility, no variety in their lives. Animals, either as visitors (animal welfare groups often take animals to visit hospital and nursing home patients) or residents, make the atmosphere more homelike, and can have a wonderful, enlivening effect on morale.

An institutionalized person who is allowed to care for a pet may become more alert, involved and sociable. As one prison psychiatric social worker put it, "the therapeutic results are nothing short of miraculous."[8] Take the story of Jed, who had been in a nursing home for 26 years after suffering brain damage in a fall. He was believed deaf and mute. When he saw Whiskey, a German shepherd-husky dog that had just been placed in his nursing home, he spoke for the first time in 26 years: "You brought that dog." He began to talk to the staff and other residents, and to draw pictures of the dog.[9]

If you're sick, a pet can help you get better faster. One study compared post-coronary survival of pet owners versus non-owners; among the pet owners, 50 of 53 lived at least a year after hospitalization, compared to 17 of 39 non-owners. Even eliminating patients who owned dogs (whose health might have been improved just from the exercise of walking the dog), the pet owners still did better. In a follow-up study, the same researcher found that pet owners' worry about their animals actually speeded their convalescence by providing "a sense of being needed and an impetus for quick recovery."

Now that scientists in the medical and psychiatric communities have accepted what pet owners have always known—that animals make people feel better—they have set about documenting the physiological effects animals have on people. When people pet dogs, especially ones they have grown attached to, their blood pressure drops. The same happens when people talk to a dog—although talking to another person usually raises blood pressure. Even the presence of a dog is comforting. In one study, people who took a standardized anxiety-measuring test when the experimenter's dog was in the room scored lower than those who took the test with only the experimenter present.

DON'T PRESCRIBE A DOG FOR THE TAXPAYER'S BLUES

You may know your dog helps keep you healthy, but don't try to tell the Internal Revenue Service that. The IRS doesn't allow you to deduct the cost of a pet as a medical expense, unless the dog is a seeing-eye or other specially trained service dog. (See Chapter 2, State and Local Regulation).

You can't claim your dog as a dependent, either: the IRS said no to a woman who wanted "head of household" rates because she lived with 25 dogs and cats.[10]

Let's let that old dog-lover Freud have the last word on the psychology of dog-people relationships. Here's how he described the "extraordinary intensity" with which he loved his dog, Topsy:

"affection without ambivalence, the simplicity free from the almost unbearable conflicts of civilization, the beauty of an existence complete in itself . . . that feeling of intimate affinity of an indisputed solidarity."

Dogs in the Law

Dogs occupy their own odd niche in the law. By the law, we mean American law and its principal predecessor, the "common law" of England. Common law is what has evolved as judges decide cases, one by one, over hundreds of years. Unlike statutes, the common law is not written down in one place, but instead is deduced from the judges' writings. The English common law came to this country with the colonists, and forms the basis for the law of every state except Louisiana (which took its law from France's Napoleonic Code).

Under English common law, dogs were not considered to have any intrinsic value. They were kept, in the eyes of the law, merely for pleasure. Only "useful" domestic animals (ones you could eat or make work for you) such as cows, horses, sheep and chickens, were considered to have value. This reasoning seems especially odd when you look at how many dogs were kept to catch rats, herd sheep or guard houses, but that's the way it was.

Because dogs weren't "property," it wasn't illegal to steal them under the common law. It took an act of Parliament (or a state legislature, in this country) to make stealing a dog a crime. And even when a legislature did act, the result wasn't always a paragon of logic: in England at one time, it was a felony to steal a dog's collar but a misdemeanor to steal the dog.[11]

Nowadays, however, the law in most places and for most purposes treats dogs just like other kinds of property. That creates its own complications. Because a dog is property, it has no legal rights of its own. So a dog can't inherit property, or sue in its own name. Those rights are reserved for its owner.

It doesn't have to be that way. It's been proposed that dogs be treated more like children than like property, so that instead of owners they would have guardians. Their guardians would have to meet certain minimal standards of responsibility and care; if they did not, the state would have power to take their animals away from them.[12] But such a radical departure from traditional law— among other things, allowing pets to own property—is extremely unlikely to happen anytime soon.

Most of the law that governs dogs today can be found in written laws: federal statutes, state statutes or local ordinances. The decisions of modern courts, which have the power to interpret what these laws mean, can be important, too, but you won't need to spend a minute worrying about what judges in powdered wigs thought about dogs.

---

[1]Murphy, "Going to the Cats," Atlantic Monthly (August 1987). The estimates of dog and cat populations come from the Pet Food Institute, a trade association.

[2]*Man Meets Dog* (Penguin, 1964).

[3]*The Dog: Its Domestication and Behavior*, by Michael Fox (Garland STPM Press, 1978).

[4]Horn and Meer, "The Pleasure of Their Company," Psychology Today (August 1984). The survey results were similar to those obtained in earlier studies by researchers at the University of Pennsylvania and University of Maryland.

[5]Quoted in Slovenko,"Rx: a dog," Journal of Psychiatry and Law, vol. 11, no. 4 (1983).

[6]In 1972, half the state psychologists in New York used some kind of pet-facilitated therapy, according to a survey by psychiatrist Boris Levinson. Cusack and Smith, *Pets and the Elderly: The Therapeutic Bond* (Haworth Press, 1984).

[7]William Geist, N.Y. Times, Feb. 14, 1987.

[8]Psychology Today (see note 4).

[9]Corson and Corson, eds., *Ethology and Nonverbal Communication in Mental Health* (Pergamon Press, Great Britain 1980), quoted in Guidelines: Animals in Nursing Homes (California Veterinary Medical Ass'n).

[10]*Davidson v. Commissioner*, Tax Court Memo. (CCH) Dec. 34, 524, 1977-232.

[11]*Law Without Lawyers*, by Two Barristers-at-Law (John Murray, London, 1905).

[12]"Rights for Non-human Animals: A Guardianship Model for Dogs and Cats," 14 San Diego L. Rev. 484 (1977).

2

STATE AND LOCAL REGULATION

licensing / vaccinations / leash laws /
lost and found dogs / pooper-scooper laws /
how many dogs you can have /dog pounds / burial

Owning a dog, which used to be a pretty simple proposition, is becoming more and more complicated as government regulation in this area mushrooms. The crackdown can be traced to urbanization: as dogs and people compete for space, the trend is for cities to put more restrictions on dogs and, sometimes, to limit the number or kind of dogs that city dwellers may have.

This chapter looks at the basic areas of government regulation that affect most dog owners.

Note on assistance dogs: Many local laws don't apply to assistance dogs trained to help disabled owners. These special rules are explained in Chapter 8, Guide, Signal, Service and Therapy Dogs.

HOW TO FIND LOCAL LAWS

Local governments are still in charge of most kinds of basic animal regulations, including limits on the number of dogs per household, license and vaccination requirements and leash laws. Laws covering these issues tend to be broadly similar everywhere, but their details vary significantly from town to town.

To find out what the law is where you live, you have to do some research. That may be as simple as calling the local Animal Control or Health Department and asking your question. If you want to read the law yourself—always a good idea—you can probably find it in the city or county ordinances, which are often called the "municipal code." The code should be available at your local public library, the law library in the county courthouse, and at city offices, usually the city clerk's or city attorney's office.

In most towns, even large ones, local ordinances are kept in a big loose-leaf binder. You can probably find what you need simply by looking in the index under "Dogs" or "Animals." (For more information, see Appendix 1, Legal Research.)

Licenses

Whether you live in the city or the country, you have to get a license for your dog. And it's important to remember that almost all laws require not only that you buy a license every year, but also that you keep the license tag on your dog at all times. There is, of course, a practical reason: the tag is the only way animal control officials have of identifying a dog that is picked up by the pound.

License Fees

In most places, annual license fees are $5 to $15. But several factors may reduce the fee you pay:
- Almost everywhere, fees are lower for spayed and neutered animals.

- Licenses for specially trained guide, signal, or service dogs that help their disabled owners are usually free. (See Chapter 8, Guide, Signal, Service and Therapy Dogs.)
- Disabled or older people are sometimes given free dog licenses. Free licenses may be limited to dogs that have been spayed or neutered. Some cities also require that household income be below a certain amount.
- You may be able to buy a "lifetime license"—valid for the dog's lifetime, not yours. Pennsylvania makes such licenses available if the dog has been tattooed with an identification number.[1]
- If you have a lot of dogs, you may be able to (or be required to) get a kennel license that covers all the dogs—a sort of quantity discount. (See Chapter 3, Buying and Selling Dogs.)

Where To Get a License

City governments regulate animals within their borders; in unincorporated areas, the county takes responsibility. No matter where you live, you can probably get your license by mail. Check the phone book under city or county offices for a licensing department, or just call a general city hall or animal control number.

To get a license in most places, you must produce a current rabies vaccination certificate. This explains why puppies are usually exempt from the license requirement until they get their adult rabies vaccination, at about four months old. Vaccination records, by the way, are sometimes how a local government keeps dog owners honest; the veterinarian administering the shot must send a record to the county, stating whether or not the dog is licensed.

If your town offers reduced license fees, you'll need proof of whatever makes you eligible: for example, a veterinarian's certificate stating that the animal has been spayed or neutered, or a document from a training institute that says your dog is a trained guide dog.

If you move from the city or county that issued the license, you may have to get a new one. In some states (New Jersey, for one), a license is good anywhere in the state. If you move out of state, you almost certainly will need to get a new license, within about 30 days after you arrive in the new state.

If You Don't License Your Dog

What happens if you don't buy a license for your dog? Well, it's sort of like driving a car without bothering to get a driver's license. If you're never stopped by the police or hit by another car, no one will be the wiser. And if your dog is never lost, stolen or nabbed by the dog catcher, never bites anyone, and never bothers someone's livestock, you may get away with not having a dog license. But if any of these things happens, having a license can make a big difference, because licensed and unlicensed dogs are often treated very differently under the law. And as with driver's licenses, the penalty for not having a dog license is bigger than the price of buying one in the first place.

When a licensed dog is picked up and impounded by animal control personnel, the pound can check the city's license records to identify—and notify—the owner. Unlicensed dogs are often euthanized (put to sleep) sooner than dogs with license tags. (See "Impounding Dogs," below.) If you go away for the weekend, and your dog escapes from the back yard, the two or three extra days a licensed dog is given at the pound could mean the difference between getting it back and losing it for good.

It's also still fairly common to find legislation that makes stealing only *licensed* dogs a crime—implying that stealing an unlicensed dog is legal.[2]

How Many Dogs Can You Keep?

In rural areas, how many dogs you keep is pretty much your own business, as long as the dogs aren't a nuisance. But many cities restrict residents to two or three dogs per household, not counting puppies less than a certain age, usually eight weeks to four months or so. The goal is to cut down on the problems that dogs cause in urban areas. People are understandably suspicious of the noise, smell and even danger that may be created if a neighbor is allowed to keep 12 dogs in one small lot.

Violating the law will probably earn you a fine and possibly even a jail sentence. A judge in Holland, Michigan—which has a two dog per household maximum—sentenced a man to 90 days in jail for refusing to give up any of his three dogs. The dog owner spent a few days in jail before agreeing to part with one of his animals.

You may wonder how these rules are enforced. After all, animal control officials don't (at least not yet) go door to door taking a dog census. They rely, for the most part, on complaints or chance observation. So as a practical matter, someone who has more dogs than is allowed under the law, is likely to get in trouble only if the dogs cause problems and a neighbor complains. The moral: no matter how many dogs you have, don't let them be a neighborhood nuisance. And if there are problems, work them out before the neighbors go to the authorities. (See Chapter 7, Resolving Disputes with Neighbors.)

Flat limits on the number of dogs per household are increasingly popular but are by no means universal. In Oakland, California, dog owners banded together to defeat a proposed ordinance that would have required people with more than three pets to get a city permit. Households with more than seven (dogs and cats) would have been designated kennels, meaning that they could not keep the animals within 100 feet of another house. The pet owners were joined by the Oakland Society for the Prevention of Cruelty to Animals and a local American Civil Liberties Union chapter. With the defeat of the ordinance, Oakland remains one of the only cities in the crowded San Francisco Bay area without a ceiling on pet ownership.

There are variations on this kind of straightforward limit. You may, for example, have to get a special kennel license if you have more than three or four dogs. That means extra fees, rules and, often, inspections by city officials. (See Chapter 3, Buying and Selling Dogs.)

Pooper-Scooper Laws

Dog droppings have become a scourge, a form of environmental pollution no less dangerous and degrading than the poisons that we exude and dump into our air and water.

—New Jersey Superior Court[3]

Anyone who has stumbled into the particular form of pollution dogs are prone to leave is likely to become, instantaneously, a committed environmentalist. While dog droppings on the bottom of a shoe isn't the most serious urban problem we face, the experience doesn't brighten anyone's day, either. Many local governments have declared that enough is enough and have passed ordinances making owners responsible for dogs that hit and run. Crowded cities such as New York led the way, but many other municipalities, small and large, have followed suit.

A typical ordinance simply requires dog owners to immediately dispose of, in a sanitary manner, droppings deposited anywhere except on their own property. If they don't, they face a fine of about $20 to $50.

Still, as anyone who's walked around the block lately knows, many dog owners neglect this law, not to mention basic good manners. People who would never dream of dropping a soft drink can in a park literally look the other way as their pets deposit unsightly and unsanitary droppings in public places. Is it any wonder that owners are giving dogs—who, after all, are only doing what comes naturally—a bad name?

Note on assistance dogs: Owners of guide, signal and service dogs are often exempt from pooper-scooper laws. See Chapter 8, Guide, Signal, Service and Therapy Dogs.

POOPER-SCOOPERS IN THE BIG CITIES

The New York statute requiring dog owners to clean up after their pets was challenged on the ground that it was unconstitutional. Stumped? The argument was that it interfered with the free exercise of religion because Orthodox Jews are forbidden from picking up litter on the Sabbath. The court said the law was reasonable, anyway.[4]

There are no pooper-scooper laws at all in Paris, where dogs are welcome at most fine restaurants—including Maxim's, where many humans aren't welcome. Instead, the city regularly sweeps the sidewalk with vehicles specially designed to scoop up droppings.

Leash Laws

Whatever may be said about the affection which mankind has for a faithful companion, modern city conditions no longer permit dogs to run at large.

—*California Court of Appeal*[5]

Long gone from most of America are the days when you could answer a longing whine from your dog by opening the back door and letting it roam the neighborhood at will. Besides the fact that many people live in apartment buildings where back doors open onto upper-story balconies, roaming dogs are considered outlaws almost everywhere, either by state law or by city or county ordinance.

"Leash laws" generally require dogs to be on a leash and under control whenever they're off their owners' property, unless a specific area is designated for unleashed dogs. Many large parks with wild, natural areas allow dogs to run, if accompanied by their owners. And some cities have parks designed just for dogs. Larkspur, California, for example has an "experimental dog park." It's a fenced-off area of a city park, complete with pooper-scoopers, where people can turn their pets loose and then, like parents at the edge of a playground, watch, scold, and applaud the results. The city will pay for clean-up costs, but dog lovers will chip in half of the estimated $18,000 cost of construction.

Even if dog owners who let their dogs off a leash only because they're confident they have complete control over them are probably in violation of the law. As a practical matter, no one is likely to be cited if the dog really is under voice control and not bothering anyone. But it happens.

LAW AND ORDER IN SUBURBAN LOS ANGELES

Here's a legal interpretation problem for you: If the law requires a dog to be on a leash, does the owner have to be holding on to the other end?

Jean Bessette of Van Nuys, California was ticketed for walking his Labrador retriever, Rex, without a leash. Bessette protested that the dog was on a leash. The problem was that Bessette wasn't holding the other end of the leash—Rex was, in his mouth.

Bessette and Rex went to court, where Rex balanced dog biscuits on his nose to show how well-trained he is. The pair got off with a warning.

In some places, leash laws are still lenient. Some apply only at night, because dogs tend to do the most damage to livestock at night, when the dogs form packs. Some apply only to female dogs in heat (that is, physically ready for breeding).[6] Male dogs are strongly attracted to females in heat, and a pack of noisy, aggressive males will quickly form around a female running loose.

A dog running loose can be picked up and taken to the pound by municipal or county animal control officers. The owner will be fined and charged for the cost of impounding the dog. (See "Impounding Dogs," below.) If the dog is unlicensed, there will be another fine as well.

There are other risks to allowing a dog to run at large. Of course, there's the obvious danger that the dog will be hit by a car. You are also letting yourself in for financial liability if the dog causes trouble—bites someone or makes a bicyclist fall, for example. To take an extreme example, in 1983, two men were severely injured when the driver of a truck in which they were riding swerved to avoid hitting a dog that had run into the street. They sued the dog's owner, and a judge awarded them $2.6 million.[7] (Liability is discussed in detail in Chapter 11, Personal Injury and Property Damage.)

Dogs who damage property or injure livestock while running at large may be subject to other laws—including the "shoot first, ask questions later" rule that prevails in most rural areas, allowing a farmer to kill any dog that's threatening livestock. (See Chapter 9, If a Dog is Injured or Killed.) And if a dog threatens or injures a person, it may be classified as a "vicious dog" and made subject to strict regulations. (See Chapter 12, Vicious Dogs and Pit Bulls.)

Off-Limits Areas

Dogs, on or off a leash, are simply not welcome in many places. Usually, taking a dog to a beach, zoo, restaurant, or farm won't make you any friends and may get you a quick and stern request to leave. State and local laws ban dogs, for health reasons, from places food is prepared, served or sold.

Surely, though, you can let your dog run in wide-open spaces? It depends. On federal land, the rules change from area to area. In officially designated "wilderness" areas, dogs are allowed on a leash, but the leash requirement is rarely enforced where there are few people and even fewer park rangers. Some National Parks and National Monuments allow dogs on leashes; some don't allow dogs at all. In National Forests, dogs are usually allowed in at least some areas.

State and local rules are unpredictable. Most trails and campgrounds of the California State Park system, for example, are closed to dogs. Check the rules before you load your backpack (or your dog's) with kibble and set off.

Note on assistance dogs: Guide dogs, and sometimes, other specially-trained assistance dogs, are allowed many places other dogs aren't. (See Chapter 8, Guide, Signal, Service and Therapy Dogs.)

Vaccinations

Rabies—the dreaded "hydrophobia" of "Old Yaller"—has been greatly diminished but not eliminated in domestic animals. In 1988, a California boy died of rabies; health officials first thought his infection came from a bat (bats are notorious carriers of the disease), but later attributed it to a dog bite.

Most states require dogs to be vaccinated against rabies. Three-year vaccines are available for dogs more than four months old, making compliance easy. Many cities offer low-cost vaccinations at permanent clinics (such clinics usually offer spaying and neutering for a low cost as well), or special one-day clinics where you merely have to show up to get your pet vaccinated. Washington, D.C., for example, holds an annual clinic, at which dogs can get free rabies vaccinations. Usually, to get a dog license you must have proof that your dog has an up-to-date rabies vaccination.

Don't think your dog is safe from rabies because you live in a city and rarely come into contact with wild animals. Common species of "urban wildlife"—skunks, raccoons, and bats—can spread the disease to pets. Healthy wild animals usually avoid domestic animals, but sick ones may not, and they are also more likely to be out in the daytime.

Cities sometimes impose additional vaccination requirements. In Los Angeles, for example, anyone who sells a dog must first immunize it against distemper, a relatively rare but very contagious and usually fatal disease in dogs.[8] Washington, D.C. and some other cities also require distemper vaccinations.[9]

You may need to have proof of recent vaccinations for your dog before you can take it into another state or country. (See Chapter 6, Traveling with Dogs.)

Dogs in Vehicles

We've all seen dogs riding in the back of pickup trucks as the trucks fly down the highway. The dogs look to be having fun, but by living in the fast lane they risk injury from flying objects. Eye injuries are common, but there is an even greater danger: according to a California legislator, approximately 100,000 dogs a year nationwide are killed because they jump or are thrown from a pickup. There's no reliable way of estimating how much damage and how many serious accidents such incidents cause.

Many local and state governments now regulate how dogs can be carried in pickup beds. California replaced the varied restrictions of 14 counties and more than 100 cities in that state with a statewide law.[10] It requires dogs in the open back of a pickup to be either in a cage or cross-tied to the truck unless the sides of the truck are at least 46 inches high. The law doesn't apply to cattle or sheep dogs used by farmers and ranchers. Violators can be fined $50 to $100 for a first offense and up to $250 for a third offense.

Note on dogs inside cars: If you're worried about your dog bouncing around inside the car, or if you just want to keep it out of your way while you're driving, many pet stores and mail order companies sell seat belts and car seats designed just for dogs.

Parked Cars. Dogs in parked cars are also at risk in hot weather; an enclosed car heats up amazingly quickly, and the heat can kill a dog. Owners can be punished for leaving a dog in a car, under anti-cruelty statutes or laws that specifically forbid leaving a dog in a parked vehicle without adequate ventilation. (See Chapter 13, Cruelty.)

Lost and Found Dogs

If a dog turns up on your doorstep, you are not free to decide that "finders are keepers" and do whatever you want with it.

If you don't want the dog, you must turn it over to animal control authorities, who have the responsibility of trying to find the owner. You should not, unless there is an emergency, take it upon yourself to have the dog destroyed.

Example: A Louisiana man found a sick puppy, which wasn't wearing a collar, in the front yard while he was visiting his father one morning. He took the pup to a vet and, given a discouraging prognosis, two days later asked the vet to humanely destroy the dog. Only later did the dog's owners find out that the dog had been taken and destroyed. They sued and won the value of the dog.[11]

What if you do want to keep the dog? In some places, a local or state law may require you to turn it over to the animal control authorities. If you do, ask for the first chance at adoption. But even if you're not required to notify the pound, you must try to find the owner yourself. If you don't, you could be liable to the owner for the dog's value.

Here are some basic steps to take:

- If the dog has a license tag, call the animal control department and get the owner's name.
- Ask the people who live around where you found the dog.
- Put a notice in the newspaper, and notify local radio stations if they read lost dog announcements on the air.
- Post signs near where you found the dog.

Common sense should tell you what to do: if the dog is healthy and well-fed, someone is probably looking desperately for it. If it looks like it hasn't had a good meal or a bath in a while, it's unlikely that an owner is worried about it—or that it will be adopted if you leave it at the pound.

Animal Burial Restrictions

Used to be, you could lay Fido to rest in the field he had happily run through during his life. But no more—at least, not legally. Although enforcement is spotty, most towns and cities prohibit burying an animal anywhere but in an established cemetery. Outside the city limits, you may be allowed to bury an animal as long as you meet county health regulations. That means, in all likelihood, that you must bury the dog fairly deep, and away from water supplies. Contact your county health or animal control department for specifics.

Most people ask their veterinarian to take care of disposing of their dog's remains. Many cities will also, for a fee of about $10 to $40, pick up and dispose of a pet's remains. You can find out local policy by calling your city or county health department, or the dog pound.

PET CEMETERIES

According to one estimate made several years ago, American pet cemeteries gross about $3 million annually.[12] That may or may not be accurate, but it is true that having a pet buried in a cemetery can cost several hundred to several thousand dollars. For example, at the Pet's Rest Cemetery in Colma, California (just south of San Francisco), burying a medium-sized pet in a pine box, with a small redwood plaque, costs $495 (not including pick-up of the dog's body). For a custom casket and granite headstone, the tab rises to $800.

Cremation is a less expensive option, just as it is for humans. At Pet's Rest, the bottom of the line is mass cremation, which runs $40. Individual cremation and an engraved solid bronze urn for a medium-sized dog cost $235.

If you've got a coon dog—a dog used to hunt raccoons—it's
eligible for burial in the Coon Dog Cemetery of northwest
Alabama. More than 100 coon dogs are buried in the
cemetery, which was begun in 1937. The dogs don't have to
be purebred, but they must be genuine coon dogs. The
cemetery doesn't accept household pets—and went so far
as to dig up an imposter whose owner had tried to pass it off
as a coonhound.

Impounding Dogs

Many dog control ordinances attempt to give animal control
authorities the power to pick up, impound, and sometimes even
destroy dogs. But the government's authority is limited by the U.S.
Constitution. Here's where the dog's legal classification as
"property" comes in handy: the constitution says the government can't
deprive you of your property without giving you due process—that is,
notice and a chance to have a hearing. There are, however,
important exceptions to this rule; if a dog is unlicensed or running at
large, you've probably lost your right to get a notice before the dog is
picked up or, in some cases, destroyed.[13]

Dogs that Are Unlicensed or Running at Large

If a dog is running at large without a license or poses an
immediate danger to the public, most courts agree that the
government has the power to impound and destroy it, without first
notifying the owner. If a dog is in the act of attacking a person or
livestock, anyone, including government employees, may lawfully do
anything necessary to stop it. (That's discussed more fully in Chapter
9, If a Dog Is Injured or Killed.)

States, however, may *not* pass laws that give animal control
authorities excessive power to act without first notifying an animal's
owner. For example, an Idaho statute that said that any dog "running
at large in territory inhabited by deer" was a nuisance and could be
killed by a game warden was ruled unconstitutional by the state
supreme court.[14]

FALSE IMPRISONMENT?

If your pet is picked up by overzealous animal control officers and locked in the doggie slammer for the weekend, chances are it will spend the time there frightened and nervous, and will come home smelly, flea-bitten and hungry. Can you recover from the city or county for its "wrongful arrest" of your innocent dog? Probably not. The law acknowledges only injury to you, not your dog. So you may be able to collect some money for your mental distress, but not your dog's. If, though, the dog becomes sick or is injured as because of the wrongful stay at the pound, you may be able to sue successfully.

Remember that you have a chance of winning a lawsuit only if the pound was wrong to pick up your dog, or kept it after you tried to bail it out. If your dog just got caught running around unleashed, and the pound didn't break any of its own rules about notifying you or releasing the dog when you paid your fine, you've got nothing, legally, to complain about. You should also keep in mind that going to court is expensive (except in small claims court) and no fun, and proving "mental distress" can be difficult.

Dogs in Owners' Possession

Occasionally, animal control authorities seize a dog that isn't running loose. Only dogs that have bitten someone or, even more rarely, proven to be an incorrigible nuisance, are taken from their owners this way. (The "vicious dog" laws that allow this are discussed in Chapter 12, Vicious Dogs and Pit Bulls.)

Unless a dog is running at large, or an emergency requires immediate action, most courts would agree that an owner who has possession of a dog is entitled to:

• be notified before the dog is seized;
• be notified before the dog is destroyed; and
• a chance to argue, in court, that the dog shouldn't be destroyed.

Most courts, then, would rule unconstitutional any law that allows animal control officials to seize or destroy a dog (in its owner's possession) without giving its owners notice and a hearing.[15] The case of Missy, a black Labrador with an unfortunate tendency to bite children, provides a good example. Because the dog had bitten three children, the San Luis Obispo County, California Department of Animal Regulation ordered the dog's owner to confine Missy to an enclosed kennel. Several years later, the owner had to go into the hospital, her son and daughter-in-law took the dog to their house. When Missy bit another child, the department ordered the dog seized and destroyed.

The county ordinance did not provide for any notice or hearing before destroying a dog, but the county conducted a "courtesy" hearing at the request of Missy's owner. The hearing officer ruled that Missy should be destroyed. A trial judge agreed.

Finally, an appellate court reversed the lower court ruling and declared that Missy "shall live and 'enjoy the noonday sun.'" The county ordinance was unconstitutional, the court said, because it didn't require a hearing before a dog was taken and destroyed. The "courtesy hearing" was not enough to satisfy the law.[16]

Note on Enforcement by Humane Societies: Local animal regulations are usually enforced by city and county Animal Control, Health, and Police Departments. Sometimes, however, a humane society or Society for the Prevention of Cruelty to Animals (SPCA) provides animal control services under a contract with the city or county. Or it may have limited powers—for example, to take charge of injured or abandoned animals, or arrest people at an organized dog fight without first getting a warrant. When it is acting in an official capacity, a quasi-public organization such as a humane society is subject to the same constitutional requirements as any other government agency. That means it must respect dog owners' due process rights, discussed above.

What Happens to Impounded Dogs

So many dogs show up at a dog pound every day—strays, dogs abandoned by their owners, dogs declared vicious by courts—that many facilities are strained to the breaking point. They can't keep all those animals forever; many dispose of dogs after only three to seven days. For a dog there are only four ways out of the pound: it may be reclaimed by its owner, adopted, sold or destroyed.

Reclaiming a dog. If your dog is impounded, you can probably bail it out by paying a fine and a per-day charge for its keep at the pound. If you don't have one already, you'll also have to buy a dog license and get any necessary vaccinations for the dog before it will be released to you.

Finding out that your dog has been picked up may be the tricky part. All shelters are supposed to notify owners whose dogs they impound. Of course, unless yours is an exceptionally smart and articulate dog, the only way the pound knows you're the owner is to read the dog's identification or license tag. Both you and the dog may be out of luck if it comes to the pound tagless. Many pounds also have some procedure for making a public announcement about dogs they pick up. This may be posting a list at the shelter, city hall and police station, or publishing descriptions in the newspaper, or, in small towns, even on the local radio station.

If you think your dog may have been picked up, remember that some cities have several dog shelters, and call all the places the dog might have been taken: humane societies, SPCAs, city and county shelters. Some pounds don't give out information over the phone. In any case, it's much better for you to go in person. Leave a picture or description of the dog at each pound. And if you don't get a satisfactory answer, keep asking. It's all too common, unfortunately, to hear stories of people who were told on the phone that their dog wasn't at the pound, and who found out too late that the dog had in fact been there.

Adopting a stray. Most pounds try, of course, to find new homes for dogs they take in—private homes, or nonprofit agencies that will train them as assistance dogs—but they are usually defeated by the sheer numbers. There just aren't enough owners to go around.

Many pounds, in an attempt to cut down on the number of abandoned animals they take in, require new owners to have the dog spayed or neutered. Commonly, new owners must put down a deposit toward the cost of the surgery. In Eugene, Oregon, the adoption fee covers the sterilization surgery as well as the first rabies and distemper shots. That way, there's no reason for the new owner not to have the surgery done: it's already paid for. Another smart technique followed by the Eugene shelter is a 24-hour waiting period before prospective owners can take their chosen dog home. That cuts down on the "impulse buying" that is inevitable when people—even people who are in no position to take care of a puppy—see homeless and irresistibly appealing puppies in a dog pound.

What if someone adopts your dog? You might get it back—if you act quickly and animal control officials are sympathetic. If the pound made a mistake—didn't notify you although it could have, or let the dog be adopted too quickly—you should have the right to your dog.

If you don't act promptly, however, the dog may be gone for good. A Georgia man, for example, couldn't get back his purebred Keeshond, which was found wandering loose without a license tag and turned into the humane society. Nine days later, someone adopted it. The owner finally got around to asking the dog pound if they'd seen his dog; when they told him one answering the description had been adopted, but refused to tell him the new owner's name, he sued. The court stood firm for the pound, ruling that the city had properly used its power to dispose of dogs.[17]

Selling impounded dogs. Many pounds are allowed, by law, to sell dogs that aren't adopted within a certain time. Who buys stray dogs? Research labs. Allowing public pounds to sell dogs for research is, of course, an emotional and controversial issue. (See Chapter 13, Cruelty.) Lawsuits challenging such policies on animal cruelty grounds have failed. But public pressure can be an extremely effective tool; working on legislators to change the laws, instead of fighting them in court, is probably a better strategy.

Some cities, and some states, prohibit their pounds from selling animals for research. In Hawaii and Pennsylvania, for example, state law forbids any pound to sell or give a dog for vivisection or research.[18] And in Iowa, only institutions approved by the state health department may get animals from pounds.[19]

If you have to turn a stray dog over to a pound, ask what happens to the dogs; shelters are unlikely to volunteer the information that dogs surrendered may end up in a lab. California law, however, requires any animal shelter, public or private, that turns dogs over to a research facility to prominently post a large sign, stating that "Animals Turned Into This Shelter May Be Used For Research Purposes."[20]

Destroying impounded dogs. Shelters across the country must destroy thousands of dogs every year; some are so crowded that they can only hold unlicensed dogs for a single day. Licensed dogs, as mentioned above, usually are granted a few more days. The law often specifies only that the dogs must be destroyed in a "humane manner"; most are given a very quick and humane death by lethal injection. Some laws, however, specifically prohibit certain methods, such as decompression, which inflicts a hideous and painful death.

What to do if your rights are violated: If the government injures or destroys your dog without giving you the notice and hearing required by law, you can sue and collect for your damages. (How to sue the government is discussed in Chapter 9, If a Dog Is Injured or Killed.)

---

[1]Pa. Stat. Ann., tit. 3, § 459-201.

[2]For example, see Mich. Comp. Laws § 287.286b.

[3]*Town of Nutley v. Forney*, 283 A.2d 142, 116 N.J. Super. 567 (1971).

[4]*Schnapp v. Lefkowitz*, 101 Misc. 2d 1075, 422 N.Y.S. 2d 798 (1979).

[5]*Brotemarkle v. Snyder*, 99 Cal. App. 2d 388, 221 P.2d 992 (1950).

[6]For example, see Penn. Stat. § 459-304.

[7]Los Angeles County Superior Court, January 1987.

[8]Los Angeles Public Safety Code § 53.15.2(b)3.

[9]D.C. Code § 6-1003.

[10]Cal. Veh. Code §§ 23117, 42001.4.

[11]*Lincecum v. Smith*, 287 So. 2d 625 (La. App. 1973).

[12]Slovenko, "Rx: a dog," Journal of Psychiatry and Law, vol. 11, no. 4 (1983).

[13]Some courts, however, stick stubbornly to the old view that legally, dogs aren't property in the same way a car or house is. Under that view, dog ownership is a limited right, granted by the state. One Georgia appeals court, in 1985, said dogs "may be subjected to peculiar and even drastic . . . regulation by the State without depriving their owners of any constitutionally protected property rights." (*Johnston v. Atlanta Humane Soc.*, 326 S.E.2d 585 (Ga. App. 1985)). What does this mean in the real world? Not too much, apparently. Almost everywhere, the rules are the same: dogs running at large, unlicensed, are picked up. And if the pound follows its own rules about notifying owners (if possible) and keeping the dog for a prescribed length of time, it is then free to dispose of the dog however it wants, consistent with state law.

[14]*Smith v. Costello*, 77 Idaho 205, 290 P.2d 742 (1955).

[15]For example, see *Fucelli v. American Soc. for Prevention of Cruelty to Animals*, 23 N.Y. Supp. 2d 983 (1940) (court ordered dog returned to owner after it had been seized by New York City Department of Health without a hearing).

[16]*Phillips v. Director of the Dept. of Animal Regulation*, 183 Cal. App. 3d 372, 228 Cal. Rptr. 101 (1986).

[17]*Johnston v. Atlanta Humane Soc.*, 326 S.E.2d 585 (Ga. App. 1985).

[18]Hawaii Rev. Stat. § 143-18; Pa. Ann. Stat. tit. 3, § 459-302.

[19]Iowa Code § 351A.2.

[20]Cal. Civ. Code § 1834.7.

BUYING AND SELLING DOGS

what sellers must tell buyers / contracts / warranties

The laws can be divided into two general categories: those that restrict how sellers can operate, and those that protect buyers, giving them warranty rights and requiring sellers to disclose certain information before the sale. In this chapter, we look at what the law requires sellers to tell buyers, how to put a sales agreement in writing, and what to do if you're unhappy after you buy a pet.

Regulating Sellers

Many of the laws controlling dog sellers are aimed at pet shops, but some also affect anyone who puts an "adorable puppies for sale" classified ad in the paper after the family dog has a litter of pups. Here are the basics.

Special License Requirements

If you keep more than a certain number of dogs, or if you breed or sell even one of them, you may need a kennel or breeder's license from

022613

Shoals Community College
Learning Resource Center

your city. Letting your dog have a litter of puppies just might make you a dog breeder under your local laws; check them first if you plan to sell any dogs. Even if you don't make money from your kennel, you may need a "hobby kennel" license if you keep a certain number of dogs, although puppies less than a few months old usually aren't counted for this purpose.

The city of Los Angeles, for example, requires anyone "who sells or offers for sale any dog or cat" to buy a $25 annual breeder's license. It also forbids advertising a dog for sale unless the ad contains the owner's license number. If you breed more than one litter a year, Los Angeles law requires you to have a kennel license, which carries its own set of restrictions and requirements. (Licenses are discussed in Chapter 2, State and Local Regulation.)

Health and Age of Dogs Sold

It is illegal to sell dogs that are diseased. Anyone who does may be penalized, and will at least have to return the buyer's money. (See "Warranties," below).

Some states do not allow puppies to be sold before they are a certain age, usually about six to twelve weeks. Pennsylvania, for example, forbids selling or even giving away a dog that's less than seven weeks old; in Illinois, the minimum age is eight weeks.[1]

Regulating Pet Shops

Pet shops—which handle an estimated half a million puppies a year—are notoriously bad places for animals. Often, puppies are isolated at a time in their lives when normally they would be around their littermates, which may affect their dispositions. They may be confined to a cage and subjected to bright lights, noise and handling by strangers all day. They may be exposed to disease. Employees come and go, and although they may have the best of intentions, it's obvious that even a well-run retail store in a shopping mall isn't the best place for a puppy.

Laws usually impose only the most basic requirements on pet shop operators: sanitary conditions, proper heating and ventilation, enough food and humane treatment of animals. Violations are usually misdemeanors and can be punished by fines and short jail sentences. (Anti-cruelty laws that apply to pet stores and "puppy mills" are discussed in more detail in Chapter 13, Cruelty.)

Get a Sales Agreement in Writing

You can do one simple thing to avoid problems when you buy or sell a dog: get your agreement in writing. Even if you think you and the person you're dealing with agree on everything, it is always useful to spell out the understanding on each side. You may not know until you sit down with pen and paper that the other person expects something quite different from what you do. And even if you don't sign a formal contract, you should think about the topics listed below before you buy or sell.

What Sellers Must Tell Buyers

Some states require people who sell dogs to disclose certain facts about the dog's health, age and history. These disclosures, while a step in the right direction, are no substitute for a complete contract (discussed below), but you should know if you are legally entitled to certain disclosures.

California, for example, requires every retail seller of a dog to fill out and give the buyer a written form, which is provided by the state Department of Consumer Affairs. The form lists:
- where the dog came from, if it came from a licensed dealer;
- its birth date;
- its immunization record;
- a record of any known sickness the dog has.

The seller is also required to tell the buyer orally about any sickness.[2] Violations may be punished by a fine of up to $250.

In Virginia, an animal dealer must give a buyer a special form only if the dealer says the dog is purebred and has been or can be registered with an animal pedigree organization such as the American Kennel Club. The form contains information about the dog and tells the consumer that if a veterinarian says the dog is unfit for purchase within ten days of when it was bought, the dog can be returned for a refund or another dog of equivalent value.[3]

Note on vicious dogs: In Ohio, someone who knows a dog is vicious and sells or gives it away must give the new owner, the local board of health, and the county dog warden a form which contains the answers to several specific questions about the dog's behavior, including: "Has the dog ever chased or attempted to attack or bite a person? if yes, describe the incident(s) in which the behavior occurred."[4] (For more on the specific laws controlling vicious dogs, see Chapter 12, Vicious Dogs and Pit Bulls.)

LOOKING FOR A DOG

If you've got your heart set on a particular breed—if you've always loved the sad eyes of a basset hound, or the clean lines of a Dalmatian—do some research before you take a puppy home.

Many breeds have characteristic problems. Some lines of Dalmatians, for example, are prone to deafness. Several large breeds, such as German shepherds and Great Danes, have a tendency to develop hip dysplasia in their hind legs. You can find out about these potential problems by reading dog magazines, looking at breed-specific books (try the library), and talking to experts. And if you see someone in the park walking the dog of your dreams, stop and chat. Is there a dog owner alive who doesn't like to talk about his pet?

When you actually choose a dog, have it checked out by an expert—a veterinarian, or someone who knows the breed well.

What to Include in a Contract

What belongs in a contract depends on why the buyer is purchasing the dog. If a buyer wants a purebred dog that can be registered with the American Kennel Club, that belongs in the agreement. If the buyer just wants a healthy mixed-breed dog, obviously there's no need to worry about pedigrees.

People who are in the business of buying and selling dogs may have their own contracts, covering all the subjects they've found important over the years. If you're not in the dog business, here are some areas to think about when drawing up an agreement:

- **Health.** This is important to everybody. The seller should set out any health problems the dog has or may have, and should guarantee that the dog is otherwise healthy.
- **Vaccinations.** List the vaccinations the dog has had, and when they were given. It's also helpful to say what further vaccinations the dog will need, and when. Listing the veterinarian or clinic that gave the vaccination is good in case the buyer needs

documentation—which may be the case when it's time to buy the dog a license.

- **History.** Where did the dog come from? If you're buying it at a pet shop, it may have come from one of the big "puppy mills." As their name implies, these places churn out puppies like factories turn out auto parts. And their purpose is the same: to make money. Dogs that come from them are often bred from inferior animals, and may suffer from malnutrition, disease or genetic defects.
- **Training.** If the dog is supposed to be trained for a particular purpose (hunting, obedience, guiding the blind), the extent of the training should be documented in the contract.
- **Pedigree.** If the dog's lineage is important to the buyer, spell it out in the contract, and attach a copy of the parents' pedigrees.
- **Quality.** If the dog is purebred but of only "pet quality"—that is, not up to competition in dog shows—you should specify that in the contract.
- **Price.** Does it include vaccinations, or the cost of spaying or neutering?
- **Warranties.** What kind of guarantees is the seller making? (Warranties are discussed in detail in the next section.)

Here is a sample bill of sale, adapted from the bills of sale in *Make Your Own Contract* (Nolo Press), that may be modified for your needs.

▲
_____

Sample Bill of Sale

1. _____, Seller, sells
   to _____, Buyer, the dog
   described in paragraph 2.

2. The dog being sold is:
   Name _____
   Breed _____
   Sex
   _____
   Birthdate_____

3. The full purchase price is $_____.

4. Buyer has paid Seller:
   [ ] the full purchase price.
   [ ] $_____, balance due on _____.

5. Seller is the legal owner of the dog described in
   paragraph 2.

6. Seller believes that the dog is healthy and in good
   condition except for the following:
   _____
   _____.

7. The dog has had the following vaccinations:
   Vaccination   Date   Veterinarian

   _____
   _____
   _____
   _____
   _____

The dog will need these vaccinations next:

Vaccination   Date

_____

_____

8. Seller obtained the dog from: _____

    on _____.

9. The dog has had the following special training:

    _____

    _____

10. The dog [ ] is purebred   [ ] is not purebred
             [ ] is registerable   [ ] is registered
    with the American Kennel Club.

11. [   ] Buyer agrees to take possession of dog immediately.
    [   ] Seller will ship dog to Buyer.
    Date of shipment: _____
    Method: _____
    To be paid for by: _____
    [   ] Dog will be insured for $_____.

12. Other terms. _____

    _____

    _____

    _____

    _____

_____   _____
Seller   Date

_____   _____
Buyer   Date

▼

After the Sale

A buyer who is dissatisfied after buying a dog may have a few choices on how to get the purchase money back or get a new dog. Obviously, it will be easier if the buyer and seller had a written contract, but even if they didn't, the law offers some guidance on how to proceed.

Special State Laws

Following the example set by "lemon laws," which give car buyers a procedure to get a refund or a new car if theirs turns out to be a hopeless lemon, some states have adopted similar laws for pet buyers. So far, only a few states in the east—New York, New Jersey, Connecticut, Virginia, Massachusetts and New Hampshire—have such laws.

The New York law gives owners the choice of returning an unhealthy dog to the seller, and receiving a refund or another animal, or keeping the animal and billing the seller for veterinary costs. The buyer must give the seller a certificate from a veterinarian, stating that the dog has a serious disease or congenital defect.

Warranties: What Did the Seller Promise?

Even if your state doesn't have a specific law for dogs, general warranty law applies when dogs are sold. Because dogs are considered property, their sale is subject to essentially the same rules as the sale of a washing machine or a lampshade. These rules, however, vary from state to state.[5] Usually, the result depends on what promises, if any, the seller made to the buyer.

Express Warranties

If someone who sells a dog promises the buyer something—say, that the dog is a rare purebred Albanian lizard hound—and the buyer bases the decision to buy on that promise ("I would *never* have bought the dog if I knew it were half Albanian lizard hound and half poodle!"), the promise is called an "express warranty." If the express warranty is violated, the buyer can sue to get back the purchase price.

Example: A man paid $3,000 for a dog he intended to enter in bird dog field trials. He claimed the seller had expressly promised that the dog was trained and ready to compete in major field trials. Once he had the dog, however, he discovered that it was infected with heartworms and was not well enough trained for major competition. A jury believed him and gave him back what he'd paid.[6]

What's the difference between an express warranty and mere sales talk? Not surprisingly, buyers and sellers sometimes disagree. The general rule is that if something the seller said really becomes part of the reason the deal is made, it's a warranty. But if the seller just natters on and on about how his dogs are the smartest (or prettiest or happiest) dogs in the world, most courts wouldn't hold him to that promise. But who wants to argue about such things? You'll save your breath, and lots of time, money and aggravation, if you get all of the agreement in writing.

Implied Warranties

Even if a seller doesn't make explicit promises, implied promises often float about when a sale is being negotiated. If you're an unhappy buyer, you can rely on an implied promise just like you can rely on an express one—that is, you can sue to get your money back if the promise isn't kept. But take our word for it: you don't want to. Implied promises are by their nature hard to prove, and you'll spend a lot of time fighting over who said what.

You may, however, be stuck with an unsatisfactory dog and only the seller's implied promises. So, briefly, here are the two kinds of implied warranties:

Merchantability. One promise that is implied in most sales is that whatever is being sold will perform as well as items of its type should. In the context of the sale of a dog, this means that the dog should be healthy, not suffering from any kind of abnormal defect. For example, it doesn't matter that a seller doesn't state, specifically, that a dog doesn't have mange; the buyer has the right to expect that a dog offered for sale is healthy.

Fitness for a particular purpose. This kind of implied promise arises if the seller recommends a certain product for a certain purpose. Let's say you want a guard dog to roam around your used car parts lot at night, and a kennel owner recommends a Doberman named Spooky. By making the recommendation, the seller impliedly warranties Spooky as a guard dog. Spooky looks fine to you, so you buy him. If it turns out later that the seller neglected to tell you that Spooky, traumatized as a pup, turns tail and hides if anyone so much as looks crossly at him, he breached the implied warranty of fitness. You're entitled to your money back.

What to Do If You're Unhappy After the Sale

Again, warranty and breach of contract laws differ from state to state. But some advice generally applies:

- If you are dissatisfied after buying a dog, promptly tell the seller so, in writing. If you have a written agreement, refer to it. Keep a copy of your letter.
- If the seller doesn't make things right by giving you a new dog or your money back within about 30 days, think about bringing a suit in small claims court.
- If you file in small claims court, don't worry about learning all the ins and outs of warranty or contract law. The judge will probably decide more on the basis of fairness than on legal technicalities.[7]
- You can help the judge come to the conclusion you want by bringing to court any evidence you have of the warranties you think have been breached. You may want to take an advertisement, or witnesses who heard what the seller told you. For example, if you bought your dog after answering a classified ad that offered "AKC-registered, champion-sired Brittany spaniels for sale," but the pups turn out to lack a pedigree, bring the ad with you.

(For more on how small claims court works, see Chapter 7, Resolving Disputes With Neighbors.)

---

[1]Pa. Stat. Ann. tit. 3, § 459-215; Ill. Rev. Stat. ch. 8, § 302.2.

[2]Cal. Health & Safety Code § 25995.3.

[3]Va. Code § 3.1-796.78.

[4]Ohio Rev. Code Ann. § 955.11.

[5]Both state and federal law may affect what happens when a buyer is unhappy after a sale. State laws are based on the Uniform Commercial Code (U.C.C.), a set of laws that every state (except Louisiana) has adopted, with small changes. A federal law that applies everywhere, the Magnuson-Moss Consumer Warranty Act, requires warranties to be written in understandable language.

[6]*Brown v. Faircloth*, 66 So. 2d 232 (Fla. 1953).

[7]Warranties are discussed in *Everybody's Guide to Small Claims Court*, by Ralph Warner (Nolo Press).

LANDLORDS AND DOGS

negotiating a lease / no pets clauses /condominiums /
public housing / landlord liability

The conventional wisdom is that dogs and apartments don't mix. This is a particularly unhappy state of affairs as households shrink, house prices rise, and more and more people live in apartments. If you haven't given up and gotten a gerbil, read on. And take heart: with a little cooperation among landlord, tenant and dog, many dog-owning tenants can live happily in rental housing.

In this chapter, we discuss how a landlord and prospective tenant can work out a lease or rental agreement that's fair to both sides. We also look at no pets clauses in leases: when they apply and when they don't.

Note on assistance dogs: In many states, landlords may not refuse to rent to disabled tenants who have specially trained guide, signal and service dogs. See Chapter 8, Guide, Signal, Service and Therapy Dogs.

RESEARCHING LANDLORD-TENANT LAW

Throughout the chapter, we mention state and local laws that affect tenants' rights to keep pets. One good way to find out if your town has laws that affect your situation is to call your local Rent Control Board (sometimes called Rent Stabilization Board) and ask if a rent control or other ordinance regulates landlords and tenants. Another good source of information is a tenants' or landlords' association.

Copies of the city ordinances should be available in the public library or the law library in the courthouse. If you end up going to the library, look up "Landlord-Tenant" and "Animals" in the index of your city's ordinances and in the index of your state's statutes. (Tips on how to make sense of what you find are given in Appendix 1, Legal Research.)

Negotiating a Fair Lease

A few landlords prefer to rent to pet owners, finding them a more responsible class of tenants. Some allow small dogs. And some will make an exception to their usual no dogs rule if they become convinced that they're dealing with a responsible owner—which means that an official no-dogs policy isn't always the final word.

A word to dog owners: If you want to negotiate something with a property owner or manager, be realistic. It's obvious why many landlords are reluctant to rent to dog owners: dogs can cause serious damage to apartments and yards, they can be a nuisance if they bark and a menace if they bite or frighten people. Landlords are worried that the place will be damaged, other tenants or neighbors will be disturbed, or that the dog will hurt someone. Their concerns are reasonable; they risk losing time and money and, in some instances, may even face legal liability if the dog injures someone. Often, however, you can get a landlord to rent to you and your dog if you deal with these concerns up front.

Before agreeing to rent to a tenant with a dog, a landlord has a reasonable right to expect:

- convincing evidence that the dog won't cause problems, and

- some provision, in the lease or rental agreement, that if the dog does cause problems, the owner will make good any loss the landlord suffers.

Evidence that the Dog Won't Cause Problems

What can a tenant do to assure a skeptical landlord that a dog won't be a problem? Praise from the obviously prejudiced dog owner is not the best evidence. References from previous landlords or neighbors are great; a brief letter saying what a nice, well-mannered pet the tenant has should go a long way with a prospective landlord. It's also a good idea for the tenant to bring the dog along on a second visit to the new place, if the landlord agrees. If the dog makes a good impression at this "audition," the landlord may let it stay.

Some other factors that may enter into the calculation:

- Is the dog spayed or neutered? Many problems are caused by female dogs in heat, which attract noisy and persistent suitors.
- How big is the dog? Even the nastiest dog of a toy breed isn't likely to cause the problems of a rambunctious malamute. A tenant should at least bring a snapshot.
- How old is the dog? A puppy is an unknown quantity, and more likely to be destructive, but an adult or older dog has a track record that can be verified.

The tenant should give the landlord something more concrete to go on, too. For example, if the tenant offers to put down a substantial damage deposit, over and above what the landlord usually charges, this show of confidence in the dog's good behavior should impress the landlord enough to allow the tenant's dog. A slightly higher rent may also be justified; after all, a landlord might charge more for a human roommate.

Note on deposit limits and rent control: Some state and local laws limit the amounts of rent and security deposits a landlord may collect. California law, for example, limits security deposits to twice the amount of the monthly rent (or three times the rent, for a furnished apartment).[1] But because most landlords don't charge the legal maximum, there's usually room for both sides to maneuver.

Note on mobile home parks: Special laws may apply to mobile home parks. For example, in California a mobile home park cannot charge a fee for keeping pets unless it actually provides special facilities or services for pets.[2]

Writing a Lease or Rental Agreement

Whatever agreement a landlord and tenant work out, it should always be clearly set out in writing—no exceptions. A tenant with a dog should never sign a lease that still contains a standard "no pets" clause, even if the owner or manager has offered oral assurances that it's all right to have the dog. If the landlord later reconsiders, or sells the property to a new owner, the dog owner could land in the middle of a legal battle. (This is discussed more fully in "No Pets Clauses," below).

Here are some clauses you can modify to fit your situation and add to a standard rental agreement or lease.

- "Tenant may have one dog, his Miniature Schnauzer named Pepper, on the premises."
- "Tenant may have one dog, which weighs less than 50 pounds, on the premises."
- "Tenant will remove dog droppings from the yard daily [or, if the yard is private, weekly]."

- "Tenant will repair, or pay for repair of, any damage done to yard or house by dog."
- "Tenant will keep the dog inside between the hours of 10 p.m. and 7 a.m."
- "Tenant will pay a $300 refundable security deposit, in addition to the standard security deposit of $500, to cover any damage that may be caused by the dog."
- "In lieu of paying an increased security deposit, tenant will pay for steam cleaning of the carpets when she moves out."
- "Tenant will keep $100,000 of liability insurance to cover injuries or damage caused by the dog." This clause is necessary only if there's some reason to fear the dog might injure someone. (See section on "Landlord Liability," below.]

PETS WELCOME

A few landlords are bucking the no pets trend and actively encouraging tenants to own pets. A model is Kennen Court Apartments in San Jose, California, a two-and-a-half acre development that caters to families with pets and children. The name is a combination of kennel and children, and the tenants of the 40 units have 25 pets and 60 children among them.

There are 10 buildings, each with four 2-bedroom apartments. To keep the environment clean and quiet, regulations are detailed and strictly enforced. Kennels, which are attached to each apartment, must be cleaned daily. Tenants can do it themselves or pay the apartment management to do the cleaning. If they lapse, they are warned and then fined. Dogs must be kept indoors overnight. Tenants must also buy renter's insurance, at about $150 to $180 a year, that protects them and the owner against liability for damage the pets might cause.

David Raskin, the owner, isn't a pet-owner himself. He's in business to provide a service and make a reasonable profit, he says, and believes his facilities make it possible to attract higher-quality tenants: "people who are stable and responsible." Before a lease is signed, both the prospective tenant and pet are "interviewed," says Raskin. He wants to make sure the dog has a good disposition and will obey its owner's commands while off a leash. To that end, Raskin offers the fringe benefit of some free obedience lessons for the dog.

There's another advantage to the dogs-welcome policy, Raskin notes: since it began encouraging dogs, Kennen Court Apartments hasn't had a single burglary.

Kennen Court Apartments are at 472 Lewis Road, San Jose, CA 95111. To contact Raskin, write to 15466 Los Gatos Blvd., Suite 109-248, Los Gatos, CA 95030.

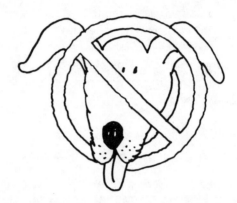

Special Rules for Tenants in Public Housing

Older people, living in government housing, being forced to give up pets that are almost their only companions—it doesn't make for good press for the bureaucrats responsible. Pressure on those government officials has yielded results in several states.

In California, residents of public housing developments (those owned and operated by a state, county, city, or district agency) who are over the age of 60 or disabled may keep up to two small pets per apartment.[3] Arizona has a similar rule; it allows elderly or handicapped people to have pets, but doesn't specify a limit on the number of animals.[4]

The laws allow the public agencies to make reasonable regulations about pets, but specifically instruct them not to impose any requirement that makes keeping a pet "financially prohibitive." The Arizona statute forbids requiring a tenant to pay a deposit of more than one month's rent.

Enforcing 'No Pets' Clauses

As all pet-owning tenants know, most standard leases and rental agreements contain no pets clauses. Such provisions are legal everywhere, and courts generally enforce them by allowing a landlord to evict a tenant who gets a pet in violation of a lease clause and refuses to give it up. There are, however, situations in which a no pets clause may not be enforceable if a tenant and dog are already living in a rental unit and:

- The tenant can prove that keeping a dog is necessary for security or health reasons; or
- The landlord agreed, no matter what the lease says, that the tenant could have a dog; or
- The landlord tries to add a no pets clause to a rental agreement, or enforce an existing no pets clause, after knowing about but not objecting to a tenant's dog for a significant period.

We discuss each of these situations below. But first, a common sense note: You don't want to go to court to argue about any of these theories if you can possibly avoid it. So if a landlord tries to get rid of you or your pet, sit down together and try to work things out. Calmly go over the issues discussed earlier in this chapter and see if you can't make the dog acceptable. You may end up paying a little more rent, or putting down more of a security deposit, but it will be cheaper than court.

LANDLORD-TENANT MEDIATION

Before you run to court to hash out a disagreement with your landlord or tenant, remember that usually, everyone loses when fights go to court. You lose money and time, and legal procedures have a way of escalating tension so that even petty differences start looking like life-and-death matters of principle.

The only exception to that dire rule is small claims court, which provides a relatively quick and painless way of resolving disputes over small amounts of money. But we still recommend trying the alternatives first.

One good alternative to court is mediation—getting people together with a neutral third person who helps them work out a problem. The mediator doesn't have power to impose a settlement, but is trained to help people come up with their own solutions. Mediation is quick and usually cheap or free.

Many cities have free programs specifically designed to mediate landlord-tenant disputes. The mediators are familiar with the common problems that crop up between landlords and tenants—and dogs are certainly one of them. To find out if such a program is available in your area, call your local Rent Control Board, if your city has rent control, or a Tenants' Union, Landlord's Association, bar association, or community mediation organization.

(For more on how mediation and small claims court work, see Chapter 7, Resolving Disputes with Neighbors.)

Separate Agreement With the Landlord

What if a landlord or manager tells a tenant it's all right to move in with a pet, even though the standard printed lease they signed says no pets are allowed? If the tenant relied on the landlord's promise that it was all right to have a dog (bought a dog, or moved into the apartment just because dogs were allowed there), a court might rule that the landlord could not later try to get out of the agreement. In the end, it comes down to basic fairness.

For example, in 1985, a New Jersey court ruled that tenants who had a dog for more than 10 years could not be kicked out of their apartment because they refused to accept a no pets clause when they renewed their lease. The apartment manager had told the tenants that they could have a dog because they were such good tenants. The court found that because the tenants had relied on that promise, buying and becoming attached to a purebred dog, they should not have to get rid of their pet "on the basis of a landlord's whim or caprice."[5]

When a Lease Runs Out or a
Rental Agreement is Changed

Sometimes, a tenant moves in with a dog and everything's fine—until another tenant complains, or the owner sells the building. Suddenly, the landlord announces that the tenant has 30 days to get rid of the dog or move out. What happens next depends on whether the landlord and tenant signed a rental agreement or a lease.

- A **lease** is an agreement that lasts for a specified time. Neither the landlord or tenant can unilaterally change the terms of the lease while it is in effect. Generally, however, a landlord is free to change the terms of a lease when it comes up for renewal. But, as discussed just below, a landlord who hasn't objected to a dog for a long time may have lost the chance.

- A **rental agreement** is an open-ended agreement. Commonly, it runs from month to month, and allows the landlord to change the terms of the rental agreement with 30 days' notice to the tenant. Local rent control ordinances, or the rental agreement itself, may limit the landlord's right to make such changes. (Note on oral agreements: If the landlord and tenant didn't sign anything, but simply agreed that the tenant would pay a certain amount of rent every month, the law says that they have a month-to-month rental agreement.)

When it comes to adding no pets clauses to a rental agreement or an expired lease, some special rules may apply. Some cities, recognizing that adding a no pets provision is often just a way to get rid of a tenant for another reason, have restricted the practice. Los Angeles, for example, forbids a landlord from adding a no pets clause and then evicting the tenant for keeping a pet if the pet was allowed before the change, unless the pet is a nuisance. Even if the dog is a nuisance, the landlord must give the tenant a chance to correct the problem—either get rid of the pet or change the circumstances so it isn't a nuisance—before beginning eviction proceedings.[6]

Some states (New Jersey, for example[7]) and cities require any lease change to be "reasonable." If a tenant's dog hasn't created any problems, a court would likely rule that it is unreasonable to later add a no-dogs provision to the rental agreement.

Enforcement After a Landlord
Has Allowed a Dog

If there's already a no pets clause in a lease, but it has been ignored for months or even years, the landlord may have lost the right to object to a tenant's pet. Some leases, however, say that a landlord who fails to enforce a lease clause when it's violated can still enforce it later. But if a lease doesn't have such an "anti-waiver" clause, how long a landlord can wait to enforce depends on the circumstances. A few days, obviously, isn't too long, as an Indiana tenant found out when his landlord told him to get rid of a cat three days after he moved in.[8] But a tenant who has had a pet for several months or a year may have a strong legal argument for getting to keep it.[9] It may be enough, by the way, that the landlord's agent—the apartment manager, if there is one—knows of the pet.

In New York City, a landlord has three months, after finding out about a tenant's pet, to start enforcing a no pets clause in a lease. If the clause isn't enforced during that period, the landlord loses the right to enforce it (again, of course, unless the pet is a nuisance).[10] The ordinance only mentions leases; it doesn't say whether or not a landlord who has allowed a pet can add a no pets clause to a month-to-month rental agreement.

LOOKING DOWN ON DOG OWNERS

Grumpy landlords aren't the only ones who treat dog owners like second class citizens. August Strindberg, a notorious curmudgeon, once wrote: "I loathe people who keep dogs. They are cowards who haven't got the guts to bite people themselves."

Tenants with Special Needs

Even a tenant who is not physically disabled in a way that requires a dog to help with everyday chores may have a special need for a dog, and that need may prevail over a landlord's wish to enforce a no pets clause. A tenant may, for example, have a particular emotional need for the psychological comfort that having a dog gives, or may have a well-grounded fear of crime and need the dog for protection.

It's hard to generalize about what special circumstances allow a tenant to keep a pet in violation of a no pets provision. There aren't many court decisions on record, and when the issue does go before a court, usually the judge's decision is based on general principles of fairness rather than on specific laws. Some things a court considers are:

- **Emotional attachment.** When weighing a landlord's claim against a pet owner's, courts increasingly listen to expert testimony about the emotional and psychological value of pets. In New Jersey, which requires changes in leases to be "reasonable," a court ruled, after hearing testimony from psychologists, that enforcing a no pets clause would be unreasonable when the tenants would suffer significant health problems if they lost their pets.[11]

And in an old English case, a doctor actually "prescribed" a dog for a woman who was nervous and depressed. "I advised her to have the company of a dog," the doctor said. "If she did not have one, she would definitely be more depressed and lose weight again which she can ill spare."[12] The court held that the woman's deliberate violation of the no pets clause in her lease did not merit eviction.

- **Protection.** Security is a big factor in many people's decisions to get dogs, and it can be a big factor in a judge's decision as well. A tenant who can prove that a dog is necessary for personal safety and peace of mind because of well-grounded fears of crime may be able to override a no pets restriction. Evidence of a well-founded fear is a history of crime in the neighborhood, drug deals in the building, or break-ins at the apartment.

If the dog is not a nuisance, the tenant will probably at least get a chance to argue that the no pets clause is unreasonable and shouldn't be enforced. As a New York court put it: "In the present circumstances of rampant crime, the inability of landowners sufficiently to police their properties may indeed give rise to a right in occupants to take such steps as may be necessary to protect themselves, including the possession, as here, of [a dog]."[13]

Condominiums and Planned Developments

People looking to buy a condominium or planned subdivision unit frequently called planned unit development or P.U.D.) should be prepared for rules. Lots of rules, covering everything from the kind of shutters you can have on the windows to how many pets you can have and what color you can paint the doghouse.

These rules can be found in a development's "Covenants, Conditions and Restrictions" (CC&Rs), the bylaws or declarations of a condominium owners' association, or other document. They often forbid or strictly limit the number of animals that residents can have, and residents can do little to get around them. If a resident violates a no pets rule, the condominium governing body can get a court order (injunction) that prohibits the resident from keeping the pet.[14]

A resident who wants to challenge a no pets rule successfully must prove one of three things:
- the rule is unreasonable;
- it was not adopted by the proper procedure; or
- it is being enforced arbitrarily or unfairly.

Reasonableness. This avenue of attack is not promising when it comes to a condominium rule that forbids pets, or allows only one small pet. Courts always say no pets restrictions in condominiums are reasonable, given residents' concerns about "potentially offensive odors, noise, possible health hazards, clean-up and maintenance problems, and the fact that pets can and do defile hallways, elevators and other common areas."[15] Rules that allow residents to keep the dogs they have, but not to replace them if they die, have also been upheld in some states.[16] Outright bans on dogs in subdivisions, where residents are more widely spaced, are rarer, and might be more vulnerable to a reasonableness challenge.

Improperly adopted rules. Every condominium has a decision-making group made up of some or all the unit owners. Whatever its form, it must follow its own rules when it adopts regulations that affect all the unit owners. That means following the requirements for voting, notice to owners, and holding meetings. As a practical matter, it may not matter that a rule was improperly adopted; after all, the rule-makers can probably just go do it again, this time getting the procedure right. But if the improper procedure really did make a difference—so that a new owner didn't know about the rule, for example—it's possible that a resident might get to hang on to a pet as a result.

Unfair enforcement. If a no pets rule isn't enforced evenly—if, for example, some owners are singled out for enforcement and others are left alone—the targeted owners may be able to challenge the enforcers. In most cases, this is the strongest tack to take. For example, a Florida man won the right to keep his dog after a condominium association tried to enforce a pet restriction retroactively. The association passed a rule that residents could not keep dogs unless the pets were replacements for dogs that had been registered with the association a year earlier. A court struck down the rule.[17]

Landlord Liability for Illegal Evictions

A tenant who is evicted illegally, in violation of a state statute or local rent control ordinance, may be able to sue the landlord for the damages suffered as a result. And a tenant who is forced to give up a dog because of an eviction may be able to recover money specifically for that loss. A landlord in Hayward, California recently agreed to pay a 10-year-old boy $5,000 for the emotional distress the boy suffered when he had to give up his dog. The landlord had evicted the boy's family from their apartment in violation of the city's rent control ordinance, and the dog was not allowed in their new apartment. (How to put a dollar figure on the emotional distress you suffer when you lose a dog is discussed in Chapter 9, If a Dog Is Injured or Killed.)

Landlord Liability for Tenants' Dogs

One of the reasons landlords are reluctant to rent to tenants with pets is that in some circumstances, a landlord may be financially responsible for damage or injury caused by a tenant's dog. In other words, if the injured person sues the landlord, the landlord, as well as the dog's owner, may end up paying. Courts are not eager to extend liability beyond the owner of a dog, but it happens. And tenants must be prepared to deal with the landlord's fear of liability, even if that fear is exaggerated.

Just leasing premises to a tenant with a dog usually isn't enough, by itself, to make a landlord legally responsible for a tenant's dog. For example, if a tenant's apparently friendly dog bites someone, the landlord isn't liable for the injury.[18]

In general, when a tenant's dog injures someone, courts hold the landlord liable only if the landlord:

- knew the dog was dangerous and could have had the dog removed; or
- "harbored" or "kept" the tenant's dog—that is, cared for or had some control over the dog.

If a landlord is found financially liable, the liability coverage of the building owner's insurance may cover the loss. (Liability insurance is discussed in Chapter 11, Personal Injury and Property Damage.)

Knowing About and Having
Power to Remove Dog

Under this rule, which is used by many courts, someone trying to hold a landlord liable for injuries caused by a tenant's dog must prove both that the landlord knew that dog was dangerous and that the landlord had the power, legally, to make the tenant get rid of the dog or move out. Sometimes, courts put this requirement in terms of the landlord's general duty to keep the property in a safe condition.[19]

But not all states use this rule. Under some laws, landlords are not liable even when they know a tenant's dog is likely to hurt someone. A Montana rancher, for example, knew that a dog belonging to his foreman (who lived on the rancher's property) had bitten someone. But when the dog later bit a utility company meter-reader, the rancher wasn't held liable. If, however, the rancher had exercised some control over the animal—was a "keeper" under the law—he would have been liable.[20]

Actual knowledge. To be held liable, a landlord must actually know that a tenant's dog is a danger to others. Dogs aren't presumed to be dangerous, although there is a possible exception for pit bull terriers, in cities that have enacted breed-specific restrictions. (See Chapter 12, Vicious Dogs and Pit Bulls.) So only a landlord who has specific knowledge of the dog's dangerous disposition is legally responsible if it injures someone. In practice, that means the landlord must know that the dog has already threatened or injured someone.

For example, a landlord who knows only that a tenant's dog is kept chained and barks at people who approach probably will not be held liable if the dog bites someone. A New York court, given those circumstances, did not hold a landlord liable for the injury her tenant's dog had inflicted. Especially in light of the town's leash law, the court ruled, the landlord shouldn't be expected to infer that a dog is vicious just because it is kept enclosed in a yard.[21]

If the dog is particularly threatening, however, that may be enough evidence of a vicious tendency, as a Colorado landlord found out. Before signing a lease, the landlord took care of two dogs that belonged to a prospective tenant. During the two weeks he had the dogs, they threatened his grandchild. Nevertheless, he rented to the tenants. When the dogs later severely injured a child, a court found the landlord liable for the injuries. The court ruled that by leasing the premises to the tenants, the landlord knowingly created a "clear potential for injury."[22]

(For a more detailed discussion of what kinds of facts put someone on notice that a dog is dangerous, see the section on "The Common Law Rule" in Chapter 11, Personal Injury and Property Damage.)

In some cases, a landlord's actions may be so outrageous—in the eyes of a jury—that the landlord is punished by being made to pay extra damages (called punitive damages), over the amount needed to compensate the victim. That's what happened in a 1986 Alaska case. A six-year-old girl was mauled by two dogs that belonged to her next-door neighbor in an Anchorage trailer park. When she sued the trailer park, a jury awarded her $235,000 in compensatory damages and $550,000 in punitive damages. On appeal, the court ruled that the trailer park's inaction, after it knew of incidents involving the tenant's dogs, had been such "blatant disregard of its tenants' safety" that it justified the extra damages.[23]

Courts generally say that a landlord who rents to a tenant with a dog doesn't have to observe the dog's behavior or check public records for complaints about the dog. For example, a California company rented a house to a family and specified in the rental agreement that they could keep a German shepherd named Thunder. The 100-pound dog chased a cable television installer out of the yard, making him injure his shoulder as he dove headlong over a fence to get away. The landlord was not held liable for the injury. There was no evidence that the landlord knew the dog was dangerous, and the court ruled that the landlord didn't need to assume that a German shepherd called Thunder would be vicious. After all, the court said, "it is not uncommon for an owner of a St. Bernard or a Great Dane to name the dog Tiny."[24]

Power to remove the dog. Obviously, it wouldn't be fair to hold a landlord responsible for a dog he is powerless to control or have removed. A landlord who buys a building that is already occupied by a tenant who has both a one-year lease and a dangerous dog won't be liable for any injuries the dog causes, because the landlord may not be able to order the dog removed. But if the tenant has a month-to-month rental agreement, which can be terminated on 30 days' notice, the landlord who does nothing after finding out the tenant has a vicious dog may be liable if the dog later hurts someone. (Remember, however, that local laws may restrict a landlord's ability to terminate a rental agreement.)

A landlord who acquires a potentially dangerous or troublesome dog along with the property can still take measures to avoid liability and be fair to the tenants. Eviction may be possible if the dog is a nuisance, or the tenants are violating a law that prohibits keeping a vicious dog. But getting rid of the dog isn't always necessary; the landlord can require liability insurance, a bigger damage deposit, or establish reasonable regulations, as discussed in the first section of this chapter.

'Harboring' a Tenant's Dog

Someone who "keeps" or "harbors" a dog—that is, cares for or exercises some control over it—is usually treated just like the dog's owner when it comes to liability for injury the dog causes. So a landlord who does more than merely rent to a tenant who has a dog—for example, by letting it have the run of the property—may be considered a "keeper" for purposes of liability.

Example: An Illinois landlord rented half of his building to a tenant and occupied the other half himself. The tenant's dog, which was kept to guard the building, roamed all of it. When the dog bit someone, the landlord and the tenant were both held liable.[25]

Another example: A landlord who lived off the premises hired a manager to take care of his Illinois apartment building. The manager allowed one tenant to fence in the building's back yard, which all the tenants used, and keep his dog there. One day the 65-pound dog leaped over the fence and bit a boy's nose, requiring plastic surgery to repair the damage. The Illinois Supreme Court ruled that the landlord had not harbored the dog within the meaning of the law. "Harboring," the court ruled, means more than simply allowing the tenants to keep a dog on the premises. Without "some degree of care, custody or control," the landlord was not liable.[26]

(The liability of owners and those who "keep" or "harbor" dogs is discussed more fully in Chapter 11, Personal Injury and Property Damage.)

[1]Cal. Civ. Code § 1950.5.

[2]Cal. Civ. Code. § 798.33.

[3]Cal. Health & Safety Code § 19901.

[4]Ariz. Rev. Stat. Ann. § 36-1409.01.

[5]*Royal Associates v. Concannon*, 490 A.2d 357 (N.J. Super. 1985).

[6]Los Angeles, Cal. Rent Stabilization Ordinance, Muni. Code § 151.09.

[7]N.J. Rev. Stat. § 10:5-29.2

[8]*Chuchwell v. Coller & Stoner Building Co.*, 385 N.E.2d 492 (Ind. App. 1979).

[9]For example, see *Mutual Redevelopment Houses, Inc. v. Hanft*, 42 Misc. 2d 1044, 249 N.Y.S.2d 988 (1964) (Landlords aware of tenants' dog for many months); *Capital View Realty Co. v. Meigs*, 92 A.2d 765 (D.C. Mun. Ct. 1952)(Tenants kept dog for almost two years with knowledge of resident manager).

[10]New York City Admin. Code § D26-10.10.

[11]*Young v. Savinon*, 492 A.2d 385 (N.J. Super. 1985).

[12]*Bell London & Provincial Properties, Ltd. v. Reuben*, 2 Ct. of App. 547 (1946).

[13]*East River Housing Corp. v. Matonis*, 309 N.Y.S.2d 240 (Sup. Ct. 1970).

[14]*Gesemyer v. State*, 429 So. 2d 438 (Fla. App. 1983).

[15]*Dulaney Towers Maintenance Corp. v. O'Brey*, 418 A.2d 1233 (Md. App. 1980).

[16]*Wilshire Condominium Assoc., Inc. v. Kohlbrand*, 368 So. 2d 629 (Fla. App. 1979).

[17]*Winston Towers 200 Assoc., Inc. v. Saverio* (Fla. App. 1978).

[18]See, for example, *Georgianna v. Gizzy*, 483 N.Y.S.2d 892, 126 Misc. 2d 766 (1984) and *Gilbert v. Christiansen*, 259 N.W.2d 896 (Minn. 1977).

[19]See, for example, *Nelson v. United States*, 838 F.2d 1280 (D.C. Cir. 1988)(U.S. government liable to girl injured by serviceman's dog on air force base; base security knew the dog had attacked children before and should have gotten rid of it to keep the base safe).

[20]*Criswell v. Brewer*, 44 Mont. 1408, 741 P.2d 418 (1987).

[21]*Gill v. Welch*, 524 N.Y.S.2d 692 (1988).

[22]*Vigil ex rel. Vigil v. Payne*, 725 P.2d 1155 (Colo. App. 1986). A similar result was reached in a New York case, *Strunk v. Zoltanski*, 62 N.Y.2d 572, 479 N.Y.S.2d 175, 468 N.E.2d 13 (1984).

[23]*Alaskan Village v. Smalley ex rel. Smalley*, 720 P.2d 945 (Alaska 1986).

[24]*Lundy v. California Realty*, 170 Cal. App. 3d 813, 216 Cal. Rptr. 575 (1985).

[25]*Edelstein v. Costelli*, 85 Ill. App. 2d 81, 229 N.E.2d 557 (1967).

[26]*Steinberg v. Petta*, 114 Ill. 2d 496, 103 Ill. Dec. 725, 501 N.E.2d 1263 (1986).

5

VETERINARIANS

animal health insurance / injuries to a vet / euthanasia /
malpractice / dogs abandoned with a vet

For many people, finding a veterinarian they trust to take care of
their animals ranks close behind finding a good family doctor. This
chapter discusses the legal relationship between pet owner and vet,
gives some tips on how they can maintain a good relationship, and
suggests what to do if something goes wrong.

The Owner-Veterinarian Relationship

Disputes between pet owners and veterinarians are likely to arise
for the same reason most other disputes arise: a failure of
communication. Owners misunderstand diagnoses, instructions and
fees, and busy vets are often guilty of not explaining things as well as
they should.

The most important thing for owners to do is to find a vet they
trust and establish a personal relationship. As one veterinarian put
it, some people expect to use veterinary services like they use a dry
cleaner or fast food outlet—and then get upset when their animal is
treated like a piece of laundry or a hamburger.

Pet owners should ask questions. Make sure you understand just what the vet thinks is wrong with your pet, what the dog needs, how serious the problem is, and how much time, effort and money you will have to spend correcting it. If you're embarking on a long-term or expensive course of treatment, such as surgery and follow-up therapy, get an agreement about fees in writing. You may not be able to set exact amounts, but it will help to put down estimates. If you're unhappy with your vet, because of inadequate or excessive treatment, high bills, or for any other reason, get a second opinion from another vet.

Veterinarians should take the time to explain what they're doing, and make sure the owner understands completely. It will avoid a lot of misunderstandings and unpleasantness. And remember that satisfied pet owners recommend a competent and accessible vet to their pet-owning friends.

Here is a sample agreement between a client and vet concerning extensive fees and treatment for a sick dog. The agreement could be modified to suit most circumstances. It addresses not only the issue of fees, but also builds in full disclosure from the vet about the likelihood of the dog's complete recovery.

▲

Sample Agreement

Geoffrey Livingstone and Alice Schweitzer, D.V.M. agree that:

1. Dr. Schweitzer is treating Mr. Livingstone's dog, Stanley, for a serious hip condition. Treatment will probably require surgery, followed by several months of examinations and medication.

2. Dr. Schweitzer estimates the cost of this treatment will be between approximately $700 and $1,200. Her office will bill Mr. Livingstone monthly.

3. Mr. Livingstone will pay up to $1,200 for Stanley's treatment. If Dr. Schweitzer discovers that the cost will exceed $1,200, she will notify Mr. Livingstone as soon as is reasonably possible. When $1,200 in fees has been billed to Mr. Livingstone, Dr. Schweitzer will not proceed with treatment without authorization from Mr. Livingstone.

4. Because of the dog's injury, the proposed course of treatment may not completely restore Stanley's leg to normal condition. The dog may always have a slight limp. The dog will suffer some pain from the surgery and recovery, but this will be kept to the minimum level reasonably possible.

_____   Date:_____

Geoffrey Livingstone

_____   Date:_____

Alice Schweitzer

▼

If you do get into a dispute, try to work something out between you, or with the help of a third person, before turning the problem into a legal battle. Filing a lawsuit should always be a last resort.

Disputes over fees. If your problem is with a veterinarian's bill for services—if, for example, you think it's excessive, or you didn't authorize the treatment—talk to the vet. If you haven't paid the bill, pay what you think is fair and include a written explanation with your check. If you have paid, you should send the vet a letter explaining exactly why you think the bill was excessive and how much money you think should be returned to you. If you and the vet don't come to an agreement, you can always sue in small claims court.[1]

Disputes over treatment. If a dog owner has lost a pet through what may have been the vet's carelessness or incompetence, it's difficult to discuss the matter dispassionately. The same goes for a veterinarian who is wrongly accused of incompetence or worse. That's why a mediator, who can help people work something out themselves, may be a great help. At this stage, a lawyer probably won't be helpful. Although a good lawyer should try to settle a dispute before it gets to court, involving a lawyer often instantly raises tension and acrimony. (Chapter 7, Resolving Disputes with Neighbors, discusses the mediation and small claims court process in detail.)

A REMINDER FROM UNCLE SAM

You may think of your dog as a dependent, but the IRS doesn't. That means you can't deduct your dog's medical expenses from your federal income tax.[2]

Health Insurance for Dogs

Health insurance for dogs and cats was virtually unheard of a few years ago, but it's looking better and better to pet owners who have paid big veterinary bills. According to one estimate, Americans spend $5 billion each year on health care for dogs and cats.[3] Operating on a cancerous tumor, for example, costs $300 to $1,000. One reason for getting insurance is that it reduces the chances that you'll have to put a dollar value on the life of your pet. That unhappy task can arise if you are forced to choose between paying for the sophisticated and extremely expensive procedures now available (laser treatment, CAT scans, chemotherapy) and destroying a dog that might be saved.

The chart below compares the main features of animal health insurance policies offered by two companies, Animal Health Insurance Agency (AHIA) and the Veterinary Pet Insurance (VPI).

Before you decide on a plan, read the actual policy carefully and be sure you understand all the fine print.

ANIMAL HEALTH INSURANCE POLICIES

	AHIA Comprehensive	AHIA Catastrophic	VPI 20		VPI 40	
Age of Dog	3 mos. to 9 yrs.	3 mos. to 9 yrs.	1-4 yrs.	5-8 yrs.	1-4 yrs.	5-8 yrs.
Cost per Year	$89	$36	$37	$69	$54	$47
Coverage Limit	$1,000 per injury or illness	$2,500 per injury or illness	$750 per incident $5,000 per policy year			
Deductible	$40	$250	$20		$40	
Amount Paid By Policy	70% of covered expenses		80% of first $180 per incident 100% of everything over that			
Things Not Covered	Vaccinations, elective neutering, checkups, pre-existing conditions and illnesses, hereditary and congenital conditions, and whelping.		Congenital or hereditary defects, elective procedures, vaccinations, food, grooming, behavioral problems, parasites, orthodontics, routine teeth cleaning, and conditions present prior to the policy effective date.			

Animal Health Insurance Agency: 1-800-345-6778
Veterinary Pet Insurance: 1-800-VPI-PETS (CA)
                                   1-800-USA-PETS (Nat'l)

Euthanasia

Euthanasia—"putting a dog to sleep"—is something that almost every pet owner must eventually consider. Many veterinary clinics have rules that govern the circumstances under which they will euthanize a dog. For example, many veterinarians will not euthanize healthy animals on demand. They ask the owners why they want the dog destroyed, and try to suggest alternatives. Sometimes behavioral problems can be corrected, or the dog can be found a new home.

If a Dog Injures a Veterinarian

Whether or not you want to believe it, there are circumstances in which your dog would bite someone. With some dogs, of course, the biting threshold is relatively low. But even if your dog patiently suffers all sorts of indignities without protest (children pulling its tail, having its toenails clipped), if a dog is frightened, threatened, or hurt enough, it will bite.

Veterinarians know this; many pet owners do not. So owners usually aren't legally liable if their dog injures a vet while being treated. The law generally recognizes that veterinarians, and their assistants, know what they're getting into when they handle sick or scared dogs. They take the risk of injury as part of the job, and should know from experience how to guard against it. As one court put it, "a veterinarian cannot assume a normally gentle dog will act gently while receiving treatment."[4]

The same rule applies to veterinary assistants and others who knowingly take the risk of handling animals in the course of their jobs. A veterinarian's employee might, however, be able to sue a vet who is negligent and exposes the employee to an unnecessary risk.

So even if you assure the vet that your puppy wouldn't dream of biting, the vet is still responsible for knowing that it may bite. Of course, there may be exceptions. If, for example, a dog was known to be dangerous, but its owner concealed that from the vet, the law might hold the owner responsible if the dog injures the vet.[5]

Even dog-bite statutes, which make owners liable for any injury their dog causes, don't usually apply when veterinarians are injured. Courts have ruled that because veterinarians deliberately and knowingly take the risk of injury, these statutes do not apply to them. (Dog-bite statutes are discussed in Chapter 11, Personal Injury and Property Damage.)

Another way to think about this legal rule is that a veterinarian, by treating a dog, provokes it to bite; provocation is a defense under most dog bite statutes. Provocation doesn't have to be deliberate or cruel; it can be completely innocent, as when you accidentally step on a dog's tail. A Florida appeals court, overturning a $25,000 jury verdict awarded a veterinarian's assistant, said that the conditions under which a dog had been treated—"in strange surroundings . . . held by two people he had never seen"—constituted provocation. The court concluded that the legislature had not intended that a dog owner should have to pay for injuries under such circumstances.[6]

THE COLLAR PURPLE

"Where retailers used to carry a basic leather leash, today customers want fine nylon leashes, and in a spectrum of colors so they can color-coordinate. If your dog has a red sweater, you wouldn't want to take him out in public with a green leash."[7] Except at Christmas, of course.

Veterinary Malpractice

The law of veterinary malpractice is pretty much like that of its theoretical ancestors, medical and legal malpractice. And following the trend in those areas, more veterinary malpractice suits are filed every year. The increase, however, is nothing compared to the explosion in the number of medical malpractice lawsuits, especially if you look only at cases involving dogs. The fact is that for a dog owner, the cost of going to court will probably exceed the amount eventually recovered—another reason for working out differences outside the courtroom.

What's Malpractice?

Malpractice is an error that a professional, who is expected to have a certain level of competence because of special training and experience, shouldn't make. For example, if a veterinarian looks at a dog with mange and treats it for heartworm, that's probably malpractice, because the vet should know better.

If you're considering a malpractice claim, either from the perspective of pet owner or veterinarian, stop and think if it's really malpractice that's on your mind. Many claims against a veterinarian aren't really malpractice suits and shouldn't be labeled that way. Only issues of a veterinarian's professional competence and judgment are malpractice issues. Acts of simple negligence for which anyone, not just a vet, would be liable do not constitute malpractice.

Some examples illustrate the point:

MAY BE MALPRACTICE
- Misdiagnosing a dog's illness
- Prescribing the wrong course of treatment
- Stopping treatment while a dog still needs veterinary attention

MAY BE SIMPLE NEGLIGENCE

- Leaving a dog on a heating pad too long[8]
- Letting a dog escape through a door carelessly left open
- Failing to turn over a dog's body to funeral organization

The distinction between negligence and malpractice is important for two reasons:

- **It's easier to sue a veterinarian for malpractice.** Someone suing a vet for negligence must show that the vet acted unreasonably—that is, not as an average, reasonable person would have acted. In a lawsuit for malpractice, the vet is held to a higher standard of conduct: to escape liability, the vet's behavior must measure up to that of the average veterinarian (taking into account education and experience) under the circumstances.

  Example: Robin takes her dog Sherlock to the vet, afraid that the dog sprained a hind leg jumping for a frisbee. That's the vet's diagnosis, too, but he's wrong; the dog actually has a fracture. Is Robin's vet liable for malpractice? Yes, if the average vet would have correctly diagnosed the problem.

  Now let's say that after this bumbling vet keeps Sherlock for observation, he goes off for the weekend and forgets to leave the dog any food. Is that more malpractice? No. It is, however, simple negligence, if the average reasonable person wouldn't have done it under the circumstances.

- **How long you have to file the lawsuit.** State law may set different time limits for bringing a lawsuit for malpractice and bringing one for negligence. (This issue is discussed in the next section.)

Who Can Be Sued

Obviously, a veterinarian can be sued for veterinary malpractice. But the veterinarian may also be legally liable for the actions of employees—the technicians and assistants who may be responsible for much of the hands-on treatment of a dog. And it may be a kind of malpractice if the vet lets untrained or unsupervised employees take care of animals.

When Lawsuits Can Be Brought

When a suit can be brought may depend on how it is classified according to state law. In most states, both malpractice and simple negligence cases must be filed within one to three years of the injury. If you don't discover the injury until later, you may be able to start counting the one- or three-year period from the time you discover the injury.

Be sure to check the law in your state. As a rule, lawsuits do not improve with age; if attempts at settlement don't work, file promptly. If you are in doubt about when you must file, see a lawyer.

Suits against a government agency (for example, if the vet at a city-run clinic neutered a dog but bungled the surgery) must usually be preceded by a claim against the government made within about 100 days. If the claim is denied, a lawsuit may be filed.

Where Lawsuits Can Be Brought

What court a lawsuit belongs in depends on how much money is being sued for. Small claims court is available, and advisable, for smaller disputes. Most states allow claims up to $1,500 or $2,500 to be filed in small claims court.

(Small claims court procedures, and the limits for each state, are discussed in more detail in Chapter 7, Resolving Disputes With Neighbors.[9])

How Much an Owner Can Sue For

Putting a dollar value on the death or injury of a pet is difficult, to say the least, and the rules are different in different states. Here is a summary of what a pet owner may be able to sue for and collect:
- cost of treatment necessary to fix damage caused by the malpractice;
- market or replacement value of the pet;

- sentimental value (in some states only);
- emotional distress (under certain circumstances); and
- punitive damages (if the veterinarian's conduct was outrageous or intentional).

(Chapter 9, If a Dog Is Injured or Killed, discusses the law in detail and gives examples of cases, including cases against veterinarians, in which dog owners recovered damages for each of these items.)

What an Owner Must Prove

To win a malpractice lawsuit, a pet owner must prove in court that:
- the veterinarian acted incompetently or carelessly; and
- the incompetence caused an injury.

Proving Incompetence

A veterinarian is responsible for exercising "the care and diligence . . . of a careful and trustworthy veterinarian." One who doesn't is liable for any injury that results.

The standard of conduct for veterinarians. We've said that a dog owner must prove that the vet acted incompetently—that is, not as competently as other veterinarians. Then the question is: what other veterinarians? The ones in the town, state, or the whole country? Specialists, or general practitioners? The most highly skilled vets, or the hypothetical "average" one?

In general, a veterinarian's skill and diligence are judged against those of an average practitioner, not a specialist or unusually skilled one. A vet who is certified as a specialist by one of 14 veterinary specialty boards, as more and more are these days, is held to a higher standard.

Example: Let's say that Robin's frisbee-chasing dog Sherlock, mentioned earlier, actually had just a hairline fracture of his leg, and that a veterinarian of ordinary competence could have missed it. But this time, assume Robin took Sherlock to Bones-R-Us, a clinic staffed by vets who specialize in orthopedics and charge extra for their expertise. A specialist there who missed the fracture, when a competent orthopedic vet would have caught it, would be guilty of malpractice.

Some states (Utah, for one) say that a veterinarian's competence is to be judged against that of other veterinarians "in the community."[10] This can cause problems at trial, because only another local vet can testify as to community standards of care. Especially insmall towns, it can be tough to find a vet willing to testify against another practitioner. Also, a local standard may not promote competence; instead, it may protect vets who don't live up to statewide or national standards.

Some states have rejected the community standard in favor of comparing vets to others "similarly situated," though not necessarily in the same community. This reduces the standard of care in the community to just one factor for a jury to consider.[11] Other factors include available facilities and size and location of the town.

Evidence of incompetence. In some cases, it is obvious that a veterinarian made a serious mistake. If a dog has fleas which the vet treats for ringworm, that obviously falls short of professional competence. Very often, however, it's necessary to get an expert witness—that is, another veterinarian—to testify about the appropriateness of the first veterinarian's actions. Only a veterinarian can testify about another one's professional judgment, which is usually the critical issue.

For example, a negligent misdiagnosis can be malpractice.[12] But the fact that a veterinarian doesn't correctly diagnose an animal's illness doesn't mean that the vet fell below the required standard of "care and diligence." Perhaps it was a difficult case, with contradictory symptoms, and would have confused any veterinarian of normal competency.[13] If that's true, the veterinarian was as competent as the law requires.

Small claims court evidence rules: In small claims court, letters and similar kinds of evidence are admissible. If you can take the dog to an out-of-town vet and get a written second opinion, the vet won't have to show up at your court hearing in person to testify. In some states, including California, testimony can even be taken over the phone.

Proving the Malpractice Caused the Injury

It's not enough to show that a vet did something and your pet was injured; the connection between the act and the injury must be proven. Again, expert medical testimony is often necessary.

Example: A woman sued a veterinarian, claiming that her horse turned into a "killer" after the vet negligently operated on its leg. She offered no proof of a connection between the surgery and the change in disposition except that the horse's behavior deteriorated after the operation. She lost her case.[14]

Other Lawsuits Against Veterinarians

Not every complaint against a veterinarian is necessarily a malpractice case. Before you get into a malpractice frenzy, check to see if your situation falls into one of the categories discussed here. But be warned that this short list doesn't come close to covering all the possible kinds of lawsuits veterinarians might come in for. If you have a situation that doesn't fit in any of our pigeonholes, you may want to find out your options from a lawyer.

If a Dog Dies at the Vet's

If your dog dies at the vet's, and you don't know why or how—or what happened at all—the law in most states helps you by making the vet responsible for proving that the death wasn't caused by malpractice or negligence.

The way you take advantage of this rule is by suing for negligent "bailment." Bailment is the legal term for the relationship that results when some item of property—in this case, a dog—is left in someone else's care. Under the law of bailment (which may vary from state to state), if a dog is left with a vet and the dog dies, the vet is presumed, legally, to be negligent. The vet must then prove otherwise or be liable to the dog's owner for the value of the dog.

Example: A woman boarded her healthy, eight-year-old dog with a New York veterinarian. When she returned two weeks later, she was told the dog had died a few days before. The vet gave no satisfactory explanation of the dog's death, so the owner was entitled to recover for the value of the dog.[15]

When Vets are Liable for Taking a Dog

A veterinarian who takes your dog without permission is liable to you for the value of the dog. The vet may also be guilty of theft, but that's a criminal matter to be handled by the police and district attorney. You can bring a civil lawsuit for "conversion." (No, this doesn't mean you can sue your vet for kidnapping your Protestant poodle and converting him to canine Catholicism.)

Example: An Oregon woman asked a vet to humanely destroy her dog, which had been shot and was in extreme pain. Instead, the vet gave the dog to two assistants who had grown attached to it. The original owner sued when she found out, and was awarded $500 for the vet's conversion of the dog. She was also awarded $4,000 for her mental anguish and $700 in punitive damages.[16]

Veterinarian's Duty to Treat Animals

In most cases, a veterinarian is under no legal duty to treat an injured animal. But once a vet agrees to treat a pet, stopping while the animal still needs attention may lead to malpractice liability.

Stray Dogs

Many vets treat injured or sick strays that wander in, just because they love animals. Some states reimburse a vet a nominal amount for taking in a stray dog that is sick or injured. The state of Maine will pay a vet who accepts a stray or abandoned dog $2.50 a day for eight days—hardly enough to pay for the food bill, not to mention the time and treatment.[17]

A vet may humanely destroy (euthanize) a dog without the owner's consent in an emergency. If, for example, a critically injured dog is taken to veterinarian, and the owner is unknown or unreachable, the veterinarian will not be held liable for damages for euthanizing the dog.

Maine statutes include a procedure for a veterinarian to follow when making such a decision. It requires the vet to authorize euthanasia in writing and to:

- keep the dog for at least 48 hours (unless the dog is severely injured or sick);
- notify the city clerk;
- decide the dog probably does not appear to have rabies; and
- decide the dog's recovery, given reasonable time and reasonable care, is doubtful.[18]

A vet who meets all these requirements is protected from a lawsuit if the owner does turn up and wants to sue for euthanizing the dog.

Abandoned Dogs

Some owners bring pets to a veterinarian, leave them, and never return. But the vet is not responsible for feeding and caring for an animal indefinitely if the owner doesn't show any intention to pick up the dog or pay for its care. To be fair to both vet and owner, many states now have laws that set out a procedure for veterinarians to follow.

California law, for example, deems an animal abandoned if its owner doesn't pick it up within 14 days of the time agreed on by the vet and owner. The law requires a veterinarian to try, for at least 10 days, to find a home for the animal. A vet who can't place an animal with a new owner may humanely destroy it. The vet may not turn the dog over to a pound or let it be used for scientific experimentation.[19] Dog owners are to be notified of these rules by a prominent sign in the vet's office or a conspicuous notice on a receipt.

Complaining about a Vet

Veterinarians, like doctors, contractors, architects and other groups, are licensed by the state. Without a license, it's illegal for them to refer to themselves as veterinarians or to perform certain acts, such as operating on animals or prescribing medication.

A pet owner who is unhappy with a veterinarian's services may complain to a local veterinary association or the state licensing agency, which will investigate the vet and may bring disciplinary proceedings. Many state laws provide that "gross malpractice," as well as many other forms of misconduct, may justify suspending or revoking a vet's license to practice veterinary medicine. But again, trying to resolve problems without resorting to formal complaints or legal action is likely to bring a much more satisfying result to a dog owner who feels wronged by a vet.

---

[1]You can find lots of helpful information about bill problems in *Billpayers' Rights* (Nolo Press).

[2]*Schoen v. Commissioner*, T.C.M. (P-H) 1975-167.

[3]U.S. News & World Report, Sept. 12, 1988.

[4]*Nelson v. Hall*, 165 Cal. App. 3d 709, 211 Cal. Rptr. 668 (1985).

[5]See *Willenberg v. Superior Court*, 185 Cal. App. 3d 185, 229 Cal. Rptr. 625 (1986).

[6]*Wendland v. Akers*, 356 So. 2d 368 (Fla. App. 1978).

[7]Terry Boyd, President of the Pet Industry Distributors Ass'n.

[8]*Knowles Animal Hospital, Inc. v. Wills*, 360 So. 2d 37 (Fla. App. 1978).

[9]For detailed, state-specific information on small claims court procedures, claims limits, and strategy, see *Everybody's Guide to Small Claims Court*, by Ralph Warner (Nolo Press).

[10]*Posnien v. Rogers*, 533 P.2d 120 (Utah 1975).

[11]*Ruden v. Hansen*, 206 N.W.2d 713 (Iowa 1973).

[12]*Boom v. Reed*, 23 N.Y.S. 421 (1923).

[13]*Brockett v. Abbe*, 3 Conn. Cir. 12, 206 A.2d 447 (1964) (suit for misdiagnosis dismissed because no evidence that misdiagnosis was negligent).

[14]*Southall v. Gabel*, 293 N.E.2d 891 (Ohio 1972).

[15]*Brousseau v. Rosenthal*, 110 Misc. 2d 1054, 443 N.Y.S.2d 285 (1980).

[16]*Fredeen v. Stride*, 525 P.2d 166 (Or. 1974).

[17]Me. Rev. Stat. Ann. § 3406.

[18]Me. Rev. Stat. Ann. § 3406.

[19]Cal. Civ. Code §§ 1834.5, 1834.6.

TRAVELING WITH DOGS

airline regulations / airline liability limits / problems with flying /
advice for travelers / international restrictions

When novelist John Steinbeck set off to drive through America in 1960, his only companion was a big poodle named Charley. "He is a good friend and traveling companion, and would rather travel about than anything he can imagine," Steinbeck wrote in *Travels With Charley*. "A dog, particularly an exotic like Charley, is a bond between strangers. Many conversations en route began with 'What degree of a dog is that?'"

Today's travelers, if they want to take their dogs with them, are probably still best off to imitate Steinbeck and take to the highways. You may have to use more modern modes of transportation, such as commercial jets, if you need to cover a long distance in a short time, but we don't recommend them if you have a choice.

The Not-So-Friendly Skies

Commercial airlines are not deliberately cruel or even particularly careless when it comes to shipping dogs; they just aren't set up to deal with pets efficiently. Unless your dog is small enough to carry on board the plane, air travel is a risky way for it to go.

The basic problem is that animals are treated as baggage. More than a million people fly every day in the United States, and as we all know, baggage slip-ups are inevitable, given connecting flights scheduled too close together, long delays, and good old human error in a stress-filled, overloaded system. When a mistake means your luggage goes to Minneapolis while you go to Atlanta, you'll survive the inconvenience. If your dog goes to the wrong city, or is forgotten on a luggage carousel, it may not survive.

The Problems with Flying

No one knows how many animals are shipped on commercial airlines each day or each year,[1] so no one knows what percentage of those animals make it through unharmed. Few complaints are received by the U.S. Department of Agriculture, the agency charged with enforcing federal animal welfare regulations, but that doesn't say much. Unsurprisingly, few people think to complain to the Department of Agriculture when an airline mishandles a pet.

The USDA's enforcement activities are largely limited to investigating the complaints it does receive, many of which are forwarded from the Humane Society of the United States in

Washington, D.C. The USDA says it doesn't have the money to inspect airline procedures on a regular basis. Airports that are hubs of animal shipping activity (Kansas City, Missouri, for example, handles lots of laboratory animals) are supposed to be subject to more frequent drop-in inspections.

Penalties for violating the USDA's animal welfare regulations include warning letters and fines. In extreme cases, the airline's license to carry animals may be suspended. United Airlines was fined $11,000 in 1988 for an incident that resulted in the death of three dogs and a large number of monkeys.

Put simply, a lot of things can go wrong when a dog goes on a commercial flight. Most problems occur on the ground, not during a flight. (Conditions on the plane are described in "How Dogs Travel on Airlines," below.) Here are some of the more common problems you should be aware of before you ship a dog.

- **The dog escapes from a cage.** This can lead to tragic results, as it did in 1988 for a small dog named Loekie. Loekie, on a TWA flight from Dallas to Los Angeles, got out of his cage during a stopover in St. Louis. The dog's body was eventually found near an airport road; it had been killed by a car.
- **The cage gets tipped or crushed during transport.** Sturdy kennels alleviate this problem to some degree, but mishandling— for example, putting a pet carrier on a regular baggage carousel— can toss an animal around.
- **The plane is delayed on the ground, with the dog in it.** During flight, the cargo area in which pets travel is pressurized, and the temperature is controlled. But on the ground, no fresh air gets in, and the temperature can fluctuate dramatically in a short time. If you've ever sat in a hot, stuffy plane on a runway during the summer, waiting to take off or pull up to a gate, you can imagine how an animal feels in the even hotter baggage compartment.
- **Baggage handlers remove the dog from the plane during a stopover and then forget to load it on again.** Animals are shipped in a compartment near the door of the plane where baggage is loaded. Thus, unknown to the owner sitting on the plane, they may be removed during a stopover (so that other

baggage can be unloaded more easily), and inadvertently not re-loaded.

- **The dog is shipped to the wrong place.** Just like a suitcase, a dog can end up in the wrong place. Because few airports are equipped to handle animals well, a dog flown to the wrong destination can have a bad or even life-threatening experience waiting for another flight or for you to show up and claim it.

- **The dog is left in the heat, cold or rain.** An animal left outside at an airport may obviously be subject to extreme heat or cold. An English bulldog died of apparent heat stroke in 1984 during transport; the dead dog was sent out on a conveyer belt with other baggage, where it was found by the owner.[2] Winter conditions can be just as devastating.

- **The dog is left unattended, without food or water, in a "lost luggage" storage area.** Because most airlines don't have special places for live animals, animals can sometimes end up abandoned with misplaced baggage. Usually, employees care for the dog as best they can. But if a dog is scared and snappish, as it may well be, it may get little care. Employees may not even know a pet is there.

Even if you plan carefully and everything goes as planned, air travel is frightening and stressful for a dog. And you often can't cope with problems as they come up, because you and your dog are separated during the critical times.

AIRPORT 'ANIMALPORTS'

Notable exceptions to the generally deplorable conditions for animals at airports are the "Animalports" now operating in a few major cities, including New York, Houston and Dallas.

The Animalport at Kennedy Airport in New York City, which is operated by the American Society for the Prevention of Cruelty to Animals (ASPCA), was the first facility of its kind. It's open 24 hours a day and takes care of pets until their owners can get them. The ASPCA will pick up and drop off animals, and will also provide shipping crates. It has weather-proofed outdoor dog runs and a clinic, and a veterinarian is always on call.

A private company runs Animalports in Houston and Dallas, and plans to open one in Miami soon. It will pick up your animal at your door, take it to the boarding facilities at the airport, and make sure the dog gets on the right flight. Employees handle all paperwork, including health certificates if necessary. If animals are stranded at the airport because of flight delay, or because they haven't gone through customs, the airlines deliver them to the Animalport, which takes care of them until they are picked up or put on another flight. The Animalport bills the airline for the cost of care.

How Dogs Travel on Airlines

There are three ways to transport a dog by commercial airline. Your choice will be determined, primarily, by your dog's size. From most to least desirable, the options are:
- carry-on luggage,
- excess baggage, or
- air freight.

Special rules for assistance dogs: Assistance dogs travel with their owners, in the airliner's cabin. (See Chapter 8, Guide, Service, Signal and Therapy Dogs.)

Warning on commuter flights: Some commuter airlines don't accept animals. If you're making connections from a major airline to a commuter line, call first to find out its policy.

Carry-on luggage. If your dog is tiny enough to be comfortable in a pet carrier that fits under an airline seat, you can take it on the plane with you. You can find out the exact measurements of the under-seat space from the airline. Most airlines allow only one animal in the cabin per flight, so don't just show up with your dog; make arrangements when you purchase your own ticket. A travel agent can handle it, or you can talk to the airline directly.

Most airlines currently charge about $30 or $35 for the animal's one-way fare, regardless of destination. Many will also rent or sell you a kennel that will fit under the seat. For example, you can buy a "pet-liner" from United for $15.

This is by far the best way to fly with your dog. Aside from being stuck in a carrier for a while (and not being able to stick its head out the window), it's not much different for the dog than a car ride.

Excess baggage. When you're traveling with your dog, the dog can usually travel as excess baggage. The dog travels on the same plane you do, in a cargo compartment that's pressurized, lighted, and heated. It's where all kinds of fragile items (flowers and musical instruments, for example) travel, according to airline officials.

Most airlines use the USDA regulations for commercial animal shippers as a guide for all animals they accept for shipment. These regulations require animals to be shipped in individual carriers big enough for them to sit, stand, turn around and lie down in.[3] TWA's rules say a dog must be in a leak-proof kennel and must further be "harmless, odorless, inoffensive and require no attention during transit." (Kennels are discussed below.)

Many airlines require a veterinarian's certificate, saying that the dog is healthy and has had a rabies vaccination, before they will accept a dog to be shipped as excess baggage. You must present the certificate when you check in with the dog before your flight. The airlines that demand a certificate also vary on how recent it must be; Pan Am says only that it must be dated within a "reasonable time," while United won't accept one older than 30 days. This requirement is imposed by the airline, not by the law. The federal law that requires health certificates for animals shipped by air applies only to commercial animal shippers (dealers, exhibitors, research facilities, and others).[4]

Even if you are all set with a health certificate and carrier, you should notify the airline in advance that you want to ship a dog as excess baggage. Each plane will only carry a few animals, and certain items—things being kept cold with dry ice, for example—can't be put into the compartment with live animals.

Shipping a dog as excess baggage currently costs about $30 to $50, no matter what the destination. (Some airlines base their charge on the dog's size or weight.) You must also buy a carrier, or rent one from the airline. United, for example, will rent a 27" x 20" x 19" carrier for $35. You can pick up the carrier at the airport when you go to catch your flight.

By now, you doubtless sense a recurring theme: to an airline, your pet is just an especially bothersome piece of luggage. And the size and weight limits that airlines impose on excess baggage apply to animals just like they apply to suitcases. That means if you have an extra-large dog, you may have to classify it as air freight instead of excess baggage—which means you're going to pay an extra-large price to ship it. On TWA, for example, anything over 100 pounds (counting the dog and the carrier together) must go air freight. A large carrier (26" x 42" x 30") weighs about 25 to 30 pounds. Air freight is discussed just below.

DOG CARRIERS (standard sizes)

width	depth	height	suitable for
12"	20"	15"	toy breeds
17	24	20	beagles, Pekingese, dachshunds
21	30	24	Shelties, bulldogs, springer spaniels
23	35	26	Dobermans, Labradors, collies
26	42	30	Malamutes, Afghan hounds

The carrier must be labeled both "Live Animals" and "This End Up" in one-inch or bigger letters. The ASPCA recommends lining the bottom of the carrier with shredded paper or other absorbent material.

Air freight. If you're not traveling with your dog, or if your dog is too big to meet excess baggage size limitations, the only alternative may be air freight. It's a poor option, for lots of reasons.

First of all, air freight is tremendously expensive. If you think of it as sending an overnight mail letter—one that weighs 100 pounds or so—you'll get the idea. That doesn't even count the cost of the carrier, which for big dogs can be close to $100.

The price is based on either the actual weight or the "dimensional poundage" of the carrier and dog, whichever is greater. Dimensional poundage is usually more than the actual poundage. TWA figures dimensional weight by multiplying the three dimensions (height, length, and width) of the carrier together and dividing by 194.

For example, say you want to ship a 100-pound dog from Chicago to San Francisco. Your carrier measures 30" x 40" x 28." With the dog in it, the carrier weighs 125 pounds. The dimensional poundage is calculated like this:

30 x 40 x 28 = 33,600

33,600/194 = 173 lbs. dimensional poundage

The shipping rate is $240 per 100 pounds. You must use the dimensional poundage figure (173 pounds) because it's greater than the actual poundage (125 pounds). That means you're going to be paying $415.20 to ship the dog one way.

If you're only using air freight because you want to send a dog somewhere without you, and it could travel as excess baggage if you went, too, it may be cheaper just to fly along. Your fare plus the excess baggage rate could be less than the cost of air freight. And in light of the problems in air travel discussed earlier, it's obviously a good idea to be around to check up on how the airline is handling your pet.

Additional regulations may apply to dogs shipped as air freight. TWA, for example, requires a health certificate (signed by a veterinarian within the previous 10 days) and rabies vaccination certificate for animals shipped air freight, but not for those carried as excess baggage.

Airline Liability Limits

Whenever you ship a dog, you run the risk that the dog will be injured. What you may not realize is that unless you buy extra liability coverage for a dog you ship by air, and something does happen to the dog, you may get stuck with the airline's decision about how much it will pay for your loss—probably just a few hundred dollars, no matter how much you lose.

Note on International Flights: Claims for damage that occurs during international flights are covered by special rules. (See "International Travel" below.)

How Liability Limits Work

The "NOTICE OF BAGGAGE LIABILITY LIMITATIONS" on the back of the ticket below says that the airline's liability for loss, delay, or damage to baggage is limited to a certain amount unless the passenger declared a higher value for the baggage and paid an additional fee to transport it. Remember, your dog is classified as baggage (carry-on or excess) unless you ship it air freight. Similar liability limits also apply to air freight.

ADVICE TO INTERNATIONAL PASSENGERS ON LIMITATION OF LIABILITY

Passengers on a journey involving an ultimate destination or a stop in a country other than the country of origin are advised that the provisions of a treaty known as the Warsaw Convention may be applicable to the entire journey, including any portion entirely within the country of origin or destination. For such passengers on a journey, to, from, or with an agreed stopping place in the United States of America, the Convention and special contracts of carriage embodied in applicable tariffs provide that the liability of certain carriers parties to such special contracts for death of or personal injury to passengers is limited in most cases to proven damages not to exceed U.S. $75,000* per passenger, and that this liability up to such limit shall not depend on negligence on the part of the carrier. For such passengers traveling by a carrier not a party to such special contracts or on a journey not to, from, or having an agreed stopping place in the United States of America, liability of the carrier for death or personal injury to passengers is limited in most cases to approximately U.S. $10,000 or U.S. $20,000.

The names of carriers parties to such special contracts are available at all ticket offices of such carriers and may be examined on request.

Additional protection can usually be obtained by purchasing insurance from a private company. Such insurance is not affected by any limitation of the carrier's liability under the Warsaw Convention or such special contract of carriage. For further information, please consult your airline or insurance company representative.

*The limit of liability of seventy–five thousand United States Dollars above is inclusive of legal fees and costs except that in case of a claim brought in a State where provision is made for separate award of legal fees and costs, the limit shall be the sum of fifty–eight thousand United States Dollars exclusive of legal fees and costs.

NOTICE OF BAGGAGE LIABILITY LIMITATIONS

Liability for loss, delay, or damage to baggage is limited, unless a higher value is declared in advance and additional charges are paid. For most international travel (including domestic portions of international journeys), this limit is approximately $9.07 per pound ($20.00 per kilo) for checked baggage and $400 per passenger for unchecked baggage. Pursuant to TWA's tariff regulations, the weight of each piece of your checked baggage shall be deemed to be the maximum acceptable weight of 70 pounds (32 kilos), unless otherwise stated on the baggage check. This establishes a standard limitation of liability for international travel of $640 per piece of checked baggage. This limit may be lower where the passenger utilizes connecting carriers.

For travel solely between U.S. points, Federal rules require any limit on an airline's baggage liability to be at least $1250 per passenger which is the maximum limit of liability for a TWA passenger. Excess valuation may be obtained for both Domestic and International travel. TWA is not responsible for jewelry, cash, camera equipment, or other similar valuable items contained in checked or unchecked baggage and excess valuation may not be declared on such items. Carriers assume no liability for fragile or perishable articles. Further information may be obtained from the carrier.

The airline can't declare itself free of all financial responsibility for its carelessness toward baggage. It can and does, however, limit its liability to a few hundred dollars. In general, for a liability limit written in fine print to hold up in court, the passenger must have had:
- notice of the limit, and
- an opportunity to declare a higher value for the baggage.

That rule is a compromise, reached by the courts. The theory is that you agree to the liability limit in exchange for getting to pay the relatively inexpensive baggage rate to ship the dog. The airline can charge the low rate because it doesn't risk being liable for a huge amount of money if something goes wrong. And you have the chance to declare a higher value if you want.

That's the theory. The reality is that this "agreement" exists mostly in lawyers' minds. After all, it's not as if you bargain with the reservation clerk every time you buy a ticket, and finally agree that you'll accept a certain limit on the airline's liability in exchange for a certain fare. Most people never even glance at the back of their airline tickets. Not surprisingly, they assume that if an airline damages their baggage—luggage, animals, whatever—the airline will be responsible for paying a reasonable amount for the damage.

Before an airline can limit the amount it will pay, it must:

1. Notify you of the limit. If as a passenger, you honestly have no reason to know about a liability limit, it obviously isn't reasonable to bind you to its terms. Courts look primarily at two factors: first, how obvious the limit written on the ticket is, and second, the circumstances surrounding its purchase.

If the liability provision is buried in the fine print on the back of a ticket, a court may rule that you weren't given adequate notice. The limit must be clear and conspicuous, in big enough type to draw attention to itself. The language of the limit must be comprehensible. You may also be able to challenge the notice if the ticket says only that the complete liability limit rules are in a booklet that you have to ask for at the ticket counter.

If you didn't have time to read the ticket—if you bought it at the gate five minutes before your flight took off, and you're not an experienced passenger—you may not be held to its limits. But if you're familiar with flying and with baggage liability limits, and you had your ticket days or weeks in advance, you will probably be held responsible for knowing what's written on it. The same is true if you were notified in some other way—by a conspicuous sign on the ticket counter, for example, or if an airline employee told you.

2. Give you a chance to declare a higher value for the baggage. The airline must also give you a fair opportunity to declare a higher value for your dog, and pay a correspondingly higher shipping fee. If it doesn't, you won't be held to the liability limit.

Most airlines do allow passengers to declare a higher value for baggage. The ticket will probably only inform you that you have this option; to find out how much the added liability coverage will cost you, you'll have to ask the airline. (See "Getting Extra Coverage," below.)

Example: In 1983, Thomas Deiro shipped nine racing greyhounds by air from Portland to Boston. The airline left the dogs in their cages on a baggage cart in the sun, in 97° heat, during a stopover in Dallas. Seven of them died, and the others were injured. Deiro sued American Airlines for $900,000.

The court awarded him $750.[5]

The court analyzed the factors discussed above and decided that Deiro, who was an experienced traveler and regularly shipped dogs by air, should have declared a higher value for his greyhounds. Deiro had received his ticket nine days before his flight, but hadn't bothered to read all the print on the back. He paid dearly for his casual attitude.

"We find it difficult," the court stated, "to imagine how any passenger with Deiro's experience, planning to check a quarter of a million dollars worth of baggage, could have had more opportunity or incentive to familiarize himself with the baggage liability provisions." The court upheld the airline's baggage liability limit. That's how, after losing seven dogs and spending four years in legal battles, Deiro ended up getting $750 from the airline.

Getting Extra Coverage

If you don't want to abide by an airline's liability limit, you can either get extra liability coverage from the airline or buy insurance from a private insurer. Obviously, if you're shipping economically valuable dogs, it will be worth your while to investigate. You can find out how much the airline charges for extra coverage by getting a copy of the airline's "contract of carriage," which is available at the ticket counter.

To get the airline to agree to a higher liability limit, you must declare that the dog's value is over the liability limit. The airline will charge you a higher fee, and you will be covered, if anything happens to the dog, for the value you declared. For example, say you are shipping a show dog worth $10,000 as excess baggage, and the airline limits its liability to $750. Before the trip, tell the airline that you want to declare a higher value on the dog. The airline will charge you an extra fee based on the $9,250 of excess declared value.

The airline may limit the amount you can declare to a few thousand dollars. Above that amount, you will have to talk to private insurance companies to get coverage. Obviously, this all takes lots of time—another reason you should make your arrangements well ahead of time. Don't expect to take care of everything when you show up to get your boarding pass.

The same goes for air freight. Airlines limit their liability, and you have the same options to obtain more coverage. TWA's rates and coverage are fairly representative: the airline limits its liability to $9.07 per pound, and declaring a higher value costs 40¢ per $100 of excess declared value. To take the example used above, say you're shipping a 100-pound dog as air freight. The dog and carrier together weigh 125 pounds. So unless you declare a higher value, the airline's liability is limited to $1,133.75 (that is, $9.07 x 125 pounds). To increase liability coverage to $2,000 would cost just $3.47 ($866.25 worth of coverage at 40¢/$100).

How Do You Figure Damages?

If your dog performs in races or shows, it may be relatively easy to put a dollar value on your claim if the dog is injured or killed during air travel. But if you got your dog free from the pound, and its value is emotional rather than economic, what must the airline pay you in damages?

It's a difficult question, and the answer seems to be changing as more and more courts become willing to take into account non-economic factors in calculating the amount of money it takes to compensate an owner for the loss of a dog. (How to put a value on your economic loss and emotional distress is discussed in Chapter 9, If a Dog Is Injured or Killed.)

Remember that you can only sue for *your* loss—the loss of or injury to your property, the dog. The dog can't sue for its own suffering. A $50,000 law suit brought in a dog's name against USAir, for example, was thrown out by a federal court in New York. The dog had been left on a conveyor belt in the Tampa, Florida airport, after its owners' flight took off.[6]

Advice for Travelers

Phyllis Wright, of the Humane Society of the United States, deals with airlines and dog owners who complain about them. She's not encouraged by what she sees, including the rising number of complaints. She says flatly that she wouldn't ship a dog on a commercial flight, except as carry-on baggage, if there were any possible way to avoid it.

But if you must ship a dog, Wright urges a simple strategy: "Raise hell." It's no time to be a shrinking violet, she says. It's up to you to make sure your dog is on the plane every time you take off. She suggests that you ask a flight attendant for confirmation from the baggage handlers that the dog is on board—or talk to the baggage people yourself. Be polite, but be persistent.

If you can, book a non-stop flight, even if it means choosing a less convenient schedule or airport. Most problems occur in airports, not during flights. Missed connections are a prime source of complications when you're shipping a dog; make sure there is enough time between flights to get all the baggage loaded on the connecting flight. You can also do valuable research on how often a certain flight is delayed; statistics are now available from the airlines. When you tentatively schedule a flight, ask the travel agent or airline representative what the on-time percentage is for that flight. Avoiding peak times (holiday weekends, for example) may also get you more cooperation from airline personnel. During hot weather, avoid flights in the hottest part of the day. During cold weather, try to schedule a stopover in a southern city instead of a cold northern one.

Be sure to get a well-made kennel for your dog. Watch out for ones that use wing nuts to attach the top and bottom. The wing nuts have been known to come off because of the vibration of the plane. You may also want to put a note on the outside of your dog's cage. The note should include the dog's name, your name, destination, flight numbers, and any special instructions or cautions.

Don't feed your animal for six hours before the flight, but attach containers of food and water to the outside of the carrier, if possible. This will allow someone to feed and water the dog without opening the cage. Opening the cage is to be avoided as much as is possible: it not only makes the handler risk getting bitten, but also might let the dog escape.

Your dog, of course, should be wearing an identification tag—but not just one that gives the address you've just left, where there may be nobody home. Attach a tag with your destination, including a phone number where you can be reached.

What about mildly tranquilizing your dog? As a general rule, you should not tranquilize an animal unless there's a specific good reason for it. Tranquilized dogs may be more susceptible to breathing problems, especially if they get overheated. And tranquilizers slow down an animal's metabolism, which is also affected by the change in pressure during flight. A less drastic alternative is motion sickness medication, which a veterinarian can prescribe. Talk to a vet who's familiar with your animal before you decide on a strategy. The best course to follow often depends on the dog's temperament, health and metabolism.

CHECKLIST FOR AIR TRAVEL

Did you book the most direct and reliable flight?

Does the airline know you're bringing an animal, and do you know all the airline's rules?

Have you obtained health or vaccination certificates, if necessary?

Is the kennel big enough for the dog to stand up, lie down, and turn around in comfortably?

Is the kennel sturdy and well-ventilated?

Have you securely attached your name, address and phone number, and any special instructions, to the outside and inside of the kennel?

Have you labeled the kennel "Live Animals" and "This End Up" in letters at least an inch high?

Is the dog wearing an identification tag and a snug but comfortable collar (*not* a chain collar, which could get caught on something and choke the dog)?

Have you obtained adequate liability coverage for your dog, from the airline or an outside insurer?

Special Hawaii Rules

Unless you're crossing national borders, you don't usually need to worry about special restrictions on taking your dog with you. But if you want to take your pet for a tropical vacation, you need to know that Hawaii quarantines *all* dogs—including guide and service dogs—for 120 days when they enter the state. As a result, rabies is nonexistent in Hawaii.

Not only do you have to give up your pet for four months, you have to pay for it: the current cost totals $366, payable when the dog arrives in Hawaii. Airlines deliver pets directly to a state holding facility, and the state takes them to the quarantine station on the Island of Oahu. Dogs are kept in individual outdoor runs. Owners can visit their dogs daily during afternoon visiting hours, but cannot take the animals out of the kennel.

State officials stress that it's important for owners to arrange, in advance, for a private animal hospital to provide emergency veterinary care. The quarantine center handles minor ailments, but it does not have facilities for major medical problems. Unless a veterinary hospital has agreed in advance to accept an ill pet, the state will not take the animal to a private hospital.

For more information, write to:

>State of Hawaii
>Department of Agriculture
>Division of Animal Industry
>99-762 Moanalua Road
>Aiea, Hawaii 96701-3246

International Travel

International travel involves a whole new set of considerations and regulations. If you're taking a dog abroad, be sure to investigate restrictions well in advance of your trip. Here are the issues to consider:

Entrance Restrictions

Some countries require health certificates and proof of rabies vaccination before they will admit a dog; others have mandatory quarantine periods for all animals entering the country. To find out what rules apply to you, contact the nearest consulate of the country to which you want to take your dog.

INTERNATIONAL TRAVEL RESTRICTIONS

To take a dog into:	You must have:
Canada	Health and vaccination certificates no more than 3 years old.
Mexico	Health certificate from veterinarian, approved in advance by U.S. Agriculture Veterinarian Services and Mexican consulate. There is a fee for approval.
England	Must apply for import permit from Ministry of Agriculture at least 8 weeks in advance. Dogs are quarantined for 6 months.
Japan	Dogs must have veterinary certificate dated within 10 days of departure and rabies vaccination certificate dated a month to a year before entry. The certificate must be stamped by a USDA veterinarian from the animal's area of origin. Dogs coming from the U.S. are quarantined for 14 days.
United States	Must have rabies vaccination certificate (unless dog is coming from certain countries, including Great Britain, Australia and Japan), listing date of vaccination and type of vaccine.

For more information, get *Traveling With Your Pet* from the American Society for the Prevention of Cruelty to Animals, 441 E. 92d St., New York, NY 10128, for $5.

Injuries During International Flights

A person whose animal is injured during an international flight must notify the airline in writing within seven days of receiving the injured animal. If, however, the animal has been lost or killed—not just injured—such notice isn't required, according to at least one United States court.[7]

As always when flying, it's a good idea to check the airline's liability limitations before you fly. You may want to declare a higher value for your dog. (See "Airline Liability Limits," above.)

On the Road

Transporting your dog in a car instead of a plane obviously gives you more flexibility and control. It has its own problems, of course: heat, space, food and water and, especially, accommodations along the way.

A list of motels that accept dogs is available from the Gaines Dog Food Company. It's called "Touring with Towser" (no kidding) and can be ordered by sending $1.50 to Gaines TWT, P.O. Box 5700, Kankakee, IL 60902.

Guide and service dogs are allowed, under most state laws, to stay in all motels and hotels, even if they don't accept other pets.

North Carolina Note: North Carolina law makes it a misdemeanor for a motel, hotel or guest to allow a dog in a bedroom used by people.[8]

Guide dogs are exempt from this restriction. If you're going to be staying in North Carolina, check ahead to see if the motel you want to stay in has kennel facilities.

Some counties and states impose restrictions on how dogs can be transported in vehicles. California, for example, requires dogs in open pickup truck beds to be in cages or cross-tied, so that they don't get thrown from the truck. (See Chapter 2, State and Local Regulation.)

Buses, Trains and Ships

Many bus lines simply don't accept animals, except guide dogs. If you want to transport a dog by bus, train, or ship, it's best to talk to the folks in charge and conduct your own inspection of the facilities. If you can't keep your pet with you when you travel, be sure to look at the area where the dog will be confined during the trip.

---

[1]The last available estimate was from the now-defunct Civil Aeronautics Board, which estimated that 3,700 animals flew on domestic flights every day in 1973.

[2]Comment, "Air Transportation of Animals: Passengers or Property?" 51 J. Air Law and Commerce 497, 502 (1986).

[3]9 C.F.R Ch. 1, § 3.12.

[4]7 U.S.C. § 2143(f).

[5]*Deiro v. American Airlines, Inc.,* 816 F.2d 1360 (9th Cir. 1987).

[6]Los Angeles Daily Journal, Jan. 7, 1987, p. 1.

[7]*Dalton v. Delta Airlines,* 570 F.2d 1244 (5th Cir. 1978).

[8]N.C. Gen. Stat. § 72-7.

7

RESOLVING DISPUTES
WITH NEIGHBORS

mediation / animal control authorities / police /
special local programs / small claims court

[T]he very best of [dogs] can, with less effort and in a shorter space of time, make themselves more of a nuisance to the square inch than any other domestic quadruped of which we have any knowledge.

—California Court of Appeal[1]

Dogs are usually more of a nuisance than a danger, but bothersome dogs can be a serious matter. Just ask anyone who's lived next door to one. Having a dog that's a nuisance to others isn't, literally, a crime, but judges are sometimes moved to discuss these problems in the stern terms of the criminal law: barking dogs may "murder sleep," said one judge who presumably had some first-hand experience.

If a dog habitually barks, digs up the neighbor's garden, evacuates last night's kibble on lawns down the street, or is otherwise obnoxious, the neighbors can, in theory, sue the dog owner to get the nuisance stopped and to recover money damages. If your response to this news is "thanks for nothing," we understand. For either side of the dispute, substituting a major hassle with expensive lawyers for a small one with a bad-mannered spaniel isn't our idea of progress, either. It brings to mind Ambrose Bierce's definition of a lawsuit: "a machine which you go into as a pig and come out of as a sausage."

And nobody wants to get into a time-consuming and anxiety-producing lawsuit—although small claims court, if it's available, may be an exception— against a neighbor. The only things you're guaranteed to get are lawyer's bills and the everlasting wrath of the neighbor.

Luckily, there are a fair number of alternative ways to solve dog problems that should keep you out of court and on relatively good terms with the neighbors. In this chapter, we discuss the most promising ways to resolve neighborhood dog disputes.

Talk to Your Neighbor

There is no such thing as a difficult dog, only an inexperienced owner.

—Barbara Woodhouse[2]

This most basic step is either ignored or botched by a surprising number of people. Perhaps it's not all that surprising: approaching someone with a complaint can be unpleasant, and in some cases intimidating. And if the problem is that you're afraid of your neighbor's burly watchdog, which snarls at you whenever you come near its owner's house, you're probably not eager to drop by to discuss things.

If you're the target of a complaint about your dog's behavior, you should at least be willing to talk about the problem, even if you think your neighbor is being completely unreasonable. If your neighbor is threatening to call the police, or retaliating for your dog's offenses by parking in front of your driveway, it's in your interest to solve the problem quickly, before it escalates into something that can't be resolved without a legal battle.

Talking to your neighbor calmly and reasonably is an essential first step. Even if you do eventually end up in court, a judge isn't likely to be too sympathetic if you didn't make at least some effort to work things out first. So it's a no-lose situation, and if you approach it with a modicum of tact, you may be pleasantly surprised by the neighbor's willingness to work toward a solution.

Sometimes owners are blissfully unaware that there's a problem. If a dog barks for hours every day—but only when it's left alone— the owner may not know that a neighbor is being driven crazy by a dog the owner thinks is quiet and well-mannered. If you have a complaint, even if you're sure the neighbor does know about the dog's anti-social behavior, it may be better to proceed as though she doesn't: "I knew you'd want to know that Rusty was digging up my zucchini, so that you could prevent it from happening again."

SHHH! ARKANSAS GETS TOUGH

A law on the books in Little Rock, Arkansas (Ordinance 6232) says that dogs are not allowed to bark after 6 p.m. and husbands are not allowed to hammer after 6 p.m.

Some common problems, such as barking or digging under fences, may be relatively easy to correct with proper training of both the dog and the owner. Often, local humane societies offer free advice and referrals to trainers or obedience schools. The San Francisco SPCA chapter, for example, has a "hotline" owners can call. A staff member answers questions and suggests solutions for hundreds of frustrated pet owners every year. Before you talk to your neighbor, make a few phone calls and see if there are some resources you can suggest during your talk.

Here are some suggestions on how to get the most from your negotiations:

- Write a friendly note or call to arrange a convenient time to talk. Don't blunder up some rainy evening when the neighbor is trying to drag groceries and kids in the house after work.
- If you think it's appropriate, take a little something to the meeting to break the ice: some vegetables from your garden, perhaps.
- If a neighbor is complaining about your dog, and you think he's being unreasonable, try to find out the exact problem. It may be easily solved—or the real problem may not be the dog at all.
- Don't threaten legal action (or worse, illegal action). There will be plenty of time to discuss legal remedies if relations deteriorate.
- Offer positive suggestions. Once you have established some rapport, you may want to suggest, tactfully, that the owner get help with the dog. Try saying something like: "You know, my friend Tom had the same problem with his dog, and since he's been taking the dog to ABC Obedience School classes, he and his neighbors are much happier." Caution: If you make suggestions too early in the process, the neighbor may resent your "interference."
- Try to agree on specific actions to alleviate the problem: for example, that the dog will be kept inside between 10 p.m. and 8 a.m.
- After you agree on a plan, set a date to talk again in a couple of weeks. If your next meeting is already arranged, it will be easier for you to talk again. It won't look like you're badgering your neighbor, but will show that's you're serious about getting the problem solved.
- If the situation improves, make a point to say thanks. Not only is it the nice thing to do, it will also encourage more progress.

Mediation: Getting Another Person to Help

If talking to your neighbor directly doesn't work, or you're convinced it's hopeless, consider getting some help from a mediator. A mediator won't make a decision for you, but will help you and your neighbor agree on a resolution of the problem.

Mediators, both professional and volunteers, are trained to listen to both sides, identify problems, keep everyone focused on the real problems and suggest compromises. Going through the process helps both people feel they've been heard (a more constructive version of the satisfaction of "having your day in court") and often puts people on better terms.

Mediation provides a safe, structured way for neighbors to talk. Those interested in the dispute meet informally with one or more mediators. The typical procedure is first to agree on ground rules—simple guidelines as basic as agreeing not to call each other names or interrupt. Then, each side briefly states a view of the problem. The mediator may summarize the problem and its history before moving on to discuss possible solutions.

The key to mediation is that, unlike a lawsuit, it is not an adversarial process. You do *not* go to mediation to argue your side. No judge-like person makes a decision for you. So there is nothing to gain from the lying and manipulation common to the courtroom; the outcome is in the hands of the people who have the dispute. Until both agree, there is no resolution. People can become amazingly cooperative when they realize it's in their power—and no one else's—to resolve their problem.

A frequent consequence of mediation is that those involved in the dispute discover that the problem they think they have—a nuisance dog, for example—isn't the main problem at all. It may turn out that the reason one neighbor hasn't controlled her dog better is that she's upset about the other's plum tree, which drops messy fruit on her side of the fence. Mediation often brings out these hidden agendas. If one neighbor solves the tree problem by pruning a few overhanging branches, he may find that his neighbor suddenly finds a way to make her dog behave.

When two people do agree on how to alleviate the problem, it's best to put the agreement in writing. The goal is not to make it legally binding—the whole point of mediation is not to rely on some outside authority, like the courts, to make or enforce decisions. But writing down the agreement helps clarify everyone's expectations. And it's invaluable if, later, memories grow fuzzy, as they almost always do, about who agreed to do what. A sample agreement is shown later in this chapter.

Where to Find a Mediator

The best place to look for a mediator for a neighborhood dispute is a community mediation group. Many cities—unfortunately, by no means all—have such groups, which usually train volunteers to mediate disputes in their own neighborhoods.

Community Boards, in San Francisco, has served as a model for programs across the country. Volunteers undergo intensive training and then, usually in panels of four, hear disputes from residents of their neighborhoods. Mediation is free. Community Boards estimates that about one in ten of its complaints involve pets. That's another advantage of volunteer mediators: they are likely to be familiar with dog disputes. (A typical Community Boards mediation session is outlined below.)

Don't overlook sources close to home. For example, someone active in a neighborhood association, if neutral in the dispute, might make a good amateur mediator. For that matter, anyone who's respected by the people involved in the dispute might be able to help. Someone who's lived in the area a long time may have some good ideas, but you'll never know unless you ask.

It's crucial that the mediator not only be neutral about the dispute, but also understand the necessity of staying neutral during mediation. Again, the mediator's function is not to impose a solution or choose sides after hearing each side argue; it's to open communication and help develop an agreement between them.

City and county governments sometimes offer mediation services of their own, or can refer you to organizations that do. Call the courthouse information number to find out. The district attorney's office, or even radio or television stations that take "action line" calls, may also be able to refer you to a mediation service.

Another good source may be a state or local bar association, which may keep a list of organizations that offer mediation. Many state bar associations publish directories of all local dispute resolution programs in the state.

If your community doesn't have a volunteer or city-sponsored mediation service, you can look for a professional mediator. Most of them, however, specialize in some area, such as disputed divorces or child custody matters. Their fees may not be worth it to you unless your only alternative is the costly one of hiring a lawyer and going to court.

Mediating Dogfights

Here's an example of a typical mediation from Community Boards, a San Francisco organization of volunteer mediators. It's based on an actual dispute.

Maxine called the SPCA and police because her neighbor's dog frightened her and woke her with its barking. The police suggested Community Boards. Don, the dog's owner, was anxious to stop what he considered Maxine's "harassment" and readily agreed to mediation. A Community Boards volunteer talked to Maxine and Don separately, wrote a short summary ("case report") outlining the problem, and scheduled a hearing.

At the hearing, after the introductions and preliminaries, the volunteer mediator read the case report. The problem was that Don's dog growled and barked at Maxine when she came home from work late each night, and woke her in the morning when it barked at anyone who rang the doorbell of Don's house. She called the SPCA because she thought the dog barked because it was being mistreated. She hadn't approached Don directly because she was afraid of the dog.

Don was upset and embarrassed by visits from police and letters from the SPCA. He'd had his dog, Aspen, for five years without any problems. He considered himself a responsible pet owner, and Aspen a good dog and a positive addition to the community.

Maxine was the first to give her opinion of the problem. "I'm so tired of all that barking and snarling! That dog is vicious, and he ought to be put away!"

Don protested that the dog served as a watchdog in a neighborhood where that was needed, barking only at strangers and unfriendly people like Maxine. "He wouldn't need to bark if you didn't make those threatening gestures."

As tension escalated, the meditators stepped in to keep Maxine and Don, who were obviously angry and uncomfortable, talking civilly about the issues. The next phase was the hardest: getting them to talk face to face.

"We would like you to talk to each other about your conflict directly," said one mediator, Joe. "Please turn your chairs to face each other."

"I don't want to talk to him," said Maxine. "Why can't you just tell him to get rid of the dog?"

"Our job is to help both of you reach your own solution," Joe reminded her. "Please talk to Don directly."

"Well, I don't think this will do any good. I can't talk to anyone who says I am harassing him. All I want is peace in my own home without being awakened or jumped on by a dangerous dog."

"I really resent that!" said Don. "Aspen's not dangerous. He's just protecting his home. If you'd stop yelling at him, he wouldn't bark or jump at you."

Another mediator, Kate, intervened, bringing Don and Maxine back to the noise problem. "Maxine, you mentioned two noise problems, during the day while you're trying to sleep, and when you are home at night, right?"

Maxine nodded. "The dog wakes me up around 9 or 10 in the morning. It seems like every morning . . . then I can't get back to sleep."

"If those salesman and religious fanatics and political freaks would stop ringing the doorbell and leaving their literature, " Don interrupted, "that's why he barks. He's just protecting his home."

"From what?" demanded Maxine. "Someone collecting signatures on a petition? Why does he throw himself against the fence and growl and show his teeth when I come from work? It scares me so much that some nights I don't even want to come home!"

"So Don's yard is right next to your front door?" asked Kate.

"Yes," answered Maxine. "I let myself in along the side of the building, and that dog is always there in the yard. He growls while I'm trying to get my door unlocked. It's scary. I'm afraid he'll break the fence down and attack me."

"Don, can you repeat what Maxine just said?" asked Kate.

"Yes, she said she was scared. But if she would take the time to meet Aspen, he wouldn't growl because he would know her."

"Would you tell Maxine that, please?" asked Kate.

Don turned back to Maxine. "You're afraid that Aspen will attack you."

"Yes, I got bitten badly when I was growing up, and I'm afraid of dogs."

"Aspen's very gentle," said Don, more sympathetically. "He doesn't ever bark at people he knows. Maybe if he got to know you, you would see that you don't need to be afraid of him."

Joe shifted the discussion to Don's problems. "Don, please tell Maxine about having the police come to your home."

"It's so embarrassing!" answered Don. "I'm afraid that the landlady will find out and get mad, and make me move or get rid of Aspen. Also, I don't want my neighbors thinking I'm a drug dealer or something."

After some more discussion, the mediators began to help Maxine and Don clarify their progress.

"Maxine, do you understand Don's position now?" asked Joe.

"I realize that Don's dog wasn't barking or threatening me on purpose. Also I know that he wants to be a good neighbor."

"I realize now that Maxine was frightened of dogs because of her childhood experience and that she was really afraid Aspen would hurt her," said Don. "Also, she called the police because she didn't think that I would listen to her."

"Maxine, if the dog's noise bothers you again, what might you do differently?" asked Kate.

"I wouldn't call the police, at least not if I could talk to Don first," replied Maxine.

"What about you, Don?"

"I would try to take care of the noise problem, and try to make Maxine feel welcome in the neighborhood," answered Don.

Next, the meditators helped Maxine and Don work together on a written resolution. One mediator read from the notes taken during the hearing, and suggested areas of agreement. Here's what they came up with:

▲

Agreement

Maxine Green and Don Kaufman wish to settle a dispute over Don's dog, Aspen. Don recognizes that Aspen frightens Maxine and bothers her with his barking. Maxine recognizes that by her behavior she has sometimes inadvertently provoked the dog's barking, and that she has exacerbated the problem between Don and herself by calling the police when the dog barks.

Maxine and Don agree that:

- Maxine will call Don instead of the police or humane society when Aspen barks.

- Don will disconnect his doorbell during the day to prevent Aspen from barking.

- Maxine will come over and meet Aspen this week, so he will become familiar with her.

- Don will stay up a few nights next week and meet Maxine, with Aspen, when she comes home from work, so that Aspen knows Maxine is friendly.

- If they have future disputes, Maxine and Don will again try to talk, with or without a mediator, to work things out amicably.

_____   _____

Maxine Green   Date

_____   _____

Don Kaufman   Date

▼

Animal Control Authorities

If your efforts at working something out with your neighbor haven't succeeded, talk to the animal control department in your city or county. The people there are likely to be more receptive than the police or other municipal officials who, if they take the matter seriously, will most often call the offending dog owner with a warning or, if the problem persists, issue a citation.

When you call local animal control authorities, don't just make your complaint and hang up. If it's really a persistent problem, you need to be persistent, too. Find out how to follow up and get results. Ask the person you talk to—and write down his name, so you won't have to explain your problem every time you call—about the department's procedures. Find out what the department will do, and when. They sometimes work in strange ways. For example, if the problem is a barking dog, the department may need to receive a certain number of complaints within a certain time before it will act. If that's the case, you may want to discuss the problem with neighbors; if they feel as you do, enlist their help.

Barking dog problems usually aren't covered specifically by local law, although a local noise ordinance (no loud noise after 10 p.m., for example) may apply. But other common complaints are likely to be specifically addressed by a local law. You're more likely to get quick results if this is so, and if you're well-informed when you complain to the city.

The local public or law library should have copies of your city and county ordinances. Check for laws that cover:
- excessive barking;
- dogs that run at large;
- dogs that damage property or threaten people; and
- the number of dogs allowed per household.

Special Local Programs

Some cities have finally quit trying to handle dog complaints as each one comes up and have set up special programs for them. This is a great idea, for two main reasons. First, it gives a specific city official or department—usually health, police, or public safety department—responsibility for the problem. Otherwise, if it's not clear who's primarily responsible, someone with a complaint is likely to get shuffled from department to department, explaining the problem to six different people during each call. Assigning the responsibility makes the process of solving the problem more efficient and less frustrating for everybody.

A special program also lets everyone—dog owners and their neighbors—know what they can expect. Without concrete procedures and rules, neither the dog owner, the neighbor, or the city knows what is supposed to happen, legally, if a dog drives the neighborhood crazy with its barking. A predictable system of warnings and sanctions reduces anxiety and gives everyone a chance to modify his own behavior, or that of his animals. Of course, it doesn't do much good unless these rules are published and readily available—which, unfortunately, is rare.

A program that should serve as a model is the Los Angeles system, which is administered by the city's Department of Animal Regulation.[3] This program, although limited to noisy dogs and dogs that run at large, is quick and easy to use, and it makes constructive use of mediation techniques.

All it takes to get the Department into action is one written complaint describing the noise and giving the name, address and phone number of the person making the complaint. The Department then sends the dog's owner a letter, saying it has received a complaint and requesting that steps be taken immediately to abate the noise.

The Department also notifies the person who complained that a letter has been sent to the dog owner. It asks the person to wait 15 days and then, if the situation hasn't improved, to call the Department. About 75% of barking dog problems are solved by the first letter.

If the dog doesn't stop being a nuisance and the neighbor does complain again, the Department sends an officer to the problem dog's house. The officer listens to the dog and looks at where the dog is kept in relation to the neighbor's windows. Next the Department schedules a mandatory meeting of an animal control officer, the dog owner, and the neighbor. The animal control officer makes more suggestions about stopping the noise. The Department estimates that another 15% of problems are solved by this stage.

The most stubborn cases—the remaining 10%— are resolved at a hearing. The officer who conducts the hearing has the power to fine the dog owner, but that's rarely done. Most often, the officer has the dog license reissued with conditions attached. For example, the owner may be required to keep the dog inside at night, or get training for the dog, or have it neutered. If the conditions aren't met, the license is revoked and the owner must get rid of the dog.

Police

The police aren't very interested in barking dog problems, and you can't much blame them. Unless you live in an exceptionally quiet and peaceful place, police have lots more serious problems on their hands. Another reason to avoid the police, except as a last resort, is that summoning a police cruiser to a neighbor's house obviously will not improve your already-strained relations. But if none of the options already discussed works, and the relationship with your neighbor is shot anyway, you might as well give the police a try. The police may be your only choice, too, if you don't know who owns the offending dog, as can happen on crowded city blocks where you just can't tell whose dog is making the noise.

As when you're dealing with animal control people, don't be afraid to ask the police questions about procedures and requirements. Find out exactly what you and other neighbors must do to get the problem addressed. You may well have to make more than one call or written complaint.

Small Claims Court

If nothing you've tried helps, and you decide to go to court, the least painful route is through small claims court. Small claims court procedures are simple and designed to be used without a lawyer. In some states, including California, lawyers are barred from small claims court. Even if they aren't banned, you will rarely see one there because most people find it too expensive to hire them. Fees in small claims court are also low, and the process is relatively fast—which means you'll get to court in a few weeks or months, not years.

What to Find Out Before You Sue

Before you begin, you need to check a few things.

- **Whether you must try to negotiate with the dog's owner.** Many states require proof that you have tried to reach some settlement of the dispute, or at least that you have demanded payment, in writing, before you sue.

- **When you must bring your case.** There is always a limit on how long you have to file a lawsuit after an incident occurs. Usually, it's a year or two. If the problem you want to sue about is ongoing, you have the right to sue as many times as you want (or are willing to) until it stops.

- **How much you can sue for (the "jurisdictional limit").** This varies greatly, from a few hundred to a few thousand dollars. Most states limit the amount you can ask for in small claims court to about $1,000 to $2,000; the chart below lists every state's limits.

- **What kinds of damages you can request.** In some states, you can only ask for compensation for actual losses or injury. Reasonable repair bills for damage to property, or medical bills, for example, are almost always allowed. A few small claims courts, however, do not allow you to request money to compensate for your pain and suffering.

- **What the court can do for you.** What you'd probably like more than anything else is an order from a judge telling your neighbor to make the problematic pooch 1) be quiet, 2) quit using your yard for a toilet, or 3) both of the above and some other things, like quit excavating in the garden, too. Unfortunately, in most small claims courts, you can't get an order (called an injunction) that requires some action to be stopped, even though it's most courts' standard remedy for nuisance. In most states, you can ask a small claims court only for a money judgment.

Still, making your neighbor fork over some money may make you feel better. More importantly, it may be even more effective than a simple court order in convincing your neighbor to clean up his (or his dog's) act. Remember, you can keep going back to court and asking for more as long as the nuisance continues.

How much money should you ask for? There is, obviously, no formula to translate your annoyance into dollars. Some general advice: start with your actual out-of-pocket losses—costs to replace a dead rose bush or damaged fence, for example. Don't spend much time computing your less tangible losses like lost sleep, or time spent cleaning up dog droppings. Small claims courts put a pretty low ceiling on what you can request, anyway, and the judge will make the final decision on what you get. If you've been suffering every day for months, even a small amount, multiplied by all those days, can add up.

IF MONEY ISN'T ENOUGH

If you absolutely must have a court order telling the neighbor to stop (the technical term for this kind of order is an injunction), you may have to go to "regular" court (often called circuit, superior or district court) instead of small claims court. For that, you'll probably need a lawyer, though you can bring a straightforward nuisance suit yourself, if you're willing to spend some hours in the law library finding out how to draw up the papers and submit them to the court. (You can find legal research help in Appendix 1.)

SMALL CLAIMS COURT JURISDICTIONAL LIMITS

Alabama	$1,000	Montana	$1,500
Alaska	$5,000	Nebraska	$1,500
Arizona	$500	Nevada	$1,500
Arkansas	$3,000	New Hampshire	$1,500
California	$2,000	New Jersey	$1,000
Colorado	$1,000	New Mexico	$2,000
Connecticut	$1,500	New York	$2,000
Delaware	$2,500	North Carolina	$1,500
District of Columbia	$2,000	North Dakota	$2,000
Florida	$2,500	Ohio	$1,000
Georgia	$3,000	Oklahoma	$1,500
Hawaii	$2,500	Oregon	$2,500
Idaho	$2,000	Pennsylvania	$5,000
Illinois	$2,500	Puerto Rico	$500
Indiana	$3,000	Rhode Island	$1,500
Iowa	$2,000	South Carolina	$1,000
Kansas	$1,000	South Dakota	$2,000
Kentucky	$1,000	Tennessee	$10,000
Louisiana	$2,000	Texas	$1,000
Maine	$1,400	Utah	$1,000
Maryland	$2,500	Vermont	$2,000
Massachusetts	$1,500	Virginia	$7,000
Michigan	$1,500	Washington	$2,000
Minnesota	$2,000	West Virginia	$3,000
Mississippi	$2,000	Wisconsin	$1,000
Missouri	$1,000	Wyoming	$750

• **Whether you can prove the dog is a nuisance under your state's law.** If you're ready to sue your neighbor in small claims court, you're already convinced that the dog you're complaining about is a nuisance. "Nuisance," however, has a special legal meaning, which has been developing since the Normans conquered England in the 11th century. And you know that anything lawyers have had their hands on that long is bound to be complicated.

Nuisance is defined broadly: it generally includes any condition that interferes with the use of someone's property. Noisy parties in the middle of the night, smelly garbage, and dogs that won't stop barking are all nuisances to the person whose enjoyment of property is affected.

Rules vary from state to state, but you will probably have to prove that the noise (or other problem) is excessive and unreasonable. You may also have to prove that the nuisance causes you actual physical discomfort and annoyance. The key question to ask yourself is this: is the activity you're complaining about unreasonable under the circumstances?

Example 1: Aaron lives next door to Flo, who has two beagles, Flash and Flood. The dogs are well-behaved and quiet, and Flo is considerate of her neighbors, never letting the dogs run loose. But beagles are hounds, and hounds howl. Whenever Flash and Flood hear a fire truck siren, they turn their muzzles skyward and let out mournful howls until the siren has faded from hearing. Sirens are a pretty rare occurrence in this quiet neighborhood. Just the same, Aaron hates the howling.

Is the beagles' baying a legal nuisance to Aaron? Probably not. It's infrequent, doesn't last long, and while mildly annoying, doesn't substantially interfere with his enjoyment of his property. After all, the siren is probably already making more noise than the dogs. Unless a court were prepared to say that it's never reasonable to have dogs in a city, it couldn't really conclude that it's unreasonable for hounds to howl occasionally.

Example 2: Mattie lives next door to Fred, who keeps two German shepherds and one unclassifiable little yapper in his relatively small back yard. The dogs are always outside, and almost always, it seems to Mattie, barking. Their favorite time to chime in together is 6 a.m., when Fred goes out to feed them. Their barking goes on a good five minutes until Fred shuts them up, by yelling at least as loudly as the dogs bark. The commotion often wakes up Mattie, who lies in bed fuming and having revenge fantasies until she can go back to sleep. Mattie is also often bothered by an unpleasant smell from Fred's yard; it's gotten so that she doesn't even open her windows on the side of the house bordering Fred's. And as if that weren't enough, the dogs sometimes leave droppings in Mattie's front yard.

Is Fred's menagerie a nuisance? You bet. The noise is persistent, at its worst at a time when many people are sleeping, and isn't reasonable by any normal community standards. The smell and the droppings are also interfering with Mattie's use of her property.

- **How you go about bringing a case.** Small claims court procedures are supposed to be simple for non-lawyers to use, and they usually are—but you've got to know where to start. Many courts have booklets that explain how to proceed with a suit. Usually, all you need do is complete a fill-in-the-boxes form and file it with a small filing fee. Be sure to get whatever materials your local court has, so you understand its special rules and way of doing things. Help on how to prepare and present your case in the most effective way can also be found in *Everybody's Guide to Small Claims Court*, by Ralph Warner (Nolo Press).

SMALL CLAIMS COURT ADVISORS

Courts in some parts of New York, California and several other states offer free professional help to people who are going to appear in small claims court. In these courts, advisors (lawyers or trained paralegals) answer questions and help people prepare for their court appearances. It's a valuable service which, unfortunately, hasn't caught on everywhere.

Preparing for Court

The most important part of your small claims case comes before you ever set foot in the courtroom. In other words, good preparation is essential.

You need to organize your case logically to present it to the judge. First, make a list of the points you want to get across. Let's take the example of Mattie and Fred, outlined above. Mattie decides she's had enough of the noise and smell of Fred's pack of dogs. She's already tried, unsuccessfully, to get Fred to agree to mediation. The city health department hasn't taken action, either, so she decides to go to small claims court.

Her first stop is the public library, for a look at her city's ordinances. It turns out the city allows three dogs per household, so that won't be any help. But the city also has an ordinance saying dogs that bark loudly and disturb neighbors are a nuisance.

Before Mattie files her claim, she writes Fred a demand letter, shown below. A demand letter is required in some states, but it's always an excellent idea. Even if it doesn't bring results, it's a good way to get your thoughts organized and make sure the person you're complaining about understands your point of view. And once you're in court, it can help you convince a harried small claims court judge that you have exhausted all your other means of solving the problem.

▲

Demand Letter

September 12, 19__

Fred Little
445 Euclid St.
Augusta, Missouri

Dear Mr. Little:

I have spoken to you several times about the problems your three dogs create for the neighborhood: the droppings left on my lawn are a nuisance, the noise and smell emanating from your yard makes it difficult for me to use my yard, and I am frequently awakened at night by the dogs' prolonged barking. This is even more bothersome in the early morning; the noise generated by the dogs' barking when fed at about 6 a.m. every day wakes me and keeps me awake.

I have also spoken to the city health and animal control departments, who have in turn contacted you. You have not responded to their requests to keep the dogs quiet and to clean your yard to eliminate the offensive smell. My attempts to work something out with you have been unsuccessful, and you have refused to try to resolve these problems with the help of a neutral mediator provided by our neighborhood association.

I am making one last formal demand that you stop the nuisance created by your dogs. If you do not correct the problem by next week, I feel I have no alternative but to take the problem to small claims court.

Sincerely,

Mattie Hinman
443 Euclid
Augusta, Missouri

▼

After waiting for a reply from Fred, which never comes, Mattie files her complaint and the court clerk sets a date for the hearing. Next, she sits down to prepare. What does she need to convince the judge of so that she will win?

1. Fred's dogs produce noise and odors that are offensive.

2. The noise, droppings and odor interfere with her use of her property.

3. She should be compensated by Fred for the inconvenience, annoyance and physical discomfort she has suffered as a result.

4. A reasonable amount of damages, figured by calculating $10 a day for the four months she's lived next door to Fred, is $1,200. The small claims court limit in Missouri, however, is $1,000, so that's all Mattie can ask for this time. She can sue again if Fred doesn't stop the nuisance.

Now that she has an outline of what she wants to prove, Mattie must see where her evidence fits. The first item on her agenda is simply to show that the dogs are offensive, loud and smelly. There are two main ways she can do this: with physical evidence (photographs, documents, tape recordings) or with witnesses who will testify to the conditions.

Mattie decides to do both. First, she will take pictures that show how close Fred's yard is to her house, how many dogs he has in his yard and how messy the yard is. Second, she will bring another neighbor, Sarah, as a witness. Sarah lives across the street from Fred, and the dogs' barking has bothered her, too. She can testify both to the loudness of the dogs and the timing of their early morning feeding frenzies. Mattie also asks her friend Jack to testify. He has been to her house and seen the conditions next door.

Then, testimony from Mattie will be the best way to convince the court that the odors and noise from Fred's yard interfere with her use of her property—that is, they constitute a legal nuisance. She should testify to specific instances, complete with dates and times, that illustrate the problem. For example, she can recount the story of a barbecue she tried to have in her back yard, but had to move inside because the dogs' barking next door made talking impossible, and the filthy conditions made breathing unpleasant. The testimony of a guest who was there would help convince the judge, too.

Live testimony is usually preferable: it has a greater impact, and is especially good if the other side has live witnesses, but written statements can also usually be admitted into the court's record of your case. A written statement, which should be brief and to the point, can be in the form of a letter to the court.

Here's a letter that Mattie gets from Jack, who can't testify in person on the day of Mattie's hearing.

▲

Letter in Support of Small Claims Case

Oct. 26, 19__

Presiding Judge
Small Claims Court
Augusta, Missouri

Re: Mattie Hinman vs. Fred Little, Case #45-77889

Dear Judge:

I have visited Mattie Hinman at her home at 443 Euclid Street several times in the four months she has lived there. Twice we tried to sit on her back patio, but both times we were driven inside by the noise and smell from Mr. Little's back yard next door. The dogs (I could see two large German shepherds, and I could hear another dog) barked whenever we came out on the patio.

I'm a dog owner myself, and I know that all dogs bark sometimes. These dogs, however, went on for probably half an hour. The noise was really nerve-wracking, and the smell was sickening.

Sincerely,

Jack Oster
849 Oakmont Ave.
Augusta, Missouri

▼

Some courts also allow testimony by telephone if a witness is unable to make it to court. You can check with the court clerk to see if the court will let a witness who is ill or out of town testify by phone. It's a good idea to have a letter from the witness, explaining why he can't be there in person.

The third item on the agenda is convincing the judge that Fred should pay for the nuisance. That should follow directly from proving that there is a real nuisance, but Mattie should bolster her efforts by showing that she's tried unsuccessfully to work things out with Fred and to get the city animal control department to do something. That way the judge knows that small claims court is her last resort, and she really needs a judgment against Fred to get him to do something. Here, copies of police or animal control department reports will document her earlier efforts to solve the problem.

When it comes to the amount Mattie is asking for, there's not too much she can do to influence the judge in addition to presenting convincing evidence about how obnoxious the dogs are. The amount that will be awarded is "within the discretion of the court"—that is, the judge will decide based on the evidence and personal judgment. There are no formal guidelines to follow. (Remember, though, that the judge is bound by the state's law limiting money awards in small claims courts.)

Going to Court

If you've never been to small claims court, try to go and watch some cases a few days before your hearing is scheduled. You'll be more at ease with court procedures, and you may learn what not to do when you're in front of the judge. A few pointers:

- State your problem in an organized way. (The person bringing the lawsuit begins by summarizing the situation.) Begin with the heart of the problem—in this case, that Fred's dogs are noisy and smelly—not the background. You should be able to state the problem in less than five minutes.
- Don't read your statement. A few notes on a 3" x 5" card should be enough to help you remember key points. You're much more likely to keep the judge's attention if you talk naturally.
- Don't overload the judge with a jumble of documents. Present relevant documents in an orderly, organized way.
- Don't argue with or interrupt the judge or your opponent. You'll get a chance to respond.

FOUR KEYS TO SMALL CLAIMS COURT SUCCESS

Be well-organized

Be polite

Present persuasive evidence (photographs, witnesses, police reports)

Be brief

Here's how Mattie's case against Fred went once they got into court.

Clerk: The next case is Mattie Hinman vs. Fred Little. Will everyone please come forward?

Judge: Good morning. Ms. Hinman, will you begin?

Mattie: I brought this case because my next-door neighbor, Mr. Little, has three dogs that are a nuisance. Their barking is a terrible annoyance because often they bark for a half hour or an hour without stopping. It's especially bad very early in the morning, about 6 o'clock, when Mr. Little feeds them. The noise wakes me up, and then I have to wait until they stop and try to go back to sleep. It also makes it nearly impossible to use my back yard, because whenever I go outside the dogs start barking.

There is also a bad smell coming from Mr. Little's back yard, because he doesn't keep the yard clean of the dogs' droppings. It gets so bad sometimes that I have to keep the windows on that side of the house closed. That's another reason I can't use the back yard. And sometimes the dogs leave droppings in my front yard.

I have here a letter from a friend of mine, who has been to my house and seen the conditions I'm talking about *(Mattie hands letter to judge).*

I've lived next door to Mr. Little for four months. I've tried to talk to him about the problem, and I wanted to get help from a community mediation panel, but Mr. Little refused. Then I called the city animal control and health departments. The health department said it would send someone out to give Mr. Little a warning, but that was two months ago and the situation is unchanged.

I have copies of my letters to the health department, your Honor, and a copy of the letter I wrote Mr. Little demanding that he stop the nuisance or compensate me for it. *(Mattie hands copies to court clerk or judge).* I also brought my neighbor, Sarah Stewart, who can testify to the noise and smell.

I'm asking for $1,000 in damages to compensate me for the discomfort and loss of sleep I've suffered for four months. And as I said, I've also all but lost the use of my back yard. All I really want is some peace and quiet, but if I'm forced to live with this nuisance, I think I should be compensated. Thank you.

Judge: Ms. Stewart, do you have something to add?

Sarah: Yes. I just want to say that Mattie is completely right about the barking and the smell. I'm not as close to it as she is, so it doesn't bother me as much, but I can still hear the barking, and sometimes it does go on for a long time. I don't know how she puts up with it. And when the wind is right, I can smell Mr. Little's house even across the street. It's not sanitary, and people shouldn't have to live next to that.

Judge: All right, Mr. Little, it's your turn to explain why you haven't responded to Ms. Hinman's and the health department's requests to keep your dogs from being a nuisance.

Fred: My dogs aren't a nuisance, your Honor! Sure, they bark now and then, but there have been burglaries in the neighborhood, and they bark when they hear something suspicious. I'd think Mattie would feel safer having my dogs next door. I've got a right to keep pets, don't I?

Judge: What about the barking early in the morning when you feed them?

Fred: Well, yeah, they do that sometimes, but I've been trying to keep them quiet ever since Mattie complained. I didn't know it bothered her until she told me, you know.

Judge: Ms. Hinman, when did you first complain to Mr. Little?

Mattie: About a month after I moved in, I think.

Fred: Anyway, I'm doing the best I can. I can't stop them from barking when I'm gone, but when I'm home I shut them up right away. I think she just doesn't like dogs, and if she were friendly to them they wouldn't bark at her when she goes in her yard.

As far as the smell, well, I live there and it doesn't bother me. I clean up the yard when I have time, but I've been real busy lately so maybe I haven't kept it quite as good as I should have.

Judge: Thank you. If no one has anything else to add, I will take the case under advisement. I'll tell you right now, however, that I intend to award Ms. Hinman some, if not all, of the damages she has requested.

The reason I'm ruling this way is that it's obvious, from the testimony presented here, that your dogs, Mr. Little, are a legal nuisance. They interfere with Ms. Hinman's use of her property and have caused her significant discomfort. Mr. Little has had several opportunities to take care of the nuisance but has not done so. You'll get my final decision on the amount of damages in the mail in a few days.

---

[1]*In re Ackerman,* 6 Cal. App. 5, 91 P. 429 (1907).

[2]Woodhouse, *No Bad Dogs* (Summit Books, 1982).

[3]Los Angeles, Cal. Public Safety Code § 53.18.5.

8

GUIDE, SIGNAL, SERVICE
AND THERAPY DOGS

exemption from regulations / tax rules / rental housing /
access to public places / transportation / dogs in the workplace

One of the happiest partnerships between humans and canines is
the use of dogs to help blind, hearing-impaired or disabled owners. A
well-trained dog can vastly improve the life of a disabled owner,
who may for the first time taste some of the independence others
take for granted. The law recognizes the special status of these dogs
and allows them places other dogs, no matter how devoted, clever or
winsome, never see.

Old laws gave privileges only to guide dogs (also called "Seeing
Eye" dogs). But some states have now amended their laws to give
other kinds of specially trained "assistance dogs" the same rights as
guide dogs, and more legislation is pending.

Types of Assistance Dogs

Four types of trained dogs are generally called assistance dogs:
guide, signal, service and therapy dogs. The most common and easily-
identified are guide dogs trained to help the blind or sight-impaired

get about. Guide dogs are matched with owners who alert them that it's time to start work by attaching them to a leather harness. They then guide their owners around cars and other people, steadfastly ignoring all outside distractions.

Signal or hearing dogs help hearing-impaired people by alerting them with a nudge to important sounds: intruders, phones, crying babies, doorbells and smoke alarms. Many signal dogs also ride along with their owners in their cars to alert them to the warnings of ambulance sirens and honking drivers.

Service dogs are the arms and legs of many physically disabled people. They pull wheelchairs, carry baskets and briefcases, open doors and even turn on lights for their owners. Those who suffer from balance problems are often paired with service dogs that help steady them as they negotiate steps and rocky terrain that were formerly off-limits.

Trained therapy or social dogs were first used in institutions such as nursing homes and schools for emotionally disturbed children. They are now gaining wider use to soothe and watch over owners with mental disabilities. Therapy dogs guide autistic or retarded people through everyday tasks, and many are trained to give calming, reassuring snuggles to owners who become agitated or withdrawn.

Because of their general temperament, size and ease of grooming, German shepherds, Labrador retrievers and Golden retrievers are the breeds most often trained as assistance dogs. While some programs differ, most dogs are bred at the training site, then spend time with skilled volunteers or families who teach them simple obedience and social skills. The dogs are then returned to the training facility, where they are spayed or neutered and put through intensive schooling. Only about half graduate. Some don't have the calm demeanor required; some just can't be trained to ignore the taunts of birds and cats.

Potential owners must pass tests, too. They are carefullly screened and interviewed to ensure that they are in fairly good health, that they want the dog for mobility and independent living and that the dog would have a good home and adequate exercise. Owners are then teamed with dogs that have the skills and temperament they require. After several weeks during which the owners stay on-site under the supervision of trainers, who teach them handling and grooming, the owner and dog team go home to live and work together.

FOR MORE INFORMATION ON ASSISTANCE DOGS

Most assistance dogs are trained in facilities that depend on outside grants and donations for their existence. If you want to find out more about their work, locate an assistance dog training program or make a donation, contact:

Assistance Dogs International
P.O. Box 446
Santa Rosa, CA 95403
707/528-0830

The Delta Society
321 Burnett Avenue South
Suite 303
Renton, WA 98055
206/226–7357

Exemptions from Local Regulations

Specially-trained assistance dogs are often granted exemptions from local requirements that are imposed on other dogs. As mentioned, some laws exempt only guide dogs, or only guide and signal dogs.

Licenses

Virtually all cities give free licenses to guide and signal dogs. The special tag that comes with the license is what identifies the dog as a trained assistance dog. If you qualify for a free license, remember that you still must go through the motions of getting the license. Only the fee is waived; you must still show that the dog has had required vaccinations. You must also renew the license when it expires.

Some states (Ohio and North Carolina, for example) make this easier, by issuing free, permanent licenses for assistance dogs. Owners don't have to worry about renewing the license every year.

Pooper-Scooper Laws

Many pooper-scooper laws (New York's and San Francisco's, for example), don't apply to guide, hearing or service dogs.[1] Unfortunately, zealous police officers trying to enforce these laws may not always know, or be willing to be told, that guide dogs are exempt. One San Francisco policeman forced a blind woman to clean up after her guide dog, even though she explained that the law exempted her. As a large lunchtime crowd gathered, the officer forced the woman to clean up the droppings and take them across the street to a garbage can. She sued, and in 1988 received a $17,000 settlement from the city for emotional trauma.[2]

Access to Public Places

Guide dogs are admitted to any building or property owned or controlled by the federal government.[3] Most states also allow guide dogs on public property. Public property, however, is more than government-owned property. In the legal sense, it usually includes anywhere the public is invited or permitted. For example, New York law allows guide, hearing and service dogs, accompanied by their owners, in:

• public and private housing;
• all modes of public and private transportation;
• buildings to which the public is invited or permitted;
• educational facilities and institutions;
• places where food is offered for sale;
• theatres (live and film); and
• all other places of "public accommodations, convenience, resort, entertainment, or business."[4]

California law is similar. Both states make it illegal to impose any extra charge for admitting a guide, signal or service dog to any place the dog is allowed by law.[5] Every state has its own minor variations. In California, for example, zoos are allowed to keep these dogs out of areas where zoo animals aren't separated from the public by a physical barrier, but the zoo must maintain free kennel facilities for the dogs.[6]

It's a good idea for people who have assistance dogs to carry copies of the state laws that allow them access to public places. If they are refused admittance to a public place, they can show the management that the law forbids such discrimination. Seeing the law in black and white almost always opens doors. Once in a while, unfortunately, it doesn't. A man denied a room in a San Francisco hotel because he had a guide dog produced a copy of the California law prohibiting discrimination by hotels, but the manager still refused to allow him to check in. Both sides called the police, who not only arrested the manager for denying access to the disabled (a misdemeanor in California, as it is in some other states) but found the man and his dog a discounted room at a much posher downtown hotel.[7]

Rental Housing

In many states, including California and New Jersey, it is illegal to refuse to rent housing to someone because that person uses a guide, signal or service dog.[8] As a practical matter, these dogs are normally so well-trained and well-behaved that a landlord has little reason to object to them, anyway. The law allows landlords to include reasonable regulations in the lease or rental agreement. The owners, like all dog owners, are liable for any damage the dogs cause.

Even if there is not a specific state statute, a court may rule that a no-pets clause will not be enforced against a disabled person. A New York court did just that, stating that a no-pets lease clause must yield to the "specific, particularized need to keep a dog, which need arises out of the handicap."[9]

Note: In some states, disabled people who live in public housing are allowed by law to have dogs, whether or not the dogs have any special training. (See Chapter 4, Landlords and Dogs.)

Dogs in the Workplace

Laws that protect a disabled worker from discrimination in the workplace may also extend to the worker's dog. New York law, for example, makes it illegal to deny a qualified person a job or promotion simply because the person is accompanied by a guide, hearing or service dog.[10]

Traveling with Guide Dogs

Assistance dogs are usually allowed by law on all kinds of public transportation, including buses, planes, and trains.

On airplanes, guide, service and signal dogs aren't subject to the rules that govern how other dogs must travel. They fly free, with their owners, in the airliner's cabin. Passengers with dogs are usually placed in the front row of a section of seats, which gives the dog room to lie down in front of the owner.

Let the airline know, when you book your ticket, that you will be accompanied by the dog. If your impairment is not obvious and the dog's presence might be questioned, it's probably a good idea to have with you some proof of your dog's special status, such as a special license tag or a certificate that documents its training.

Income Tax Deductions for Guide Dogs

Even the Internal Revenue Service has something for guide dogs: it recognizes them as a legitimate medical expense, which can be deducted for federal income tax purposes.[11]

Public Assistance

Some states assist low-income disabled people with the expenses of keeping a guide dog. New York and California, for example, give a monthly payment for dog food (in New York, it's $35 a month and up) to owners who qualify.[12]

The federal government also may pay for a guide dog for a veteran who is entitled to federal disability compensation.[13] The costs paid for may include travel expenses incurred when the veteran goes to pick up the dog from a training center.

Guide Dogs Are Safe from Creditors

In New York, a creditor cannot take a guide, service or hearing dog to satisfy a court judgment for money against the dog's owner. The dog's food is also exempt.[14] Twenty-four more states prohibit creditors from taking a debtor's "health aids," which should include assistance dogs.

STATES THAT PROHIBIT CREDITORS FROM TAKING "HEALTH AIDS"

Alaska	Iowa	Ohio
Arizona	Kentucky	Oklahoma
California	Maine	Oregon
Colorado	Maryland	South Carolina
Connecticut	Missouri	Tennessee
Georgia	Montana	Utah
Idaho	New Mexico	West Virginia
Illinois	New York	
Indiana	North Carolina	

Penalties for Injuring Guide Dogs

At least one state, Rhode Island, applies a special law when a guide dog, or a blind person using a guide dog, is injured by another dog. The Rhode Island law makes the owner of the guilty dog liable for twice the amount of damages the blind person incurs. If the dog hurts a guide dog or owner again, the tab goes up to three times the amount of damages.[15]

---

[1] N.Y. Pub. Health Law § 1310.

[2] San Francisco Chronicle, Aug. 16, 1988.

[3] 40 U.S.C. § 291.

[4] N.Y. Civ. Rights Law § 47.

[5] N.Y. Civ. Rights Law § 47-b; Cal. Civ. Code § 54.2.

[6] Cal. Civ. Code § 54.7.

[7] San Francisco Chronicle, Sept. 6, 1988.

[8] See Cal. Civ. Code § 54.1(5).

[9] *Ocean Gates Associates Starrett Systems, Inc. v. Dopico*, 109 Misc. 2d 774, 441 N.Y.S.2d 34 (1981).

[10] N.Y. Civ. Rights Law § 47-a.

[11] Treas. Reg. § 1.213-1(e)(1)(iii).

[12] N.Y. Soc. Serv. Law § 303-a; Cal. Welf. & Inst. Code § 12553.

[13] 38 U.S.C. § 614.

[14] N.Y. Civ. Prac. Law § 5205.

[15] R.I. Gen. Laws § 4-13-16.1.

9

IF A DOG IS INJURED OR KILLED

justified killing / economic loss / emotional distress /
negotiating a settlement / suing the government / insurance

What legal recourse does a dog owner have if a dog dies because of someone's deliberate or careless act? It can happen: a dog is hit by a car, shot while chasing a farmer's chickens, euthanized after being picked up by a dog pound, or carelessly treated by a veterinarian, to name just a few scenarios.

The lawyer's standard answer—"sue the bastard!"—will not be a surprise to anyone familiar with how the legal system works. We recommend a less adversarial approach. If possible, working out a settlement is less painful, less expensive and quicker than battling in court. When the dispute centers on how much money a dog is worth—which is often relatively little—going to court is unlikely to be worth your while. That's why throughout the book, we stress negotiation and mediation as alternatives to the formal legal ways to resolve disputes. (Chapter 7, Resolving Disputes with Neighbors, contains a detailed discussion of mediation; we don't repeat it here.) In general, only if those methods don't work should you consider whether or not a lawsuit makes sense. And if you do have to go to court, small claims court is usually the best choice.

This advice applies no matter which side of the fence you're on: whether your dog was hurt or you're the one who shot at a dog that was threatening your prize sheep. But only when you understand your legal options are you ready to negotiate, or sue, if it comes to that. This chapter can help.

Note on dealing with the government: Not surprisingly, special rules apply when your dog is impounded, injured or killed by a government agency. For one, you have constitutionally guaranteed rights to notice and a hearing before any government action is taken. And if your animal has already been killed and you want to sue, special rules govern when and how you can proceed. (There's a section on "Suing the Government" later in the chapter.)

When a Dog Owner Can't Win

Sometimes, killing a dog is legally justified, and the person who does it isn't financially liable to the dog's owner. For example, if someone kills a dog because it is threatening to injure a person or livestock, the action is justified by law, and the dog's owner can't sue successfully for the loss. This section discusses the common situations in which a dog owner whose dog has been hurt or killed can't expect to get any money.

Dogs Attacking People or Livestock

Generally, it's perfectly legal to do anything necessary to stop a dog in the act of attacking a person or livestock. A dog's owner is not legally entitled to any money from someone who injures or kills the dog while protecting a person or farm animal from attack. Nor is the person guilty of a criminal offense; many animal cruelty laws specifically exempt the act of injuring or killing a dog that is harassing livestock.

"Livestock" usually means only commercially valuable animals, not pets or wild animals. Some state laws include a list of the kinds of animals protected; others say only that a dog may be killed if it attacks a "domestic animal," which historically does not include dogs and cats. Dogs and cats may even be specifically excluded; for example, in Ohio it's legal to kill a dog that is chasing or injuring a "sheep, lamb, goat, kid, domestic fowl or domestic animal except a cat or another dog." Someone who does injure a dog that's chasing another dog, or a deer, may be liable for damages to the dog's owner—and the killer may also be guilty of cruelty to animals. (See Chapter 13, Cruelty.)

Essentially, the dog must be caught in the act of chasing or preparing to attack livestock or a person, actually attacking, or fleeing after an attack. As one court put it, "it is not the dog's predatory habits, nor his past transgressions, nor his reputation, however bad, but the doctrine of self-defense, whether of person or property, that gives the right to kill."[1]

Incidentally, the rules protecting livestock are often stricter than those that apply to people. In Kentucky, for example, it's legal to kill an unlicensed dog just for going into a field or enclosure where livestock or poultry are kept. And any dog that is "pursuing, worrying, or wounding any livestock . . . or attacking human beings" can be killed.[2]

WORRIED LIVESTOCK

Just exactly what do these statutes mean when they talk about dogs "worrying" livestock? Must the cattle or chickens be pacing back and forth with troubled expressions and furrowed brows? Nope. Generally, a dog is worrying animals if it is running after or barking at them. No physical injury need be shown. That means that dogs that are standing still and barking at cattle can be legally shot for worrying the livestock.[3]

Generally, a farmer may legally kill a dog only on her own property. An Illinois court ruled that a sheep farmer who followed a dog back to its owner's home (in a residential area, no less) and shot it there an hour after the dog had killed some of his sheep was not protected under the Illinois statute.[4] Instead, he should have sued the dog's owner for the value of the sheep killed. (See Chapter 11, Personal Injury and Property Damage.)

A dog is not, however, necessarily safe as soon as it leaves the farmer's property. In general, a farmer who wants retaliation is allowed to pursue a dog for a "reasonable time." What is a reasonable time under the circumstances is a question that's resolved when the lawsuit gets to court.

For example, a Kansas jury vindicated a farmer who shot and wounded a dog he found attacking his hogs. He shot at the dog, but it ran away, with the farmer in hot pursuit in his pickup. The dog ran home, where the farmer shot it twice and left it hiding, wounded, under the house. When the dog's owner came home, he rushed the dog to a veterinarian; it eventually recovered from its injury. The owner sued for almost $8,000, but the jury came back with a verdict for the farmer.[5] The Kansas statute allows a livestock owner to kill a dog that has been found injuring livestock "a reasonable time" before.

A farmer must also produce proof that a dog he injures was chasing his livestock. In an old California case, for example, the rancher's belief that his sheep were in danger from a dog was not enough, the court ruled, to absolve him of financial responsibility for shooting them.[6] The dogs' owner successfully sued for $225 (this was in 1889) for the injuries to his three highly-trained dogs. It's hard to understand, however, what evidence would have satisfied the court; testimony indicated that the dogs were following a herd of pregnant ewes, which were agitated and frightened. Most judges would have found that to be close enough to a real chase to free the rancher of legal blame for the shooting.

Dogs Running at Large

Most statutes, as mentioned, do not allow a farmer to shoot dogs that are merely running loose (at large). A North Dakota rancher, who shot a neighbor's greyhound after it ran through his cattle herd without particularly disturbing the cattle, was not protected by the state statute, which allows killing a dog only if it is "worrying" livestock. The rancher had to pay $300 to the dog's owner.[7]

Some states, however, allow farmers to shoot any dog that is, to paraphrase the Indiana statute, "roaming over the country unattended." Under this statute, an appeals court upheld the right of a farmer to shoot dogs he said were trying to get into his chicken pen in the middle of the night.[8] The dogs, two coonhounds, had been hunting with their owner but got separated from him in a heavy rainstorm about 2 a.m. (For the uninitiated, raccoon hunting is done at night.) Under the relatively severe Indiana law, it made no difference that the dogs were bothering the chickens; their hours were numbered as soon as they got away from their master.

Even if you know your dog was innocent when a trigger-happy farmer shot it, in most instances, there is absolutely no way to prove that a dog wasn't doing what the farmer or rancher who shot it says it was doing. The only other witness is likely to be the dog, and it isn't talking. If you're a dog owner, you don't want to end up quarreling over whether or not a certain law applies when your dog has already been shot. From this point of view, the moral is quite simple: If you live in a rural area or close to one, NEVER let your dog run loose off your property. As anyone who has ever lived on a dirt road knows, dogs tend to form packs (especially at night), and farmers tend to shoot first and ask questions later, if at all.

Dogs Injured Accidentally

Although we tend to forget it in these days of lawsuit mania, sometimes no one is legally at fault for an injury. If a dog chasing a cat through the house gets hurt crashing into a ladder that a painter left in a corner while on a lunch break, can the dog's owner sue the painter? Well, you can always sue, but the chances of winning in this case would be slim. Sure, the painter left the ladder that caused the injury there, but no one would say that it was   an unreasonable thing to do.

Often, of course, deciding whether or not someone acted unreasonably, and so may legally be at fault, is a tougher question. For example, was it unreasonable for federal government employees, who were trying to kill coyotes, to spread poisoned bait in a field where hunters regularly took their dogs? No, said a court when a hunter sued after his dog was poisoned. The government had the landowner's permission, and posted some warning signs; it had acted reasonably.[9]

When a Dog Owner May Win a Lawsuit

A dog owner can usually sue successfully if someone injures or kills a dog intentionally or through unreasonable carelessness.

Note on veterinary malpractice: Special legal standards apply when a dog owner sues a veterinarian who has injured a dog. (See Chapter 5, Veterinarians.)

Dogs Injured Intentionally

Anyone who intentionally injures a dog is financially liable for the injury unless a statute (like the ones discussed above, which let a livestock owner protect animals from attacking dogs) allows the actions that cause the injury.

Example: Sonia is annoyed at her neighbor Julia's dogs, Labrador retrievers that sometimes chase her cat. The next time she sees the dogs, she gets out her old heavy-duty slingshot and lets fly. She hits one dog squarely on the ear, and it yelps and runs home, badly injured. Sonia is liable to Julia for the cost of the injury to the dog. (How to figure this amount is discussed later in the chapter.)

But Julia may also be partly at fault for letting the dog run around the neighborhood., so the amount she can recover from Sonia may be reduced correspondingly. (See "If the Owner Is at Fault, Too," below.)

Here are some other examples of intentional injury to dogs, for which the dog's owner is legally entitled to compensation:

- an angry neighbor poisons a dog;
- a farmer shoots a dog, even though the dog isn't threatening livestock;
- a thief takes a dog and sells it to a research lab.

Note on criminal prosecutions: Anyone who intentionally mistreats, injures or kills an animal may also be guilty of a crime. (See Chapter 13, Cruelty.)

Dogs Injured Through Carelessness

Someone who is unreasonably careless (the legal term is "negligent") and as a result injures or kills a dog is legally liable to the dog's owner.

For an example, let's continue the saga of Sonia and her neighbor's dogs. Here are two examples of carelessness that will make Sonia liable to the dogs' owner:

- Sonia, upset over hitting the dog with the slingshot, decides to go talk to her therapist about it. She backs out of the driveway, but in her distracted state doesn't notice the neighbor's other dog behind her. The dog receives a glancing blow from the fender, which leaves it stiff-legged and in need of medication for a couple of weeks.
- Sonia decides to make it up to Julia by taking the two convalescent Labradors some hamburger while her neighbor is at work. But, hapless as always, she leaves the gate open when she goes in the yard. Both dogs, no doubt determined to get as far away from this two-legged disaster as possible, take off as fast as their sore bodies will carry them, and don't come back for a week.

Examples are more useful than abstract rules because what constitutes negligence in any given situation depends on the circumstances, and every situation is unique. It's hard to generalize about when someone will be held liable. But the basic question is always the same: did the person act reasonably, under the circumstances? If the dispute gets all the way to a lawsuit and trial, the question is given to the jurors to answer, based on the evidence they hear.

Here are some more examples of negligence that results in injury to a dog:

- A dog pound picks up a dog and destroys it the next day, not noticing that the dog is wearing a license tag, which means its owner could have been notified.
- An employee of a dog-walking service carelessly leaves a dog in a parked car on a hot day; the dog dies of heat prostration.
- A neighbor accidentally leaves rat poison out in his driveway, where he knows the dog from next door often lies; the dog eats the poison and becomes ill.

Dogs Hurt by Other Dogs

The laws that allow livestock owners to kill attacking dogs do not usually apply when it's a dog that is being attacked. So, a dog owner who injures a dog in an attempt to protect his own dog may still have to pay or the injury, or answer a cruelty to animals charge. It will be up to a jury to decide if the owner acted reasonably under the circumstances. For example, a New York man was found innocent of a cruelty charge after he shot and killed a dog that charged into a family picnic, scattering the children present, and attacked his dog.[10]

Even though the owner of a dog that is being attacked may not legally be allowed to kill or injure the other dog, he probably can sue the other dog's owner. Remember that legally, a dog is its owner's property, and the owner can sue for property damage. Whether the other dog's owner is liable depends on state law and the circumstances. In a slight majority of states, dog owners are financially responsible for all property damage their dog causes, in most circumstances. In the rest of the states, the injured party must show that the dog owner knew, or should have known, that the dog was likely to cause that kind of damage. (These rules are discussed in detail in Chapter 11, Personal Injury and Property Damage.)

A real life example: In 1919, a four-and-a-half-pound Pomeranian was being walked on the streets of San Francisco when it was attacked by an Airedale terrier. The attack was fatal. As the court put it, the little dog "crossed to that shore from which none, not even a good dog, ever returns." Its owner sued the Airedale's owner for $1,000. (This Pomeranian, according to the court, was "regarded in dog circles as possessing the bluest of blood.") The Airedale's owner was found liable.[11]

If the Dog Owner Is at Fault, Too

What if the dog's owner is partly responsible for an injury? Most states have adopted the doctrine of "comparative fault" or "comparative negligence," which roughly means that if you sue and win, your award is reduced in proportion to your fault. So if you're one-third at fault, for example, you get one-third less.

CONTRIBUTORY NEGLIGENCE STATES

A few states still follow the old legal doctrine of "contributory negligence" instead of the comparative fault rule. Under contributory negligence, someone who sues and is the least bit at fault can collect nothing.

The contributory negligence states are:

Alabama	Maryland
Delaware	North Carolina
District of Columbia	South Carolina
	Virginia

Look back at Julia and her Labradors, one of whom is hit by her neighbor Sonia's car. You can certainly argue that Julia partly caused the car accident by letting her dogs roam the neighborhood. She may have even broken a law, if her town or state requires all dogs to be kept on leashes.

Let's say Julia sues Sonia in small claims court for her dog's $78 veterinarian bill. The judge decides that Julia is 20% at fault and

Sonia is 80% at fault. The judge thus reduces the $78 verdict by 20%, and awards Julia $62.40.

In most comparative negligence states, if Julia were more than half at fault, she would get nothing. So if a jury decided she were 49% at fault, her award would be reduced by 49%, but if she were 51% at fault, she would get nothing.

Keep in mind that the owner's negligence affects the outcome of the case only if it contributed to the injury. So an owner who carelessly lets a dog run loose, resulting in its being hit by a car, obviously contributed to the risk. But if the dog is picked up by the pound, and while there a pound employee maliciously kicks the dog and injures it, the owner probably wouldn't be considered at fault. At least in the legal sense, letting the dog run loose doesn't have anything to do with the deliberate and nasty act of the employee.

How Much Can a Dog Owner Sue For?

How much is a dog worth?

"Easy," says the dog owner. "My dog is priceless."

Not so fast, say the courts, which are used to dealing in terms of economic value. Most pets couldn't be sold for much, if anything, and their upkeep—food, licenses, veterinary care—costs plenty. Those facts, of course, come as no surprise to pet owners. If you want to make money, you buy pork belly futures, not a cuddly mixed-breed puppy. The benefits a pet provides—companionship, laughter, security—are non-economic and unique.

The extent to which a dog owner may recover, in a lawsuit, for the loss of those things depends on the state's law and, to a large extent, the sympathies of the judge or jury. Some states allow pet owners to collect only the "market value" of the dog. In other states, a court may let a dog owner recover damages for "sentimental value," or "intentional infliction of emotional distress," or "mental suffering." The legal theories go by different names, but they are all attempts to compensate owners for the real, but hard to pin down, emotional loss they feel when they lose a pet.

Depending on the circumstances, state law and the disposition of the judge or jury toward dogs, a dog owner may be able to sue the person responsible and convince a court to find the person liable for:
- costs of treatment if the dog is injured;
- market or replacement value of the dog;
- sentimental value of the dog;
- emotional distress; and
- additional money damages to punish the person responsible.

Each of these is discussed below.

Remember that if the dog owner is partially at fault for the injury, whatever amount won in a lawsuit will, in most states, be reduced according to the owner's fault. (How that works is explained in "If the Dog Owner Is at Fault, Too," earlier in this chapter.)

Cost of Treatment

The first expense a dog owner is likely to suffer when a dog is injured is the veterinarian's bills. The person responsible for the injury can be found legally liable for those bills.

Generally, courts allow the owner to be reimbursed only for "reasonable" treatment. What's reasonable in a particular case depends on the dog's "injuries, condition and prognosis," in the words of one New York court.[12] A dog owner probably can't expect to recover $10,000 for extensive surgery of an 18-year-old dog if the veterinarian says the dog is likely to die soon anyway. But just because a dog is advanced in years doesn't mean that expensive treatment is never justified. In 1988, the New York court just mentioned approved an award of $300 for antibiotics and suturing of an aged, arthritic and partially deaf dog that had been injured by another dog.

To document the costs of treatment during negotiations or at trial, keep records of all bills for treatment, medication and hospitalization. But you probably can't be paid back for the time you took off from work to care for the dog or take it to the vet.

Market or Replacement Value

All dogs have a market value—that is, a price they would bring if sold on the open market. That may not be much, but whatever it is, the dog's owner is entitled to it if a dog has been killed. Some courts award the dog owner the amount it would cost to replace the dog, instead of the dog's market value. This replacement value is likely to be a larger amount.

Factors to be considered in computing market value include the dog's:

- purchase price
- age
- health
- breed
- training
- usefulness
- special traits or characteristics of value

Here are a couple of examples of how that translates into dollars in the legal world:

- An Illinois couple's show dog was run over by a visitor's car in their driveway. The dog was severely injured and had to be destroyed. In small claims court, the owners testified that the year-old dog had cost $200 as a pup, had appeared in four dog shows and won first prize in each, and had been sired by an international grand champion. The court, in this 1979 decision, awarded them the $500 they had requested.[13]

- The owner of an injured dog was awarded $200, in 1975, for the market value of the six-year-old pedigreed dog. The amount was based on the dog's age, purchase price ($125-$150), the relatively long life of the breed, training, and desirable (but unspecified) character traits.[14]

THEY DON'T GET OLDER, THEY GET BETTER

Does the fact that a dog is getting on in years—a little unsteady on its feet, maybe, with a tendency to run into table legs and door frames—mean its loss is worth less to its owner? Not at all. Listen to a town court judge from Westchester County, New York: "A good dog's value increases rather than falls with age and training."[15] Well said, your honor.

    Valuable dogs. Your average mutt may not be a high-priced item, but a pedigreed purebred of championship lineage, who can trace its ancestors many generations farther back than you can, may be worth thousands of dollars on the open market.

INSURED DOGS

Most unusually valuable dogs are insured. If the dog is injured or killed, the owner should make a claim to the insurance company, just as when an insured car or house is damaged. It becomes the responsibility of the insurance company, after it pays the owner for the covered loss (minus the deductible amount), to sue the person responsible for the injury.

If you own a valuable dog but aren't familiar with the current market, talk to people who raise and show dogs of your dog's breed. They can tell you the going prices. You can find breeders' names in dog owners' magazines, or by calling a local kennel club or the American Kennel Club.

Dogs kept for breeding are essentially business assets and may be given a monetary value based on not only their market value but also the revenue they would have brought their owners. A Palo Alto, California man who claimed his dog had been rendered sterile while in an animal shelter recently brought suit for $250,000, his estimate of the dog's stud value. A court may, however, stick to the replacement value theory, reasoning that the owner can simply replace the dog with one that will generate the same income—and cost less than a quarter of a million dollars.

Sentimental Value/Loss of Companionship

Surely an owner's affection for and attachment to a dog—not the market value—is the greater loss when a dog is killed. But as mentioned, some courts simply do not allow it to be considered; they stick to market value. An Alaska court stated flatly that the owners' "subjective estimation of [their dog] Wizzard's value as a pet was not a valid basis for compensation," and allowed them to recover only the $300 market value of their dog, which had been killed by mistake in a dog pound.[16] Other courts give up because of the difficulty in putting a dollar amount on the loss: "It is impossible to reduce to monetary terms the bond between man and dog," said one, limiting a dog owner's recovery to the cost of veterinary treatment.[17]

Some courts, however, have been willing to give it a shot. Recognizing that "the affection of a master for his dog is a very real thing . . . for which the owner should recover, irrespective of the value of the animal," the Supreme Court of Florida reversed a lower court's ruling that "sentimental value" couldn't be considered when valuing a pet.[18]

An Illinois court came to virtually the same conclusion, comparing the loss of a dog to the loss of other unique and irreplaceable items such as family heirlooms or photographs. Because these objects, which are not bought and sold, have no meaningful market value, the court ruled, damages are measured by their "actual value to the owner." Actual value can include sentimental value, at least to some extent.[19]

A state's failure to admit to allowing consideration of sentimental value when computing damages does not, of course, mean that a judge (or jury, if the case is brought in regular, not small claims, court) doesn't unconsciously consider it.

Evidence of sentimental value can be as simple as testimony about the importance of the dog in the owner's life. If the owner is someone who is cut off from family or friends, or lives alone, or is unusually dependent on a dog, a court is more likely to figure in sentimental value.

Emotional Distress

We've stressed that in the eyes of the law, a dog is just another thing: something you buy, sell, and own, like a car. Anyone who has lost a beloved pet, of course, knows that the law is simply wrong. And some courts have come around, recognizing that "a pet is not just a thing but occupies a special place somewhere in between a person and a piece of personal property. . . . To say it is a piece of personal property and no more is a repudiation of our humaneness."[20]

This change in attitude is shown by courts' willingness to let people sue for the mental anguish they suffer when they lose a pet because of malicious or extremely reckless acts. The legal theory is similar to the one that lets people sue when a child or spouse is injured; they can sue not only for lost income, but for the emotional anguish the death triggers.

The law in this area is still developing, and its boundaries are unclear. Some state courts (West Virginia, for example[21]) do not allow claims for mental suffering. Other states impose various limitations. In some places, to recover for mental anguish, the person must see the injury take place, or suffer physical injury, or require medical treatment. The rules change constantly as courts refine—or, just as often, confuse—them.

Damages Note: In states that don't allow emotional distress claims, a dog owner may be able to get punitive damages (damages meant to punish the wrongdoer) if a dog was harmed intentionally or in some truly outrageous way. Punitive damages are discussed just below.

Generally, people can sue for two types of mental distress: first, the shock and distress caused by seeing an accident or mistreatment, and second, the grief and long-term effect the loss has on their lives. The more outrageous the conduct of the person being sued, the more money that can be claimed. Proving mental suffering, which of course is in the mind of the sufferer, is not always easy. But the person suing can testify about how he felt at the death of the pet, and how the loss disrupted his life. If the person sought medical treatment or psychological counseling, that will strengthen the claims.

The best way to get a feel for what the rules are is to look at actual cases:

• A family was awarded $1,000 for the mental anguish they suffered when their 9-year-old dog died of heat prostration after state agency employees in Hawaii left it in an unventilated van in the sun.[22]

• A landlord in Hayward, California agreed to pay a 10-year-old boy $5,000 for the emotional distress the boy suffered when he had to give up his dog. The landlord had violated the city's rent control ordinance by evicting the boy's family, and the dog was not allowed in their new apartment.

- A family sued and won $13,000 after their dog was seriously injured in a Florida animal hospital and subsequently had to be destroyed. The dog had been left on a heating pad for almost two days without care, and was severely burned. The court allowed the jury, when it decided on how much to award the family, to consider their mental pain and suffering.[23]
- A New York judge gave $700 to a woman who, at her dog's funeral, opened the casket and found a dead cat inside. The animal hospital where the dog had died apparently didn't give the dog's remains to Bide-A-Wee, the organization that arranged the funeral. The judge found that the owner had suffered shock, mental anguish and despondency due to the loss of the dog's body, and was deprived of her wish for an elaborate funeral and the right to visit the dog's grave.[24]
- An Oregon woman who asked a vet to humanely destroy her dog, which had been shot and was in extreme pain, was awarded $4,000 for her mental anguish when she discovered that the vet had not euthanized the dog, but had given it away. Her worry about what her children would go through when they found the dog living with someone else justified the jury verdict, an appeals court ruled.[25] She was also awarded $700 in punitive damages.
- A judge refused to allow a claim for intentional infliction of emotional distress in a case where an Alaska couple's dog was impounded and mistakenly killed. The couple went to the pound at 4:50 in the afternoon to retrieve the dog, which they could see chained in the back of the pound, but employees said the pound was closed and refused to release the dog. When the couple went back the next day, the dog had been killed. These circumstances weren't severe enough to warrant an emotional distress claim, the trial judge ruled.[26]

Damages as Punishment

When a court orders someone who injured or killed a dog to pay the dog's owner, that money is intended to compensate the owner for the economic and emotional loss, not to punish the wrongdoer.

Usually, a court can punish, with fines or imprisonment, only someone who has broken a criminal law. If the actions were especially outrageous or deliberate, however, the judge or jury in a civil lawsuit may assess "punitive damages" against the wrongdoer. Punitive damages are like a fine, except that the money is paid to the other side in a lawsuit, not to the government. They are added on to the amount the dog owner gets as compensation for the loss of the dog.

Punitive damages are given only when someone has caused injury intentionally or recklessly. Punitive damages may, however, be especially appropriate in animal cases, where compensatory damages are likely to be low. As a Minnesota court pointed out, if compensatory damages don't make it worthwhile to sue, the wrongdoing will go unpunished unless punitive damages are given.[27]

Here are some examples:

- A jury awarded punitive damages against a man who hit a dog in the head with a large rock, giving the dog convulsions and a concussion. A New York appeals court ruled that the malicious act justified punitive damages.[28]

- An appellate court did not allow punitive damages against a Cedar Rapids, Iowa animal shelter that picked up a woman's dog and mistakenly sent it to a research laboratory, where it was killed. The court ruled that the animal shelter must pay the owner $5,000 in compensatory damages, but not the extra $5,000 the jury had awarded in punishment. Why? Because, the court said, the shelter had been merely careless—it had sent the woman's dog to the lab after a day, even though it was required to keep animals for three days—but it had not acted willfully or recklessly.[29]

- Punitive damages were allowed, however, against a Minnesota animal warden who killed an impounded cat although he knew that a city ordinance required that it be kept five days. The warden killed the animal simply because the city had no facilities to take care of it—showing, in the words of the court, "a willful disregard for both the law and the property rights of private citizens." A jury awarded the cat's owner $40 in compensatory damages and $2,000 in punitive damages. The appeal court reduced the punitive damages to $500.[30]

If you're suing a government agency: Many states do not allow punitive damages against a city government unless a state law specifically authorizes it. Individual public officers, however, are liable for punitive damages just like other individuals are.[31]

Negotiating a Settlement

It's best to avoid courts whenever possible, and instead work things out by talking with the person you've got the dispute with. Mediators may be a big help, but even if you go it alone you'll save money, time, and aggravation.

Before you try to negotiate, do some research in the law library to see if the courts in your state have decided any cases similar to yours.[32] That will give you an idea of how much a jury might award if you did get into a lawsuit. (A periodical called *Jury Verdicts Weekly* is the best source.) You'll also be more convincing if you show you know your legal alternatives.

Your next step, if your dog has been injured, should be to write a letter setting out what happened. Even if the person you're writing to knows the facts as well as you do, it's a good way to organize your thoughts and make them clear to the other person. Include how much money you think would compensate you for your loss, explain how you arrived at that figure, and mention any state statute that applies directly to your situation. Give a deadline for payment—that's a good incentive for the person to act quickly. And say if you don't work something out by then, you'll file a small claims (or other) court case. In some states, a letter to the other side demanding payment is required by law before you can file a small claims action.

Here's a sample letter, continuing the saga of bad-luck Sonia, who accidentally ran her car into her neighbor Julia's Labrador retriever, Buster. Because Julia doesn't expect Sonia to put up much of a fuss about paying the costs of the dog's veterinary care, and because she feels she may have been partly at fault (for letting Buster loose without a leash), she decides to write a fairly low-key letter. If Julia expected more resistance from Sonia, she could have written a stiffer demand letter.

▲
───

May 14, 19__

Ms. Sonia Burns
8859 Baltimore Ave.
Littleton, IL 61433

Dear Ms. Burns:

Three weeks ago, you hit my dog Buster with your car as you
backed out of your driveway. Buster's left hind leg was
injured as a result, and for two weeks he had to take pain-
killers. Only now is he able to walk normally again.

As a result of your carelessness, I incurred a veterinary
bill of $78.40 for Buster's examination and medication. I
also suffered severe shock and distress, because I was
sitting on my porch when you came zooming out of your
driveway, and I saw your car hit Buster. I thought the dog
might be severely injured, and maybe even have to be put to
sleep.

I am willing to give up any claim I might have for my own
emotional distress, but I think you should reimburse me for
the cost of Buster's treatment. If you would like to discuss
the matter further, please give me a call. If you think it
would be helpful, we could get the help of a free mediator
from the Littleton Community Mediation Program. Please get
back to me by May 25. I would prefer to work this out
between us rather than take the matter to small claims or
other court.

Sincerely,

Julia Shaughnessy
8855 Baltimore Ave.
Littleton, IL 61433
(309) 831-5755

───
▼

If you reach an agreement, be sure to put it in writing and have all
the people involved sign it. You can use type out your own agreement,

or use a pre-printed release form. Here's a sample, using the release form from *Make Your Own Contract* (Nolo Press).

Release

Form 3

1. ___JULIA SHAUGHNESSY_____, Releasor, voluntarily and knowingly execute this release with the express intention of eliminating Releasee's liabilities and obligations as described below.

2. Releasor hereby releases ___SONIA BURNS_____, Releasee, from all claims, known or unknown to Releasor that have arisen or may arise from the transaction described in Clause 4.

3. Releasor is the owner of certain property (Property) located at _____ ___8855 BALTIMORE AVE., LITTLETON, IL_____, which specifically consists of ___A LABRADOR RETRIEVER NAMED BUSTER_____ _____.

4. Releasor has alleged that Property suffered damage in the approximate amount of $_78.40_ as a result of the following activity of Releasee: ___RELEASEE BACKED___ ___HER CAR INTO BUSTER, INJURING HIS LEFT HIND LEG,_____ _____.

5. In executing this release Releasor additionally binds his or her spouse, heirs, legal representatives, assigns, and anyone else claiming under him or her. Releasor has not assigned any claim arising from the transaction described in Clause 4 to another party. In addition to Releasee, this release extends to Releasee's heirs, successors, insurers and personal representatives.

6. Releasor has received good and adequate consideration for this release in the form of: _____ ___$78.40._____

7. This release was executed on ___MAY 21_____, 19_____ at ___LITTLETON, IL_____.

___Julia Shaughnessy_____
Releasor's Signature
___8855 Baltimore Ave._____
Address
___Littleton, IL_____

_____
Releasor's Spouse's Signature
___Sonia Burns_____
Releasee's Signature
___8859 Baltimore Ave._____
Address
___Littleton, Ill._____

Witnesses:
___Vees L. Uldrian___ ___3757 E Botsford Avenue, Cudahy, WI___
Name   Address
___Cornelius P. Hornswaggle___ 1600 Pennsylvania Ave. Washington, D.C.
Name   Address

Mediation

If you can't work something out with the other person, think about getting some help from a community mediation program. A mediator's job is to help people work out their own problems; the mediator has no power to impose a decision. (The mediation process is discussed at length in Chapter 7, Resolving Disputes with Neighbors.)

Lawsuits

Sometimes the best, most conscientious efforts at settlement don't work. Your next stop: court. Which, by the way, doesn't necessarily mean a side trip to a lawyer's office.

Where and When Lawsuits Are Brought

Be sure to look at small claims court as an option. In most states, the amount you can sue for in a small claims court is limited to $3,000 or less. (A chart listing all the state limits is in Chapter 7, Resolving Disputes with Neighbors.) These limits increase regularly; you can find out if your state's limit has gone up, and probably get some guidance in the form of a booklet, from your local small claims court clerk. (You can also find lots of information in *Everybody's Guide to Small Claims Court*, by Ralph Warner, Nolo Press.

If your dog was particularly valuable, or the conduct of the other person particularly shocking, and you can't squeeze your case into small claims court, you'll have to go to "regular" court—often called superior, district or circuit court. There, you will probably need the help of a lawyer, especially if the other side is represented by one.

LAWYERS AND FEES

When you sue someone for a loss caused by careless or intentional conduct, you're suing for a "tort." Negligence (carelessness), malpractice, or intentional infliction of emotional distress are all torts.

A lawyer who takes a tort case usually charges what is called a "contingency fee." That means the lawyer doesn't charge by the hour, and instead agrees not to take anything unless you win. If you win, the lawyer gets 30% or more of the amount.

That may sound like a no-lose proposition. But before you agree, be sure to do a couple of things:

- Find out who pays for "costs." Although you aren't paying lawyer's fees, the lawyer may expect you to advance money for fees charged by the court, investigation, and depositions.

- Get your fee agreement, including who pays for costs, in writing. A written contingency fee agreement is required by the law in several states (California is one); you should have one no matter where you live. If your lawyer isn't willing to put the agreement in writing, get another lawyer.

Wherever you decide to sue, act promptly. State law limits how long you have to start your lawsuit; usually, you must file within a year or two of the incident. You can find your state's rule by looking in the statute books under "statute of limitations" or "limitations" for torts. If you are suing the federal, state or local government, you may have to act much more quickly. (See "Suing the Government," below).

At the Small Claims Court Hearing

When you get to court, you want to prove three things to the judge:
- your dog was injured by the person you're suing;
- how much your loss is worth (which you figured out in "How Much Can the Dog Owner Sue For?" above); and
- the outrageousness of the conduct that caused the loss.

Strictly speaking, the outrageousness of the other person's conduct isn't relevant unless you're asking for punitive damages. But we all know it affects the outcome of the case. And it may bear on relative fault, if the other person accuses you of being partly to blame.

To bolster your own testimony, you may want to bring:

- written statements from people who can back up what you say about the extent of your loss;
- bills and receipts (veterinary bills, burial expenses) that show your financial loss;
- witnesses who can testify about the incident or your financial loss or emotional distress;
- evidence of your attachment to the dog and the effect its loss had on your life, if your dog was killed and you are asking for damages for your emotional distress;
- evidence of the outrageousness of the other person's behavior, if you are asking for punitive damages.

(For more on how small claims court works, see Chapter 7, Resolving Disputes with Neighbors.)

ONE LAWYER'S STRATEGY

This book wouldn't be complete without one of the most famous speeches about dogs ever made, which was delivered by a 19th century lawyer during the trial of a lawsuit over a dog killed by a neighbor. The lawyer who made the speech, George Vest, later became a United States Senator from Missouri. The jury returned a verdict of $500—more than twice the amount asked for—and would have sent the defendant to prison had the law allowed it. Judges still quote Vest. And through all the overblown, melodramatic oratory, you can see why; it is a genuinely moving statement.

Gentlemen of the jury: The best friend a man has in this world may turn against him and become his enemy. His son and daughter that he has reared with loving care may become ungrateful. Those who are nearest and dearest to us, those whom we trust with our happiness and our good name, may become traitors to their faith. The money that a man has he may lose. It flies away from him when he may need it most. Man's reputation may be sacrificed in a moment of ill considered action. The people who are prone to fall on their knees and do us honor when success is with us may be the first to throw the stone of malice when failure settles its cloud upon our head. The only absolutely unselfish friend a man may have in this selfish world, the one that never deserts him, the one that never proves ungrateful or treacherous is his dog.

A man's dog stands by him in prosperity and poverty, in health and sickness. He will sleep on the cold ground, when the wintery winds blow and the snow drives fiercely, if only he can be near his master's side. He will kiss the hand that has no food to offer, he will lick the wounds and sores that come in encounter with the roughness of the world. He guards the sleep of a pauper as if he were a prince.

When all other friends desert, he remains. When riches take wings and reputation falls to pieces he is as constant in his love as the sun in its journey through the heavens. If fortune drives the master forth an outcast into the cold, friendless and homeless, the faithful dog asks no higher privilege than that of accompanying him to guard him against danger, to fight against his enemies, and when the last scene of all comes, and death takes his master in its embrace and his body is laid away in the cold ground, no matter if all other friends pursue their way, there by his graveside will the noble dog be found, his head between his paws and his eyes sad, but open in alert watchfulness, faithful and true even to death.

Suing the Government

Individuals may lawfully injure or kill a dog only in the very limited circumstances discussed earlier in the chapter. The government has far broader powers to pick up, impound, and destroy dogs. But it must respect owners' constitutional ("due process") rights, and, in most cases, give an owner notice and a hearing before taking action. (This is discussed in Chapter 2, State and Local Regulation.) If the government abuses its authority, and wrongfully injures or kills your dog, you can sue. There are special rules, however, for suing the government. They vary from state to state, but you usually have less time to file a claim than you would have to if you were suing a private person.

Typically, if you want to sue a city, county or state government, you must first file a claim with it, within a very short time after the incident—often, just 90 or 100 days. You can get a claim form from the city or county clerk, or the state attorney general. The city or county attorney, or the state attorney general, will review the claim and make a recommendation. Most claims are denied. Only after your claim is denied may you sue. If you go to small claims court, take the letter denying your claim with you.

If you want to sue a federal agency, you're going to need a lawyer. Suits against the federal government must usually be brought in federal district court, which has no small claims procedures of its own. The federal government cannot be sued in local small claims court without its consent.

Once you get to court, the issues and procedures are much the same as when you sue an individual: you must put a dollar value on your loss, and prove that the government is responsible for it.

Damages note: You may not be able to get punitive damages against the government. See the discussion of punitive damages in "How Much Can a Dog Owner Sue For?" above.

---

[1]*State v. Smith*, 156 N.C. 628, 72 S.E. 321 (1911).

[2]Ken. Rev. Stat. § 258.235.

[3]That's exactly what happened in *Failing v. People*, 105 Colo. 399, 98 P.2d 865 (1940).

[4]*People v. Pope*, 22 Ill. Dec. 802, 66 Ill. App. 3d 303, 383 N.E.2d 278 (1978).

[5]*McDonald v. Bauman*, 199 Kan. 628, 433 P.2d 437 (1967).

[6]*Johnson v. McConnell*, 80 Cal. 545 (1889).

[7]*Trautman v. Day*, 273 N.W.2d 712 (N.D. 1979).

[8]*Puckett v. Miller*, 381 N.E.2d 1087 (Ind. App. 1978).

[9]*Molohon v. United States*, 206 F. Supp. 388 (Mont. 1962).

[10]*People v. Wicker*, 78 Misc. 811, 357 N.Y.S.2d 597 (Town Ct. 1974).

[11]*Roos v. Loeser*, 41 Cal. App. 783 (1919).

[12]*Zager v. Dimilia*, 524 N.Y.S.2d 968 (Vill. Ct. 1988).

[13]*Demeo v. Manville*, 68 Ill. App. 3d 843, 25 Ill. Dec. 443, 386 N.E.2d 917 (1979).

[14]*Stettner v. Graubard*, 82 Misc. 2d 132, 368 N.Y.S.2d 683 (1975).

[15]*Stettner v. Graubard*, 82 Misc. 2d 132, 368 N.Y.S.2d 683 (1975).

[16]*Richardson v. Fairbanks North Star Borough*, 705 P.2d 454 (Alaska 1985).

[17]*Zager v. Dimilia*, 524 N.Y.S.2d 968 (Vill. Ct. 1988).

[18]*La Porte v. Associated Independents, Inc.*, 163 So. 2d 267 (Fla. 1964).

[19]*Jankoski v. Preiser Animal Hospital, Ltd.*, 157 Ill. App. 3d 818, 110 Ill. Dec. 53, 510 N.E. 2d 1084 (1987).

[20]*Corso v. Crawford Dog and Cat Hospital, Inc.*, 415 N.Y.S.2d 182, 97 Misc. 2d 530 (1979).

[21]*Julian v. DeVincent*, 155 W. Va. 320, 184 S.E.2d 535 (1971).

[22]*Campbell v. Animal Quarantine Station*, 632 P.2d 1066 (Ha. 1981).

[23]*Knowles Animal Hospital, Inc. v. Wills*, 360 So. 2d 37 (Fla. App. 1978).

[24]*Corso v. Crawford Dog and Cat Hospital, Inc.*, 415 N.Y.S.2d 182, 97 Misc. 2d 530 (1979).

[25]*Fredeen v. Stride*, 525 P.2d 166 (Or. 1974).

[26]*Richardson v. Fairbanks North Star Borough*, 705 P.2d 454 (Alaska 1985).

[27]*Wilson v. City of Eagan*, 297 N.W.2d 146 (Minn. 1980).

[28]*Rimbaud v. Beiermeister*, 168 A.D. 596, 154 N.Y.S. 333 (1915).

[29]*Schade v. Cedar Rapids Animal Shelter*, 409 N.W.2d 716 (Iowa App. 1987).

[30]*Wilson v. City of Eagan*, 297 N.W.2d 146 (Minn. 1980).

[31]*Smith v. Wade*, 461 U.S. 30 (1983).

[32]For legal research help, see Appendix 1 of this book and *Legal Research: How to Find and Understand the Law*, by Steve Elias (Nolo Press).

10

PROVIDING FOR PETS

wills and trusts / leaving money for a dog's care /
why you can't leave money to a dog / ordering a dog put to death

Most pet owners want to make sure that when they die, their pets will be well taken care of. For people who are elderly or seriously ill, this can be an immediate concern.

Some people make informal arrangements; there is an "understanding" that a friend, neighbor or relative will care for a dog if the owner can't. Often, that's enough, but not always. What if, for example, the person you've asked to provide care doesn't have much money to spare, and might be burdened by food and veterinary bills? Or what if the person you make arrangements with isn't able to care for the dog when needed?

Usually, it is better to make more formal provisions for your dog's care. But before we get into specifics, here are a few legal and practical rules to keep in mind:

- You can't leave money or other property to your dog, either through a will or a trust. (We explain why later in the chapter.)
- Instead, plan to leave your dog, and perhaps some money for expenses, to someone you trust to look out for it.
- Don't rely on the legal system to enforce your wishes concerning care of your pet after you die. Make your own arrangements with

someone you trust. The legal system, cumbersome and unreliable enough when it comes to providing for human survivors, is absolutely untrustworthy when you're concerned about the animals you will leave behind.

Strategies for Taking Care of Pets

Although you can't leave money directly to your dog, there are lots of things you can do to make sure it is well-provided for when you can no longer take care of it.

Use a Will or Trust to Leave Your Dog

Animals have these advantages over man: they have no theologians to instruct them, their funerals cost them nothing, and no one starts lawsuits over their wills.

— Voltaire

When you draw up your estate plan, make specific plans for what you want to happen to your dog when you die. Remember, legally your dog is an item of property, and when you die, it will have a new owner. Choosing that new owner is the most important thing you can do to make sure your pet is well taken care of after your death.

You can use either a will or a revocable living ("inter vivos") trust to transfer ownership of the dog at your death. With a will, you simply include a provision like: "I leave my dog Taffy to my friend Lola Marquez." Variations on this simple clause are outlined below.

Many people use a living trust, instead of a will, to transfer property. Using a trust eliminates the need for probate, which is a time-consuming and expensive process by which a court supervises the distribution of a deceased person's property. Probate costs aren't usually significant when it comes to a dog, but you may want to include your dog in a living trust if you've already set one up for other property.

To set up a revocable living trust, you sign a paper called a trust document. Usually, in the trust document you name yourself as trustee and name another person to take over as trustee at your death. You then transfer property to the trust. When you die, the new trustee takes over and transfers the property to the beneficiaries, who you also listed in the trust document. That points out another advantage of a living trust: it's easier to change the beneficiary of a trust than the beneficiary of a will. To change a will, you must sign it in front of witnesses. A living trust doesn't require that formality, although you can have it notarized just to make it more "official." A trust also remains private; a will becomes a matter of public record after you die and it is filed with the probate court.

Whether you choose a will or a trust, don't make the gift of your dog a surprise. Talk to the people you want to take the dog, and make sure they are really willing and able to do it. They may adore your dog, but if their children are allergic to it or they live in a high-rise apartment building, they simply may not be in a position to take it.

Because circumstances change—your first choice for someone to take your dog could marry someone allergic to dogs, take a job that requires lots of travel, or move away—it's always a good idea to line up a second choice. You should name this person as an alternate beneficiary in your will or trust, too.[1]

If you don't name a new owner in your will or trust, one of two generally undesirable consequences will result:

• Your dog will pass under the residuary clause of your will (the catch-all clause that disposes of everything that's not taken care of by the rest of the will); or

- If you don't have a will, the dog will go to your next of kin, as determined by state law.

This means that, absent a lucky coincidence, the person who will inherit your dog probably won't be the person you would choose.

EMERGENCY CARE FOR YOUR DOG WHEN YOU'RE UNAVAILABLE

While you're making arrangements for your dog's care after your death, also think about what would happen to your dog in an emergency, if you became sick or disabled and couldn't care for it for an extended period. Obviously, it makes sense to have a fallback caretaker. Arrange with someone to take care of the dog, and write down any needed instructions. Think about what food the dog eats, what medication it needs, who your veterinarian is, who takes care of grooming—and make sure the designated temporary caretaker has, or can easily get to, a copy of your instructions.[2]

Leave Money to the New Owner

You may not be satisfied just to name a new owner for your dog in your will or trust and leave it at that. After all, you know that it's a big responsibility to take care of a dog. One simple strategy is to leave some money, along with the dog, to the new owner. This person who, after all, should be someone you trust, can use the money toward the costs of caring for the dog.

Leaving money is particularly important if the person you are leaving the dog to isn't affluent. But if in doubt, provide the money. After all, a dog who arrives with a full dinner dish is likely to be more welcome than one who is on the dole.

A will provision might read like this:

```
"If my dog, Taffy, is alive at my death, I
leave her and $3,000 to be used for her care to
Brian Smith. If Brian is unable to care for
Taffy, I leave her, and the $3,000 to be used
for her care, to Susan McDermott."
```

You should know that although the provision leaving the $3,000 to Brian is legal and enforceable, the part about using the money to take care of Taffy probably isn't. Your friend Brian could lose the whole stash in Atlantic City, and there wouldn't be anything anybody could do about it. But this shouldn't be a big worry. You shouldn't leave your dog, and money to care for it, to someone you don't trust.

If Taffy isn't alive when you die, Brian won't get the $3,000. Any property that the will doesn't specifically give away will be given to the person named in the will to receive the "residuary" of your estate.

HELPING OTHER ANIMALS

When you make your will or trust, remember that humane societies, assistance dog training centers and other non-profit organizations depend on donations. A gift in your will can help many animals.

Putting Conditions on the Gift: It is possible, but complicated and usually impractical, to make the gift of the dog conditional on certain acts of the new owner. For example, you can put a clause like this in your will:

> "If my dog, Taffy, is alive at my death, I leave her and $3,000 to Brian Smith, on the condition that Brian care for Taffy until her death, but no more than 21 years. Should Brian stop providing necessary care for Taffy, Taffy and the $3,000 shall go to the McDonough County, Wyoming Society for the Prevention of Cruelty to Animals."3

Who will enforce the condition? If your estate is probated (these days many are not because so many people use probate avoidance techniques), the executor of your estate has the responsibility as long as the estate is still before the probate court. After probate is wrapped up and all property is distributed, it's up to the alternate beneficiary—in this example, the McDonough County SPCA. Either way, it's a lot of trouble, and we recommend against using conditional bequests. Once again the central truth appears: don't rely on the law to protect your pets. Arrange for them to be taken care of by people who know that a dog is more than another piece of property.

Leave the Dog to One Person, Money to Another

In unusual circumstances, you may want to consider leaving the dog to one person and the money for the dog's care to someone else. Let's say, for example, that your friend Brian is great with dogs and has a place in the country, but his love of animals extends to the ponies— that is, he can't stay away from the track when he's got some extra cash in his pocket. You could leave your dog Taffy to Brian, and the $3,000 to Brian's sister, Karen, with instructions to give it to Brian in chunks that he won't find quite so tempting.

It can be particularly important to consider a plan like this if the person who will care for your dog receives some kind of public assistance—Social Security or disability, for example. If that person receives several thousand dollars from you in a lump sum, it might mean the grant would be cut off until the money is spent—a situation that, obviously, benefits neither your friend nor your dog.

Here are some sample clauses:

> "I leave my dog, Taffy, if she is alive at my
> death, to Brian Smith."

> "If my dog Taffy is alive at my death, I leave
> $3,000, for her care, to Karen Smith. I desire
> that she give her brother, Brian Smith, as
> long as he has custody of Taffy, $30 a month
> for Taffy's care. I also desire that, in
> addition, she use the money to pay Taffy's
> veterinary bills, or reimburse Brian for
> veterinary bills he pays."

Again, remember that legally, the $3,000 goes to Karen outright if Taffy is alive when you die. The instructions about how to use it aren't legally enforceable—but they make your wishes clear, which should be enough if you choose the right people.

Keep Your Will or Trust Up to Date

What if your dog dies before you do, but you don't get around to changing your will or living trust, which leaves money for the dog's care? It depends on the court, but the money you intended to be used for the dog's care will probably still go to the person you named. A Colorado court ruled that way after looking at the following will clause:

> "FOURTH: Should my husband predecease me, or should we die as the result of a common disaster, I hereby give $5,000.00 to IRENE MORRISON, should she survive me, for the proper care of my dog Dutchess."

Dutchess died before her owner did, but the court ruled that Morrison should get the $5,000 anyway.[4] Other courts faced with similar situations have ruled the same way.[5] The theory is that the obligation to care for the dog doesn't arise until after the gift of the money is made. And because it's not the beneficiary's fault that she can't carry out the condition, she's entitled to keep the gift.

If you want to prevent a similar result, it's quite easy. All you need to do is follow the sample clauses we use, being sure to include the provision about your dog surviving you:

> "If my dog Taffy is living at my death, I leave her, and $3,000 to be used for her care, to Brian Smith. If Brian is unable to care for Taffy, I leave her, and the $3,000 to be used for her care, to Susan McDermott."

Make Arrangements with a Veterinarian

After you've taken care of leaving your dog, and perhaps some money for its care, to someone, you may want to use your will to arrange for the dog's veterinary care for life. You can do this by leaving money to the vet. The amount, and what is expected of the vet, should of course be worked out with the vet in advance. Any money left when the dog dies could go to a relative, a charity, or to the vet in appreciation of her services—whatever you want.

Another approach is to write out a life care contract with a vet. Then you don't have to clutter up your will with this issue. You could arrange this in at least two ways:

- Have a vet agree to provide lifetime care in exchange for a lump sum.
- Pay the vet a certain amount, as a credit toward expected services, and agree on what is to be done with any excess that's left when the dog dies.

Sample contracts, which can be modified to fit your situation, are shown below.

▲

CONTRACT (Lifetime Care)

Helen Strauss, D.V.M., and Stephen Kowalski agree that:

1. Dr. Strauss will provide veterinary care for Mr. Kowalski's dog Sparky from the time of Mr. Kowalski's death until Sparky's death.

2. The veterinary care provided shall include all necessary vaccinations, diagnosis, medications, reasonable treatment of diseases or injury, and euthanasia.

3. If Dr. Strauss determines that Sparky has a terminal condition, and that further treatment is unlikely to significantly prolong the dog's life, or that prolonging his life with treatment would mean that the dog would suffer unduly, she may decline to continue treatment.

4. Mr. Kowalski has paid Dr. Strauss $3,000 for her agreement to provide care for Sparky for life.

_____   Date: _____

_____   Date: _____

▼

▲

CONTRACT (Credit Toward Services)

Jacqueline Buckley, D.V.M., and Peter Campbell agree that:

1. Dr. Buckley will provide veterinary care for Mr. Campbell's dog Charlemagne from the time of Mr. Campbell's death until Charlemagne's death.

2. The veterinary care provided shall include all necessary vaccinations, diagnosis, medications, reasonable treatment of diseases or injury, and euthanasia.

3. If Dr. Buckley determines that Charlemagne has a terminal condition, and that further treatment is unlikely to significantly prolong the dog's life, or that prolonging his life with treatment would mean that the dog would suffer unduly, she may decline to continue treatment.

4. Mr. Campbell has paid Dr. Buckley $3,000, which shall count as a credit toward Dr. Buckley's veterinary care of Charlemagne.

5. This $3,000 shall count as a credit for veterinary services for Charlemagne's new owner. Dr. Buckley shall provide the new owner with statements, specifying services provided, their cost, and the amount of credit remaining.

6. If, at Charlemagne's death, any of the original $3,000 payment has not been used up, it shall be donated to the Phoenix, Arizona Society for the Prevention of Cruelty to Animals.

7. If the $3,000 in services is used up, Dr. Buckley may discontinue treatment of Charlemagne, or charge Charlemagne's owner for any further services.

8. If Dr. Buckley moves away from the area, or ceases to practice veterinary medicine, she shall either:

    a)   arrange with another veterinarian, subject to the approval of Charlemagne's owner, for continued care of the dog under the terms of this agreement, so that the new veterinarian extends the same credit for services as remained when Dr. Buckley quit providing services; or

    b)   refund whatever of the original $3,000 credit remains to Charlemagne's owner.

_____   Date: _____

_____   Date: _____

▼

Why You Can't Leave Money to a Dog— and What Happens If You Try

As mentioned earlier, you cannot leave money or other kinds of property to your dog. And it's not just because he can't see over the bank counter to open an account. The law says animals are property, and one piece of property simply can't own another piece.

Wills

Since a dog can't own property, obviously it can't be a beneficiary (someone who receives property) in a will. If you do name your dog as a beneficiary, whatever property you tried to leave it will go instead to the person you named as your residuary beneficiary (the person who gets everything not left to the beneficiaries named in the will). If there's no residuary beneficiary, the property will be distributed according to the "intestate succession" laws of your state, which control what happens to property if there is no will or trust to dispose of it. The point is that the dog will get nothing.

That rule can lead to results far from what the person making the will intended. Take the case of Thelma Russell, who left "everything I own . . . to Chester H. Quinn and Roxy Russell." Chester was a close friend; Roxy was a dog. Russell's niece challenged the will in 1968. The California Supreme Court agreed that the gift to Roxy was void, which left the question of what to do with half of the property. Should it go to Chester, or to the niece, who was Russell's only heir under California law? Despite a note that Russell had left, urging Chester not to let her nieces get their hands on her property no matter what it took to stop them, the court gave half the estate to the niece.[6] There's no record of what happened to Roxy, but we like to think that she settled down happily for the rest of a long life with Chester, blissfully unaware of all the human squabbling.

Trusts

With a trust, property is left to a beneficiary, but you put someone else, called a trustee, in charge of managing it and doling it out to the beneficiary. The trustee follows a written set of instructions (called trust powers) that you provide.

Sounds like just the ticket for making sure your dog has enough rawhide chews for life, but trusts don't work for animals. The legal problem is the same as with wills, because the beneficiary of a trust is considered the owner of certain interests in the trust property. The basic rule still holds: a dog, because it's property itself, can't own property. With a trust, there is the added problem that the beneficiary must be able to enforce the trust provisions—that is, make the trustee fulfill all responsibilities honestly and according to the terms of the trust. Dogs can't go to court to snitch on a dishonest or inept trustee who spends the dog chow money on lottery tickets.

Remember that you can use a trust to leave a dog to someone—you just can't use a trust to leave money to a dog.

Courts, however, have shown some sensitivity and ingenuity when faced with wills that try to set up trusts for pets. A common solution is to turn the trust into what is called an "honorary trust." That means the court allows the property left in trust to be used for the animal beneficiary, but that it won't force the trustee to perform duties according to the written terms of the trust. The trustee is free to decide how to use the money to care for the animal. Any money left over after the dog dies is distributed according to the terms of the trust; most trusts include directions for what the trustee is to do with any leftover money. From a practical point of view, you wind up pretty much where you would have been without a trust: dependent on someone's good will to care for your animals.

What about Thelma Russell's will (discussed above), which left her property to her friend Chester and her dog Roxy? The court could have salvaged her obvious intention by ruling that she had meant to set up a trust for Roxy's care, with Chester as the trustee. But the court staunchly stuck to the letter of the law, puffing that a simple bequest "in equal shares to two beneficiaries" couldn't possibly mean that a trust for one beneficiary was intended. Never mind that one of the beneficiaries was a dog—if you believe the court, Russell simply intended that half her property be dumped in front of Roxy's doghouse.

Even if it uses the honorary trust doctrine to try to provide for a dog, a court is likely to scrutinize, and perhaps meddle with, both the amount of money left for the animal and how long the trust is to last.[7] If, for example, the amount left in trust is extravagant in the court's opinion, the court may step in to reduce it. An example is the trust set up by a Pennsylvania woman in 1974, which made $40,000 to $50,000 a year available for the care of four horses and six dogs. The court ruled that as long as the animals were well taken care of, the trustee was free to give the surplus money to the alternate beneficiaries named in the will.[8]

The moral of these stories is obvious: a trust is a lousy way to provide for an animal. A trust may be thrown out by a court, and even if it isn't, a court must still interpret it, which is an expensive and unpredictable process.

Will Provisions that Order Animals Destroyed

While you're alive, your dog is, legally, your property. Aside from the restrictions of cruelty laws, you can do almost anything you want with an animal you own: sell it, give it away, or have it humanely destroyed.

What about when you die? If your will directs the executor of your estate to have your dog humanely destroyed, and the executor or a local humane society doesn't object—quickly—to carrying out your wishes, the dog will be destroyed soon after your death.

If someone does object, the probate court, which oversees the administration of your estate, will rule on the validity of the will provision. Almost always, these provisions are found to be invalid, and the court may forbid the executor from carrying out your instructions. Courts have always frowned on wills that order the destruction of any kind of property, on the ground that it goes against public policy to needlessly destroy valuable property.[9]

Generally, the court's rationale is something like this: Someone leaves instructions in a will to destroy a dog because of the worry that the dog will not be cared for properly, or will end up in a pound or somewhere worse. The owner wishes to prevent pain and suffering. So, if the dog is old and ill, or so attached to the owner that it couldn't adjust to a new home, the owner's request that it be destroyed may make perfect sense. But if an executor has found a good home for a young, healthy animal, and the animal seems well-adjusted and well taken care of, a court may decide that the previous owner's wishes are best fulfilled by not carrying out the will's order.

For example, a court faced with a will provision ordering the humane destruction of two healthy Irish setters concluded that the owner wouldn't really want them killed, because the dogs were happy and well-cared for in a country home: "There is no lack of care. There is no reason for carrying out the literal provision of the will. That decedent [the deceased owner] would rather see her pets happy and healthy and alive than destroyed there can be no doubt."[10]

One state legislature, moved to action by the public outcry over the impending death of a little mixed-breed dog (which was being temporarily protected by the San Francisco SPCA), used the same rationale to pass a special law to save the dog's life. The legislature found that the dog's deceased owner, "having the best interests of her pet dog in mind, would not wish her instructions for the destruction of the pet dog carried out" if she knew how happy the dog was now.[11]

Although courts rarely mention it, there is also overwhelming public opposition to carrying out such a will provision. In one California case in 1980, the court allowed into evidence 3,000 letters from people who opposed a will that ordered the executor of the estate to have a dog euthanized.[12] Although courts don't want to admit they are bowing to public pressure, it's hard to imagine a judge who wants to become famous for ordering the death of a happy, healthy pet that hundreds of families have offered to take in.

Many question the motives of dog owners who put such directions in their wills. Most pet owners who are truly worried about what will happen to their pets could arrange, if they tried hard enough, to have them go to loving homes. Obviously, there are exceptions: some dogs' attachment to one person is legendary, and such dogs can't be expected to adjust to new homes. The same goes for dogs that are incorrigibly bad-tempered around anyone outside the immediate family. And, of course, older dogs who are not in the best of health are not easy to place in new homes. But unfortunately, there are times when using a will to order healthy, normal pets to die when you do seems a flamboyant exercise of power, reminiscent of ancient emperors who had servants, wives and animals buried with them.

---

[1]For help in writing a will, see *Nolo's Simple Will Book* or *WillMaker*, software that lets you do your own valid will on your personal computer.

[2]Nolo's *For the Record*, a computer program, helps you record and organize this information so that in an emergency, it is easily available to those who need it.

[3]The 21-year provision is to avoid invalidating the gift—see footnote 7.

[4]*Morrison v. Prindle*, 491 P.2d 108 (1971).

[5]For example, see *In re Andrews' Will*, 34 Misc. 2d 432, 228 N.Y.S.2d 591 (Surrogate's Ct. 1962).

[6]*In re Estate of Russell*, 70 Cal. Rptr. 561, 69 Cal. 2d 200, 444 P.2d 353 (1968).

[7]If the trust doesn't specify a termination date ("until the death of the animals" isn't enough; the date must be explicit or related to a human life), a court will usually impose a time limit—21 years is the standard one—on the trust. The 21-year restriction (what dog lives more than 21 years?) is a bow toward medieval law. Using it avoids a messy argument over an arcane legal doctrine called the "rule against perpetuities."

[8]*Lyon Estate*, 67 Pa. D. & C.2d 474 (1974).

[9]This prerogative, of course, isn't exercised logically or consistently: if it were, a court could intervene whenever an owner wanted a healthy pet killed, not just when the owner tries to do so from beyond the grave.

[10]*Capers Estate*, 34 Pa. D. & C. 121 (1964).

[11]California S.B. 2509, signed June 16, 1980.

[12]*Smith v. Avanzino*, No. 225698 (Super. Ct., San Francisco County, June 17, 1980).

11

PERSONAL INJURY AND
PROPERTY DAMAGE

financial responsibility / the one-bite rule / dog-bite statutes /
injury to livestock / small claims court / liability insurance

Admit it. Some dogs can cause a lot of trouble, ranging from mildly annoying to life-threatening. As a society, we tolerate this, essentially, for the same reason we tolerate children—because many of us think the benefits outweigh the inconvenience.

Owners, like parents, have a legal responsibility to prevent their pets from injuring people or damaging property. In general, if a dog injures someone, the owner will probably have to pay the victim's medical expenses and other financial losses. The owner may also be required to take measures to prevent another incident—in the most serious cases, by destroying the dog. If a serious injury is caused by an owner who acts recklessly or deliberately—letting a vicious dog run loose around children, for example—the owner may face a fine or even a jail sentence. (Criminal penalties are discussed in Chapter 12, Vicious Dogs and Pit Bulls.)

An owner whose dog injures or kills livestock must also pay for the damage, which can be considerable. For the dog, especially if it's caught in the act of attacking livestock, the sentence is likely to be death.

For Dog Owners: How to Prevent Injuries

If you pick up a starving dog and make him prosperous, he will not bite you. This is the principal difference between a dog and a man.
—Mark Twain

The best way to avoid liability is, obviously, to prevent your dog from causing injury or damage. A few simple rules will help you avert incidents and, should your dog bite someone, keep your liability as low as it fairly should be.

- **Never let a dog run at large.** In some states, you're automatically liable for any injury your dog causes while at large, even if you might be off the hook if the same thing happened while the dog was on your property.
- **Remember that any dog can hurt someone.** Don't think that because your dog is gentle, old, or small, it can't cause an injury. You may not be scared when your Pekingese comes tearing around the corner of the house barking, but someone walking by on the sidewalk might be. If that timid passer-by falls, you could be liable for any hospital bills. And even normally docile dogs will bite when they are frightened or when they are protecting their puppies, owners, or food—not necessarily in that order.

  Dogs can also do serious damage to property. Just a few minutes' excavation in the neighbors' prize-winning rose garden can rack up a big bill.
- **Keep your dog's license and vaccinations current.** If your dog bites someone, the authorities, not to mention the victim, will view it a lot more seriously if the dog doesn't have a current rabies vaccination. The dog will probably spend some time quarantined behind bars, even if you're sure it hasn't been exposed to rabies.

- **Post warning signs.** If you have any reason to think that your dog might injure someone coming onto your property, post "Beware of Dog" signs prominently. Again, remember that your dog can easily hurt someone accidentally, by frightening or tripping them. Warning signs at least alert visitors that there's a dog about. They can't hurt, and may also discourage burglars from trying your house. Stay away from the creative variations on the traditional "Beware of Dog" signs. Someone could reasonably assume that a cartoon-like "Trespassers Will Be Eaten" sign is a joke, not a serious warning.
- **Keep the dog out of strangers' paths.** Lots of people—mail carriers, salespeople, poll-takers, girl scouts—routinely come to your front door. You may not think you invited them, but the law says you've issued an "implied invitation" unless you warn them away with locks or signs. (This is discussed in "Was the Victim Trespassing?" below.) You are responsible for making sure your dog doesn't hurt them. That means keeping the dog away from the main door. A fenced front yard isn't good enough; most people will open a gate and walk on up to the door. Putting the mailbox outside the gate may solve some problems.
- **Keep your dog securely enclosed.** If you think children are likely to be attracted to the dog, make sure the gate to your yard is child-proof. If your dog injures a child while both are on your property, you will probably be responsible if you could reasonably have expected a child to go in the yard, even though you didn't invite the child there.

If You're Hurt by a Dog

If you're attacked by a dog, or see someone else attacked, you can, of course, fight back. The laws of nearly every state authorize anyone to take whatever action is necessary, including killing, to stop a dog caught in the act of attacking a person. (This is discussed in more detail in Chapter 9, If a Dog Is Injured or Killed). Very few dogs are killed this way, because dogs rarely engage in a sustained "attack" on a person. Most dogs that bite do so quickly, out of fright, nervousness, or misdirected protectiveness.

If you're injured by a dog, there are a few things you should do right away.

- **Get the names and phone numbers of the dog's owner and witnesses to the incident.** Even if you don't think you'll be asking for any money, get the dog's owner's name and address. You may change your mind the next day, when you discover that jumping out of the way of that lunging dog has given you a swollen ankle. The same goes for any witnesses. You may need them to back up your version of what happened if you and the dog's owner later disagree.

If you don't know who owns the dog, you should still get the witnesses' names. Animal control authorities may be able to find the dog from your description.

- **Get medical attention if you need it.** If your injury is serious enough to require medical attention, get it quickly. Keep records of doctor's office or hospital visits and copies of bills.

Although it may not be the way things should be, you will probably win more money in a lawsuit if you can document a number of doctor's appointments and bills and, if appropriate, x-rays, physical therapy sessions, or other treatment.

- **Report the incident to animal control authorities.** This is especially important if the dog wasn't wearing a license tag and you don't know who owns it. City or county authorities will try to pick it up so it can be quarantined. Many cities and some states require that a dog that bites someone be quarantined, to see if the dog is rabid, for seven to twenty days, either at the owner's home or in the dog pound. Confinement may not be required if the dog has a current rabies vaccination.

The local animal control department may also have records of prior attacks by the dog. That could help you negotiate with the owner, or win a case in court if it goes that far. If the dog has been officially labeled "vicious," (as some cities and states designate dogs who have bitten people), the owner may be fined, and the dog may be ordered destroyed. (Vicious dog programs are discussed in Chapter 12, Vicious Dogs and 'Pit Bulls.')

Dog Owner Liability: An Overview

The rules that control legal responsibility for injuries caused by dogs vary from state to state. Before we get into a detailed discussion of the law, here's an overview of when dog owners are liable, and what they must pay for.

GEE, KING IS ALWAYS SUCH A FRIENDLY PUPPY...

When the Dog's Owner Is Legally Liable

In most states, dog owners are financially liable for any personal injury or property damage their pets cause. Depending on state law, they may be found liable for one of three reasons, each of which we mention here and discuss in detail later in the chapter. (See "Laws that Make Dog Owners Liable.")

- A **"dog-bite statute."** Many states have laws that make a dog owner legally liable for any injury or property damage the dog causes. Although commonly called dog-bite statutes, most of these laws cover all kinds of dog-inflicted injury, not just bites. Usually, it's easiest for an injured person to sue under a dog-bite statute, because the dog owner is automatically liable if the statute applies.

Example: Barbara lives in Minneapolis with her spaniel-mix dog Ray, who has always been gentle with people. But one day, while Barbara has it on a leash, Ray unexpectedly bites a child in a park. Barbara wasn't being careless, but under her state's law, she's financially liable if her dog "without provocation, attacks or injures any person who is acting peaceably in any place where the person may lawfully be."

STATES WITH DOG-BITE STATUTES

Alabama	Iowa	New Jersey
Arizona	Kentucky	Ohio
California	Louisiana	Oklahoma
Connecticut	Maine	Pennsylvania
Delaware	Massachusetts	Rhode Island
District of Columbia	Michigan	South Carolina
Florida	Minnesota	Utah
Hawaii	Montana	Washington
Ilinois	Nebraska	West Virginia
Indiana	New Hampshire	Wisconsin

- **The common law rule.** The "common law" rule, developed by courts over the centuries, makes an owner legally responsible for injury a dog causes only if the owner knew the dog was likely to cause that type of injury—for example, that the dog would bite, or jump on people. Even in states that have dog-bite statutes, an injured person can sue on a common law theory if for some reason the statute doesn't cover the situation. It's tougher to sue under this legal theory than under a dog-bite statute, because the victim must prove the owner knew of the dog's dangerousness.

  Example: A New Jersey man was scratched by a dog. He couldn't sue the dog's owner under the state statute, which covers only injuries from dog bites. He sued and won on a common law theory, because he proved that the dog's owner knew of the dog's tendency to jump up and scratch people.[1]

- **Negligence.** If the state has no dog-bite statute, and someone hurt by a dog can't prove that the dog owner knew the dog was dangerous, there's one more legal avenue for an injured person to try: proving the injury happened because the dog owner was unreasonably careless (negligent) in controlling the dog.

Example: Lucy brings her new dog Zippy home and puts it in the back yard, but forgets to close the gate. The dog runs out into her front yard and frightens the mail carrier, Frank, who's walking by. He wrenches his back trying to avoid the dog. Frank's state doesn't have a dog-bite statute, and he can't sue under a common law theory because he can't prove that Lucy knew the dog would frighten people. But he may be able to prove that Lucy's negligence—leaving the gate open—caused his injury.

Note on choosing a strategy: In some states, time limits on filing lawsuits may differ depending on the theory of the lawsuit. For example, in Arizona, lawsuits under the dog-bite statute must be filed within one year of the incident. But an injured person who sues under a common law theory has two years to file a case.[2]

DOGS ON DUTY

Many states exempt the police or military from liability if their trained dogs bite someone while they're working. So someone who is injured by an on-duty police dog may not be able to sue the police or city government successfully. California limits this immunity from lawsuits to situations in which the government agency in charge of the dog has a written policy on proper use of its dogs.[3]

What the Dog Owner Must Pay For

A dog owner who is legally responsible for an injury to a person or property may be responsible for reimbursing the injured person for:

- Medical bills (emergency room, office visits, hospital stays, surgery, medication, physical therapy)
- Time off work
- Pain and suffering
- Property damage

If the dog has injured someone before, or the owner's conduct was particularly outrageous (letting a dog known to be vicious run loose, for example), the owner may also be liable for:
- Double or triple damages (in some states), or
- Punitive damages (damages meant to punish the dog's owner for misconduct).

(All of these are discussed below in "How Much the Victim Can Recover.")

Who Is Responsible

Usually, a dog's owner is legally responsible for damage or injury the dog causes. But someone else may also be liable, if:
- The dog owner is less than 18 years old;
- The dog was on someone else's property, and that person was negligent in not removing the dog;
- The dog owner's landlord knew the dog was dangerous but didn't do anything about it; or
- Someone besides the owner was taking care of the dog.

If any of these fits your situation, read the section below on "Who Can Be Sued: Owners and Keepers" before you negotiate or start legal action.

Note on suing family members: In most circumstances, parents can't be sued by children who are injured as a result of parental negligence. But in at least one instance, a toddler was allowed to sue her parents after the family dog bit her severely. An Arizona court ruled that because the parents had a duty, as dog owners, to keep their dog from injuring anyone—including their own child—they were not immune from a lawsuit by their daughter [*Schleier ex rel. Alter v. Alter*, 767 P.2d 1187 (Ariz. App. 1989.)]

Negotiating with the Owner

Most dog bite disputes never get to court. Negotiating directly with a dog owner or insurance company often gets an injured person compensated much more quickly and easily than the cumbersome legal system. If you've been injured by a dog, contact the dog's owner. Write a letter setting out what happened—even though the owner may know the facts as well as you do. Include an itemized list of your expenses, and mention any local or state dog-bite laws. Give a deadline for payment—that's a good incentive for the owner. And stress that if you don't work something out by then, you'll file a small claims (or other) court case. It's also a good idea to mention that the dog owner may be covered by insurance; homeowner's insurance pays for many dog-bite injuries, but the dog's owner may not realize that. A sample letter is shown below, in our hypothetical small claims case.

If you do work out an agreement, put it in writing. The agreement you sign is called a release, because the injured person releases the dog owner from all legal claims arising out of the incident. We include a release below, in our story of The Jogger and the Beast.

SOMEHOW YOU KNEW YOU'D END UP IN COURT

"As a general rule dogs in a dream are a good omen and symbolize friends. To hear a dog bark happily signifies pleasing social recognition, but if it barked fiercely, you are being warned of possible legal troubles."[4]

Is Small Claims Court Right For You?

If you're hurt by a dog, you can probably sue the dog's owner and collect. But you don't want to get embroiled in a lawsuit if you can help it. The time and expense are mind-boggling. A few numbers: in many large cities, lawsuits routinely take two years or more to get to trial. And attorneys charge $75 to $200 an hour, or, if they work on a "contingency fee" basis, keep one-third or more of what you finally collect from a lawsuit.

Small claims court is the exception, and it's the best our legal system has to offer when it comes to disputes that don't involve too much money. It's relatively fast—you'll wait a few weeks or months, instead of years—procedures are simple and designed for laypeople, and (in many states), lawyers aren't allowed.

The problem is that the most you can sue for in small claims court is currently around $1,500 or $2,000 in most states, though these limits are creeping up slowly. (A list of every state's small claims court limit is in Chapter 7, Resolving Disputes with Neighbors.) But don't automatically give up on small claims court just because your claim is over the limit. Because of the higher cost of proceeding in regular court, you may still come out ahead by reducing your claim so it fits in small claims court.

Example: Natalie lives in Illinois, where the small claims court limit is $2,500. She is injured when a dog runs in front of her as she rides her new 15-speed bicycle down the street. The bike is totaled, and Natalie runs up more than $1,000 in medical bills. All together, she's out about $2,800. Should she abandon small claims court and get a lawyer? You probably already know the answer. By the time Natalie pays a lawyer, and the higher filing fees of regular court, she'll lose at least the $300 that she must give up if she files in small claims court.

Before you start a small claims court case, check on other limits peculiar to small claims court in your state. For example, some states do not allow people to sue for pain and suffering. Most states have free publications that explain the rules for filing a small claims court case: what papers to file, when to file them, how to schedule a hearing, and other procedures. (Valuable guidance on preparing a small claims court case can be found in *Everybody's Guide to Small Claims Court* by Ralph Warner, Nolo Press).

If you have much in the way of medical bills or time off work, small claims court may not be any help, and you may need to go to "regular" court. If that's the case, you should see an experienced lawyer. This book isn't meant to be a do-it-yourself guide to filing or defending a lawsuit based on a dog bite. Researching and applying the law to a particular dog-bite case can be tricky, and it's impossible to prepare you for a trial when the other side is represented by a lawyer.

A Small Claims Court Case

The best way to show how small claims court works is to follow a hypothetical case from beginning to end.[5] Here is how a typical case, which we call "The Jogger and the Beast," might unfold:

One Sunday morning, Jake was jogging along a dirt fire trail when he met two women and a dog. The women, Jake thought, looked friendly, but the dog looked like a cross between a large Doberman and a medium-sized wolf. Because the women and the dog took up most of the center of the road, Jake moved to the far right edge. Then, noticing that the beast was on a long leash, he moved off the path into the ditch.

As it turned out, Jake didn't go quite far enough. The dog lunged for him, fangs first. Jake tried to bound into the brush at the side of the ditch (poison oak looking like the lesser of two evils at the moment), but he wasn't quick enough. The dog bit Jake's ankle before the woman holding the leash could restrain him.

Jake yelled in pain, the woman hauled the dog back to the other side of the road, and her friend went to see how bad the bite was. Before Jake hobbled off to see a doctor—his ankle was bleeding from a good-sized gash—he got the name and phone number of the dog's owner, Allison Finley, and of her friend, Kathleen Huxley.

Because it was Sunday morning, Jake had to go to the emergency room of a local hospital to see a doctor. After sitting an hour and a half in a crowded waiting room, a doctor stitched up the bite and gave him some painkiller and orders to stay off the leg for a few days. Jake spent the rest of the day restless and uncomfortable. He didn't sleep well that night, and decided not to try to go to work on Monday. Tuesday morning, he saw his regular doctor, who pronounced the wound "healing nicely." That afternoon he limped back to work.

Meanwhile, Jake contacted officials at the county animal control department, notifying them of the incident and confirming that the dog was properly licensed and vaccinated for rabies. Jake consoled himself with the thought that at least he wouldn't start foaming at the mouth. After a few weeks, he could jog again without pain, although his fear of encountering The Beast again prompted him to choose a new route. Jake decided it was time to add up his costs and demand payment from Allison Finley.

Looking up the law

First, however, he decided to check on California law to see just what he was entitled to. Looking up "Dogs" in the general index of the California code (the state statutes) gave him a long list of laws. The most promising was under "Bite, liability of owner." Jake turned to the statute.

It read, in part: "The owner of any dog is liable for the damages suffered by any person who is bitten by the dog while in a public place . . . regardless of the former viciousness of the dog or the owner's knowledge of such viciousness."

Reading the statute closely told Jake he had to prove:

- Allison Finley owned the dog;
- The dog bit him;
- He was in a public place when bitten; and
- He suffered damages as a result.

Piece of cake, Jake thought. Allison couldn't even argue about anything but the amount of the damages. And as far as Jake could tell, she didn't have any defenses to make—nobody could say, Jake was sure, that by jogging along minding his own business, he had provoked the dog into biting him.

Adding up damages

Jake's out-of-pocket costs looked like this:

Hospital emergency room	$260
Two doctor visits	200
1 1/2 days off work	300
Torn sock	3
Medication	40
TOTAL	$803

But what about his pain and suffering? Jake had spent two very uncomfortable days, and another ten unable to do a lot of the things he enjoyed, such as running and playing tennis. His pleasure in jogging on his formerly favorite running trail had also been displaced, in part, by anxiety about being attacked again. Puzzling over a monetary amount for this, Jake decided he didn't want to ask for a ridiculously large amount, and feel as irresponsible as the dog's owner, but he did feel wronged. Finally he decided to ask for a total of $2,000, the small claims court limit in his state, California.

Negotiating

Jake's next step was to call Allison Finley, who told him she considered the whole incident at least half his fault. Her theory was that when Jake leaped into the ditch, it sent a signal to Fred, her dog, that Jake was afraid and fleeing. It's a well-known fact, she went on, that dogs naturally go for cowards. Eventually, she offered to pay Jake's medical bills, but nothing else, claiming Jake could have gone to work if he had wanted to.

Jake, his blood pressure rising, hung up and went for a walk. When he'd calmed down, he wrote a letter. In California, such a demand is required before a small claims suit may be brought. In any state, it's a good idea.

▲

December 17, 19__
Allison Finley
1143 Rose Street
Oakland, CA 94616

Dear Ms. Finley:

As you will recall, on Sunday, November 24, 198_, your dog Fred bit me on the leg for no apparent reason at about 10 a.m. on the Strawberry Canyon fire road in Berkeley. I went immediately to the emergency room at General Hospital in Berkeley, where I received six stitches and medication for the pain.

During the next two days, I experienced a great deal of pain and discomfort, so much that I missed work on Monday, November 25, and half a day on Tuesday, November 26. It was necessary that I be treated by Dr. Elizabeth Goldthwait twice (November 26 and December 2). On her orders, I was not able to exercise until December 4. I am normally an active person, and this forced idleness was frustrating and unhealthy.

My out-of-pocket expenses are as follows:

Hospital emergency room	$260
Two doctor visits	200
1 1/2 days off work	300
Torn sock	3
Medication	40
TOTAL	$803

In addition, I believe that my very real pain and discomfort, which have significantly disrupted my life, should be compensated, for a total of $2,000.

Please promptly compensate me for my losses, or have the matter taken care of by your insurance company. If I don't hear from you by January 1, 19__, I will file a lawsuit in small claims court. If you wish to discuss this matter further, you can reach me at 398-9987.

Sincerely,

Jake Kurtz
Encl: copies of all bills and receipts

▼

A few days later, Jake got a reply from Allison, who offered to pay $600 in six monthly installments. He filed his small claims court suit the next day.

Settlement

Let's interrupt this story, dramatic as it may be, and give it an alternate ending: Allison suffered a change of heart and calls Jake back, offering to pay $1,400 if he won't take her to court. Jake, rather than go through the hassle of small claims court, where he is not guaranteed to get anything, accepts her offer. Jake and Allison get together to put their agreement in writing, using a personal injury release form such as the one shown below, taken from *Make Your Own Contract* , by Steve Elias (Nolo Press).[6]

Preparing for court

To prepare for his court appearance, Jake first gathered all his emergency room, doctor, and pharmacy bills and made photocopies of them. He also got a statement from his boss, documenting the time lost from work.

He then called the only witness to the incident, Allison's jogging companion, Kathleen Huxley. She obviously felt bad about what had happened, but didn't want to testify against her friend. Finally, she agreed to write a four-sentence note confirming that Jake had not provoked the dog, had tried to avoid it, and that the dog had lunged at and bitten him. (This kind of letter is generally allowed in small claims court, but not in regular court.) Jake could have had Kathleen served with a subpoena—an order to show up and testify in court—but he decided against it, for the sensible reason that it wouldn't be wise to force an unwilling witness to come to court.

/

Form 6

Release

1. _____Jake Kurtz_____, Releasor, voluntarily and knowingly executes this release with the express intention of eliminating the Releasee's liabilities and obligations as described below.

2. Releasor hereby releases ____Allison Finley_____, Releasee, from all liability for claims, known and unknown, arising from injuries, mental and physical, sustained by Releasor as described below: Finley's dog Fred bit Kurtz on the ankle on Nov. 24, 19 ___ in Tilden Park, Berkeley, CA. Kurtz suffered severe injury and pain, and was forced to miss 1½ days of work as a result.

3. Releasor has been examined by a licensed physician or other health care professional competent to diagnose

[Choose one or more]

[X] physical injuries and disabilities.

[ ] mental and emotional injuries and disabilities.

Releasor has been informed by this physician or health care professional that the injury described in Clause 2 has mended without causing permanent damage.

4. By executing this release Releasor does not give up any claim that he/she may now or hereafter have against any person, firm or corporation other than Releasee.

5. Releasor understands that Releasee does not, by providing the consideration described below, admit any liability or responsibility for the above described injury or its consequences.

6. Releasor has received good and adequate consideration for this release in the form of _____ $400, paid today.

7. In executing this release Releasor additionally intends to bind his/her spouse, heirs, legal representatives, assigns, and anyone else claiming under him/her. Releasor has not assigned any claim arising from the events described in Clause 2 to any other party. This release applies to Releasee's heirs, legal representatives, insurers, assigns and successors as well to Releasee.

8. This release was executed on ____Jan. 12_____, 19_____ at_____.
Berkeley, CA

Releasor's Signature _____Jake Kurtz_____

Address
____1147 8th Ave_____
____Berkeley Ca. 94710_____
Releasor's Signature

Releasor's Spouse's Signature _____

Releasee's Signature ___Allison Finley_____
Address
____1193 Rose St., Oakland CA 94616_____

Witnesses:

Tom Jefferson   Old Farm Road. Monticello, Va
Name   Address
Kai Reynolds   1784 Seaview Drive, San Francisco CA
Name   Address

Thinking about what other evidence would be convincing to a small claims court judge, Jake decided a picture of ferocious-looking Fred the dog would definitely help. To get it, Jake sent a neighborhood teenager who was an avid amateur photographer to Allison's house, where Fred was in a fenced yard and easily visible from the street.

The only witness Jake decided to call at his hearing was a friend who had brought him homemade chicken soup when he was laid up the day after the incident. She would testify to Jake's obvious suffering.

In court, everything went just about as Jake had expected. He presented all his evidence and even did a Lyndon Johnson routine, showing the judge the scar on his ankle. Allison testified that Fred was really a sweet animal. She reminded the judge that several women had been attacked while jogging in the area, and said she needed the dog for protection. She brought along a couple of witnesses who said nice, but irrelevant, things about Fred's good disposition. (Whatever impression that testimony made, Jake thought to himself, was dispelled by the snapshot of Fred.)

What did the judge say? We gave this hypothetical to four experts: two small claims court judges and two small claims court advisors (court employees who help people going to small claims court prepare their cases). Their verdicts:

Judge #1:	$ 2,000
Judge #2:	$ 1,300
Advisor #1:	$ 900
Advisor #2:	$ 860

There's no better way to show you the inherent unpredictability of taking a dispute to court, even when a jury isn't involved.

Laws that Make Dog Owners Liable

As mentioned earlier, dog owners may be found liable for injuries their dogs cause for one of three reasons:
- a state dog-bite statute makes owners responsible for all damage their dogs cause;

- the owner knew the dog was dangerous before the injury occurred (the common law liability rule); or
- the owner's negligence (carelessness) caused the injury.

Here, we discuss each of these theories in more detail.

Dog-Bite Statutes

Twenty-nine states and the District of Columbia have statutes that make dog owners liable if their dogs cause injury. They are called "strict liability" statutes because they impose liability without fault—an injured person does not have to prove that the dog owner did anything wrong. (The only exception is Hawaii, where a victim must still prove the dog's owner was unreasonably careless.)

The theory behind these laws is that anyone who has a dog should be responsible for any damage it causes, period. It doesn't matter that the owner was careful with the dog, or didn't know it would hurt anyone, or conscientiously tried to keep it from injuring anyone.

For example, the Minnesota strict liability statute says:

```
If a dog, without provocation, attacks or
injures any person who is acting peaceably in
any place where the person may lawfully be, the
owner of the dog is liable in damages to the
person so attacked or injured to the full
amount of the injury sustained.
```

The chart below sets out some of the main features of these statutes.

DOG-BITE STATUTES

	Only Owner Liable?	Bites Only?	Other Provisions
Alabama	yes	no	Only applies if injury on owner's property.
Arizona	yes	yes	
(two statutes)	no	no	Only applies if dog at large.
California	yes	yes	
Connecticut	no	no	Victim must prove not committing tort.
Delaware			
Dist. of Columbia	yes	no	Must prove negligence, but ignorance of dog's viciousness not absolute defense. Only applies if dog at large.
Florida (1)	yes	yes	Statute is only way to sue for bites. Owner not liable if displayed sign
(2)	yes	no	including words 'Bad Dog.'
Hawaii	no	no	Victim must prove owner was negligent.
Illinois	no	no	
Indiana	yes	yes	
Iowa	no?	no	Victim must prove not doing unlawful act that contributed to the injury.
Kentucky	no	yes	
Louisiana	no	no	
Maine	no	no	Victim must prove not at fault.
Massachusetts	no	no	Victim must prove not trespassing or committing tort (unless < 7 years old).
Michigan	yes	yes	
Minnesota	no	no	Owner 'primarily liable.'
Montana	yes	yes	Only applies in city or town.
Nebraska	yes	no	Victim must prove not trespasser. Applies if dog chases, bites, kills, or wounds.
New Hampshire	no	no	Victim must prove not trespassing or committing tort.
New Jersey	yes	yes	
Ohio	no	no	Victim must prove not trespassing or teasing, tormenting or abusing dog on owner's property.
Oklahoma	yes	no	
Pennsylvania	yes	yes	Owner must pay victim's medical bills.
Rhode Island	no	no	Only applies if dog out of enclosure. On second occurrence, double damages and court can order dog killed.
South Carolina	no	no	Only applies if dog bites or attacks.
Utah	no	no	Possible criminal liability.
Washington	yes	yes	
West Virginia	no	no	Only applies if dog at large.
Wisconsin	no	no	After owner has notice that dog has caused injury, double damages & penalties.

Note: Georgia has a dog-bite statute, but it doesn't impose strict liability on owners; it's essentially the same as the common law rule.
Citations to all statutes are included in Appendix 2 of this book.

Reminder: In almost all states, dog-bite statutes operate in addition to the common law rule. That means someone who is injured by a dog often has a choice of suing under the statute, if it applies to the situation, under a common law theory (and having to prove the owner knew the dog was dangerous), or on a negligence theory.

How to Read a Dog-Bite Statute. If you want to know what your rights or obligations are under your state's dog-bite law, you're going to have to read the actual statute carefully. Before you can do that, of course, you've got to find it. (Instructions on how to find a law library and look up a statute are in Appendix. 1, Legal Research, in this book.)

Let's look at a typical dog-bite law and see what an injured person must prove to recover from the dog's owner under the statute. Here is Michigan's statute:

```
287.351  Dogs, injury by; liability of owner
The owner of any dog which shall without provocation
bite any person while such person is on or in a
public place, or lawfully on or in a private place,
including the property of the owner of such dog,
shall be liable for such damages as may be suffered
by the person bitten, regardless of the former
viciousness of such dog or the owner's knowledge of
such viciousness.
```

What the injured person must prove:

1. He was bitten (other injuries aren't covered by the statute) by a dog.

2. The person he is suing (the defendant) is the owner of the dog that bit him.

3. He didn't provoke the dog to bite him.

4. He was in a public place, or lawfully on private property, when bitten.

What the owner may try to prove to avoid liability:

1. The victim knew the dog was dangerous but took the risk anyway.

Now here's a different type of statute, this time from Arizona:

```
24-521 Liability for dog bites
The owner of a dog which bites a person when the
person is in or on a public place or lawfully in or
on a private place, including the property of the
owner of the dog, is liable for damages suffered by
the person bitten, regardless of the former
viciousness of the dog or the owner's knowledge of
its viciousness.

24-523 Provocation as defense
Proof of provocation of the attack by the person
injured shall be a defense to the action for damages.
```

What the injured person must prove:

1. He was bitten (other injuries aren't covered by the statute) by a dog.

2. The person he is suing (the defendant) owns the dog that bit him.

3. He was in a public place, or lawfully on private property, when bitten.

What the owner may try to prove to avoid liability:

1. The victim provoked the attack.

(The possible legal defenses a dog owner has if sued are discussed below in the section on "A Dog Owner's Legal Defenses.")

The Common Law 'One-Bite' Rule

The common law rule holds a dog's owner or keeper liable for injuries the dog causes only if the injured person can prove the owner knew, or had reason to know:

- the dog was vicious or dangerous to people; and
- the specific tendency (for example, a tendency to bite or to knock people down) of the dog that caused the injury.

An injured person will want to sue under a common law theory if the state has no dog-bite statute or if the statute doesn't apply (for example, if the statute only covers bites and the dog caused the injury by knocking the person down).

A dog owner may be able to escape liability by proving that the injured person provoked the injury, or voluntarily and knowingly risked the injury. (See "A Dog's Owner's Legal Defenses," below.)

COMMON LAW RULE ONLY

Alaska	Missouri	Pennsylvania
Arkansas	Nevada	South Dakota
Colorado	New Mexico	Tennessee
Georgia[7]	New York	Texas
Idaho	North Carolina	Vermont
Kansas	North Dakota	Virginia
Maryland	Oregon	Wyoming
Mississippi		

The crux of the common law rule is one question: did the owner know the dog was dangerous? An owner who knows of the dog's dangerousness but doesn't prevent the injury is legally responsible for it. The person injured by the dog must prove that the owner knew the dog was likely to cause the kind of injury suffered.

The logic is straightforward, if not unquestionable. This rule allows a person who owns a dog to assume, until there is some concrete indication to the contrary, that the dog isn't dangerous. But an owner who knows a dog is an exception and poses a risk to people must take action to prevent the foreseeable injury—or will have to pay for it.

A common misconception is that every dog gets one "free" bite (free for its owner), and from then on the owner is on notice that the dog is dangerous. This "one-bite rule" is not really an accurate statement of the common law rule. It's true that if a dog bites someone, its owner is definitely on notice that the dog is dangerous, but less serious behavior is also enough, legally, to give the owner the knowledge the law looks for. In other words, a hostile, aggressive dog usually doesn't get one free bite.

The "one-bite" label is misleading for another reason: bites are by no means the only kind of injury inflicted by dogs. But the test for liability is the same no matter how the injury was caused: Did the owner know of the dog's dangerous tendency? For example, if a dog jumps up and knocks someone down, the question is: Did the owner know of the dog's tendency to knock people down? If so, he's liable for it.

Terminology note: Judges often say that, to be liable under the common law rule, an owner must have known the dog was "vicious" or had a "vicious propensity." The term, as it's used in this context, simply means dangerous—likely to hurt someone, even if by being overly friendly. It has nothing to do with a dog's temperament.

Here are some examples to illustrate how the common law rule works. But remember that what a court decides depends on the facts of the case—and the judge's attitude.

- A Doberman pinscher, usually kept in the house or a fenced yard, barks when the doorbell rings. It also barks at, and occasionally chases, other dogs. It has never attacked a person. If it bites someone, its owners will probably not be liable, because they have no reason to think it is dangerous to people.[8] The law doesn't take into consideration, however, the prejudices of a judge or jury should a dispute actually go to court. It's fair to say that large dogs of breeds popularly believed to be mean, such as Dobermans, German shepherds and pit bulls, may be judged more severely than dogs of cuddlier breeds.

- Luke's dog often growls and snaps at people who come near, but hasn't ever actually bitten someone. Its actions, however, should reasonably put Luke on notice that the dog might bite someone. If the dog does bite, Luke will be liable.[9]

- A friendly and playful golden retriever is in the habit of jumping on guests who come to his owner's house. One day an elderly friend comes to the door and is knocked over by the exuberant dog. The dog's owner is held liable: he knew that the dog behaved this way and might injure someone because of its size.

- A collie likes to run along the fence that separates his yard from the sidewalk, barking at pedestrians and bicyclists and sometimes jumping up against the fence. A child walking along the sidewalk is so startled by the dog's sudden and noisy appearance that she darts into the street and is hit by a car. The dog's owner is probably liable, because he knew of the dog's habit of menacing people from behind the fence but did nothing to stop it.[10] At least one court, however, has ruled that an owner wasn't responsible for foreseeing that a barking dog could frighten someone so much she would run into the street.[11]

- A little terrier that is affectionate and gentle with people has a history of fights with other dogs. That's probably not enough to put the owner on notice that the dog might bite a person. Courts usually recognize that canine society has its own rules, and the way a dog behaves under them isn't a reliable predictor of how it will act toward humans.[12]

Note on Warning Signs: A "Beware of Dog" sign might be used by a judge or jury to infer that a dog's owner knew the dog was dangerous. The sign would be just one item of evidence, which the owner could refute with testimony of witnesses or other evidence.

The Dog Owner's Negligence

Negligence is the third legal doctrine under which a dog owner may be found liable for injuries caused by a dog. A dog owner who is unreasonably careless (negligent) in handling a dog may be legally responsible if somebody is hurt as a foreseeable result.

Reminder: From an injured person's perspective, the strategy of trying to prove a dog owner was negligent is usually desirable only if there's no dog-bite statute to sue under, and it doesn't look possible to prove, on a common law theory, that the dog's owner knew the dog was dangerous.

When it comes to defining negligence, broad rules are of little help. Whether or not someone acted negligently is a question that must be resolved based on the facts of a given situation. It comes down to this question: did the dog owner accused of negligence act reasonably? If so, the owner wasn't legally negligent.

Example: Lucy left her dog chained in the unfenced front yard, so that it couldn't reach the sidewalk, and posted a "Beware of Dog" sign. Frank walks up to the dog and gets bitten. Was Lucy negligent—should she have foreseen that such an injury might occur? At least one court, in Indiana, faced with such a case, has said no. The court ruled that confining the dog inside the owner's property, and posting a sign, are enough precautions against someone being injured.[13]

If a dog owner violates a law, and the violation leads to an injury, the owner may be automatically negligent—which means that the injured person must prove only that the law was violated.

Example: A California man let his dog roam, in violation of a local leash law. The dog ran into the road, and a pickup truck crashed trying to avoid it. Two men riding in the back of the truck were thrown out; they suffered serious permanent injuries.[14] A judge held in 1987 that the dog owner's violation of the leash law was negligence, and awarded the injured men $2.6 million. (The dog owner's insurance company ended up paying the whole amount, even though the owner's policy limit was $100,000. See section on "Liability Insurance," below.)

A Dog Owner's Legal Defenses

So far, we've talked about the legal rights and options of someone who's injured by a dog. But the dog owner is entitled to fight back with another set of legal theories.

The owner may not be legally liable if the injured person:
- provoked the injury from the dog;
- knowingly took the risk of being injured by the dog;
- was trespassing;
- was breaking the law; or

- was unreasonably careless, and that carelessness contributed to the injury.

   In this section, we discuss each of these defenses. It's important to keep in mind three things about them:

1. Not all defenses can be used in all states.

2. Sometimes, the defenses that can be used depend on what the dog owner is being sued for. For example, some defenses may be available if the dog owner is being sued under a common law theory, but not under a dog-bite statute.

3. Some dog-bite statutes make the victim prove that he *wasn't* at fault—the dog owner doesn't have to prove the victim was at fault. (See "How to Read a Dog-Bite Statute," above.)

Was the Dog Provoked?

A dog owner may be able to successfully defend a lawsuit by an injured person by showing that the injured person provoked the dog.

Some acts—for example, hitting or teasing a dog—clearly are the kind of provocation that will get the dog and its owner off the hook. But just as the motivation of the dog is unimportant for legal purposes—it doesn't matter that the dog that knocked you down a flight of stairs was just trying to be friendly—the motivation of the injured person is irrelevant, too. A person may innocently and unintentionally "provoke" a dog. If, for example, a child steps on a dog's tail, and the dog turns and nips the child's ankle, the dog's owner will probably not be liable for the injury, regardless of the dog's prior behavior.[15]

A general word of warning: Unique circumstances may always affect the legal outcome. If, for example, a dog were known to have a hair trigger around children, the legal result could be different.

There are many ways a person, especially one unfamiliar with dogs, can unknowingly provoke a dog. Petting even an otherwise friendly dog when it's eating, going near its special "territory," or intervening in a dog fight can provoke a hostile response. And dogs in strange surroundings are often nervous and may bite out of fear if approached.

The dog-bite statutes of eleven states require the injured person to prove the dog wasn't provoked. (See chart above on "Dog-Bite Statutes.) In two of those states (Massachusetts and Connecticut), if the injured person is a child less than seven years old, the law presumes the child didn't provoke the dog. In those states, an owner who wants to assert provocation as a defense bears the burden of proving it. The Ohio statute doesn't require the injured person to prove that the dog wasn't provoked in any way; it requires only proof that the dog wasn't teased, tormented or abused.

Did the Victim Know the Risk of Injury?

A dog owner may also avoid liability by proving that the injured person knew there was a risk of injury from the dog, but voluntarily took that risk. The theory is that someone who knowingly took the risk and was injured can't later hold the dog's owner responsible for such foolhardiness.

Example: You warn a visitor that your dog, who is in the back yard, might bite a stranger who entered the yard. The visitor goes in the yard anyway and gets bitten. If sued, you would have a good argument that the visitor knew of and took the risk of the dog's behavior.

The same goes for warning signs. Someone who ignores a clear, prominently posted "Beware of Dog" sign is probably not going to be able to blame the dog's owner for any injuries. For example, a Maryland deliveryman ignored a "Guard Dog On Duty" sign at a warehouse and was severely bitten by a German shepherd that most definitely was on duty. He sued but lost. A court concluded that he "voluntarily left his place of safety" and knowingly took the risk of injury.[16]

In some states that have dog-bite statutes, this defense can't be used (Ohio, for example[17]); in other words, the owner is liable for injuries to someone who knowingly risked the injury. Some other states (Illinois, for example[18]) do allow it in lawsuits based on the statute. Some state courts have yet to consider the question.

Was the Victim Trespassing?

In most states, dog owners aren't liable to trespassers who are injured by a dog. But a word of warning: the rules are convoluted, and vary significantly from state to state.

In general, a trespasser is someone who wasn't invited on the property. Unless you warn people off your property with signs or locked gates, you are considered to have given an "implied invitation" to members of the public to approach your door on common errands—for example, to speak with you, try to sell you something, or ask directions.

Without at least some such implied invitation, someone who ventures onto private property is a trespasser. In one case from Nebraska in 1983, a child visiting relatives stuck her hand through a fence to pet the neighbor's dog; she was found to be a trespasser.[19]

A general rule is that a dog owner who could reasonably expect someone to be on property is probably going to be liable for any injury that person suffers. This rule is particularly important when it comes to children, who make up a large percentage of dog-bite victims. Even a dog owner who does not explicitly invite a neighborhood child onto property will probably be held liable if it's reasonable to know the child is likely to wander in—and dogs are a big attraction to children. In other words, there is a legal responsibility either to prevent the child from coming on the property or to keep the dog from injuring the child.

Specific legal rules that determine whether or not a dog owner is liable to an injured trespasser vary from state to state. Here are the basics.

- **Dog-bite Statutes.** If the state has a dog-bite statute, the law should spell out whether or not trespassers are covered. Most don't allow trespassers to sue for an injury.

Most dog-bite statutes apply only if the person injured by a dog was in a public place or "lawfully in a private place." That means that the injured person must have a good reason for being where he was. Mail carriers, for example, are always covered. So is anyone else who has an invitation, express or implied, to be on the dog owner's property.

Some laws put the same idea another way by forbidding trespassers from suing under the statute. (Alabama, perplexingly, turns the tables and allows someone to sue under its dog-bite statute only if the injury occurred on the owner's property.)

Example: A woman going door to door to take a survey was let into a house, where she was knocked down and bitten by a dog. The front yard of the house wasn't fenced, although a cartoon-like "Trespassers Will Be Eaten" sign was displayed in the window. An Arizona appeals court ruled that the survey-taker entered the property with the implied consent of the residents, so she could sue under Arizona's dog-bite statute, which applies only if the person injured is "lawfully" in a private place.[20]

- **Common Law Rule.** If the state follows the common law rule—which, remember, imposes liability on a dog owner who knew a dog was dangerous—the fact that the injured person was trespassing technically doesn't matter. So if the common law rule rule were applied strictly, if you know your dog is dangerous, and it bites a burglar who breaks into your house, you're liable. In practice, however, courts and juries are reluctant to hold a dog owner liable to a trespasser. Many courts have softened the rule to avoid unjust results. Some have modified the rule to say that a dog owner, even one who knows a dog is vicious, isn't liable if the dog hurts a trespasser.[21] Some say that the common law rule doesn't apply to trespassers if the dog is a guard dog.[22]

Another way courts get around an unfair result is by allowing the dog owner to charge that the victim, by trespassing, either was partly to blame (see "Was the Victim Careless?" below) or knowingly took the risk of injury (see discussion above). If the dog owner can prove either of those circumstances, liability may be reduced or eliminated altogether.

- **Negligence.** The states don't agree on whether or not an injured trespasser who sues a dog owner for negligence (unreasonable carelessness) can win.

In some states, an injured trespasser can sue and win if the dog owner acted unreasonably under the circumstances.

Other states still use an old legal rule that landowners are liable to injured trespassers only if the landowner, after knowing the trespasser was on the land, intentionally harmed the trespasser or failed to warn of the danger. There is an important exception to this rule: a landowner has a duty to protect trespassing children, who don't have the judgment to avoid dangerous situations.[23]

Reminder: To cover their bases, injured people can and do sue on more than one legal theory. So someone might raise two claims in a lawsuit, one under a state's dog-bite statute and one based on the common law theory.

Was the Victim Breaking the Law?

Some dog-bite statutes apply only if the victim can prove he wasn't at fault. The victim may have to show he was "peaceably conducting himself," for example (that language is from the Illinois statute). Iowa's law applies "except when the party damaged is doing an unlawful act, directly contributing to the injury." This means it's up to the injured person to prove he wasn't doing something illegal when bitten. a victim who can't prove it can't recover from the dog's owner. The dog owner doesn't have to prove that the injured person *was* doing something illegal.

Was the Victim Careless?

In most states, a victim whose own carelessness contributed to the injury is entitled to less money from the dog owner. The amount is reduced in proportion to the victim's fault. So a victim who is 20% at fault receives 20% less than if the dog owner were completely responsible for the injury. This doctrine is called "comparative fault."

Example: Phyllis decides to visit her new neighbors down the street. When she gets to their yard, she sees a big "Beware of Dog" sign on the picket fence around the front yard, but she opens the gate and goes in anyway. The neighbors' dog rushes out and bites her ankle, and Phyllis has to pay $100 in medical bills to treat it. When Phyllis sues the dog's owners in small claims court, the judge gives her only $50, ruling that Phyllis, by ignoring the sign, was careless and half at fault for the injury. The judge decides that the owners were half at fault, too, because they kept an aggressive dog in an unlocked yard where visitors might be expected to enter.

Note: In a few states, a victim who contributed to the injury even the least bit may recover nothing from the dog owner. These "contributory negligence" states are Alabama, Delaware, the District of Columbia, Maryland, North Carolina, South Carolina, and Virginia.

Who Can be Sued: Owners and 'Keepers'

In general, whoever has control over the dog is legally responsible for the dog's actions. That usually, but not always, means the dog's legal owner must pay for damage or injury caused by the dog. It depends on the circumstances and on the law in force where the injury took place. In some cases, more than one person may be legally liable.

Keepers and Harborers. Under the common law (discussed above), someone who harbors or keeps a dog is just as liable as the legal owner of a dog, if the dog causes injury. Many state dog-bite laws also make the "owner or keeper" of a dog liable for damage or injury the dog causes.

A "keeper" is someone with care, custody, and control of a dog.[24] A Minnesota court put it this way: "Harboring or keeping a dog means something more than a meal of mercy to a stray dog or the casual presence of a dog on someone's premises. Harboring means to afford lodging, to shelter or to give refuge to a dog. Keeping a dog . . . implies more than the mere harboring of the dog for a limited purpose or time. One becomes the keeper of a dog only when he either with or without the owner's permission undertakes to manage, control or care for it as dog owners in general are accustomed to do."[25]

A dog may have more than one owner, and so more than one person may be liable if the dog injures someone. For example, if you leave your dog with a friend for six months, and the dog bites someone, the friend may be liable as a "keeper." But you're still the owner, so you may be liable, too, either because of a dog-bite statute or, if you knew the dog was dangerous, the common law rule. The injured person may decide who to sue based on who has more money to go after.

Here are some examples of keeping or harboring a dog:

- A man lets a woman and her dog stay in his house while he's on vacation. The dog bites someone. Ruled: He is an "owner" under Minnesota law.[26]
- While a woman is visiting her son, his dog injures someone. Ruled: The fact that while she was there, she gave the dog commands and let it in and out doesn't make her a keeper under New York law.[27]
- A Minnesota landlord lets a tenant have a dog in his apartment. The dog bites another tenant in her apartment. Ruled: the landlord isn't an owner.[28] (Landlord liability is discussed in detail in Chapter 4, Landlords and Dogs.)
- A dog escapes from an Illinois animal shelter and runs onto a highway, causing a motorcyclist to have an accident. Ruled: Under state law, the pound is the "owner" for liability purposes.[29]
- The owners of a restaurant rent out part of the building to a woman who works in the restaurant and has three bulldogs. The dogs occasionally wander into the restaurant for handouts from customers, and the restaurant owners pet the dogs and sometimes take them for rides in their car. One day the dogs bite a woman coming out of the restaurant. Ruled: Because they do not give the dogs shelter, protection or food, or exercise control over them, the restaurant owners are not keepers.[30]

Some state dog-bite statutes limit liability to the owner of the dog. A Washington court, for example, ruled that "mere keepers or possessors of a dog" aren't liable under the Washington statute, which limits liability to owners.[31] But be careful not to take these statutes at face value. Sometimes another section of the statute, or a court interpreting it, defines "owner" as anyone who cares for or harbors the dog. For example, the Illinois statute says that if a dog injures a person, "the owner of such dog" is liable for the full amount of the injury. But another Illinois statute defines "owner" as anyone who keeps or harbors a dog.[32]

Local ordinances may define "owner" more broadly than state laws. Under the Oklahoma statute, for example, "owner" is given a limited meaning. A Tulsa ordinance, however, defines owner as anyone "having the care or custody of or harboring, keeping or maintaining" a dog. Tulsa residents are subject to the broader local meaning, the Oklahoma Supreme Court has ruled.[33]

Minors. If the dog is owned or cared for by someone less than 18 years old, that minor's parents are probably legally liable in place of the minor. The dog-bite laws of Connecticut, Massachusetts and Maine say that explicitly. Some other states have laws that make parents responsible, to a limited extent, for damage their minor children cause. In California, for example, parents are liable for their children's deliberate misconduct, up to $10,000.[34] In other states, courts are likely to rule that the child's parents, who allow the dog on the premises and give it food and shelter, are liable because they are "keepers" of the dog.

Property Owners. In some circumstances, landlords may be held financially responsible for injury or damage caused a tenant's dog. (The special situation of landlords whose tenants have dogs is discussed in Chapter 4, Landlords and Dogs.)

Anyone who lets a dog stay on his property may be liable for injury the dog causes if not removing the dog is unreasonably careless. For example, a New Jersey store was sued after a dog, tied outside the store by a shopper, bit a girl on her way inside. The court said that if a jury decided the store should have foreseen that the dog might bite someone, it would be liable for the injury. (*Nakhla v. Singer-Shoprite, Inc.*, 500 A.2d 411 (N.J. Super. A.D. 1985).)

Calculating an Injured Person's Damages

Most dog-bite cases are settled out of court. But to negotiate a settlement, both sides need to have a rough idea of what a jury might give someone injured by a dog.

A dog owner who is found legally liable for a dog-inflicted injury may end up paying for:

Medical bills. The most obvious expenses of dog-inflicted injuries are medical bills. They include all costs that are a result of the injury, which can include bills for doctors (including specialists such as plastic surgeons) and hospital services, medication, physical therapy, and in some cases, even visits to a counselor or psychiatrist.

If the injury aggravates a victim's pre-existing medical condition, the final tab may be much more than would be expected from the dog-inflicted injury alone.

Example: Muffy the Lhasa Apso trips an elderly visitor to her owner's house, Mr. Leonard. The fall wouldn't be serious for a healthier person, but Leonard's back has been in bad shape for years, and the fall puts him in the hospital. The common legal rule is that if you hurt someone, you are responsible for all injuries that flow from your action, even if those injuries are made worse by some condition the victim already had. That means some big medical bills for Muffy's owner, who can't get away with paying only for what the injury would have cost a normally healthy victim.

Time lost from work. If someone injured by a dog must take time off from work, for medical diagnosis, treatment or recuperation, the dog's owner must reimburse the injured person for any lost income.

Pain and suffering. The pain that an injured person suffers is very real—but it's very hard to put a dollar value on it. Jurors, and lawyers who are trying to settle a lawsuit before it gets to the jury, do it, but the amounts they award injured people vary tremendously. Some states have limited the amounts that can be awarded for pain and suffering, but the limits are too high to affect most dog-bite cases. Here are some factors to consider:

• A child may suffer more from a dog bite than an adult. The child may, for example, become terrified by dogs or have recurring nightmares of attacks.

- If a dog that isn't vaccinated for rabies bites someone, that person will spend at least a few anxious days wondering if the dog (which is probably quarantined) is going to start showing symptoms of the fatal disease. A jury may compensate the person for that suffering.
- An unofficial rule is that damages for pain and suffering are often between two and four times, depending on the circumstances, as much as the actual medical damages.
- If the injury was caused by a vicious and completely unprovoked attack, a sympathetic jury is likely to award more money to the victim. The same goes for injuries caused by breeds commonly viewed as vicious, such as Dobermans or pit bulls.

Loss of Services. A few states allow spouses or close relatives of an injured person to sue for loss of the person's services. It's hard to pin down what these services are, but they don't necessarily have to be economic; they may refer to companionship. For example, a New York woman whose nine-year-old son was bitten by a dog sued for the loss of his services, and was awarded $4,500.[35]

Multiple Damages. Some dog-bite statutes (Wisconsin's, for example) allow an injured person to collect double or triple damages if the dog has bitten someone before. And if a dog has been officially labeled "vicious" under local or state law because of its prior behavior, the victim is probably entitled to multiple damages. (See Chapter 12, Vicious Dogs and Pit Bulls.)

Punitive Damages. An owner whose conduct was truly outrageous—for example, repeatedly letting a dog known to be dangerous run loose—may be punished by having to pay an extra amount, over and above the amount needed to compensate the victim. A jury is free to base these "punitive damages" on the wealth of the person being punished. For example, to make a big company feel some pain, it must be stung with a bigger verdict than would be assessed against the average person.

Note on Excessive Verdicts: If a dog-bite case goes to trial, and a jury gives an injured person an unrealistically huge amount of money, a judge (in the trial court, or an appellate court if the verdict is appealed) may reduce the amount. For example, a New York woman who had been bitten on the arm by a dog received a $240,000 verdict from a jury. Her husband also got $70,000 for loss of his wife's services. The dog owner appealed the decision, and an appeals court ruled that the damage awards were excessive. After all, the court said, the injury consisted of only a bite that healed quickly and left a faint scar. The court discounted testimony that the woman had developed a dog phobia after the bite, and ordered a new trial on the amount of money the victim should get.[36]

Note on insurance: A homeowner's or renter's insurance policy may cover damage caused by the policyholder's dog, even if it happens off the owner's property. (See section on "Liability Insurance," below.)

Injury to Livestock

In the eyes of the law, injuring economically valuable livestock is traditionally a more serious matter than injuring a person.[37] In at least one state, Minnesota, a dog owner is even guilty of a minor criminal offense—a petty misdemeanor—if the dog kills or pursues domestic livestock.[38]

The two cardinal rules, which apply almost everywhere, are:

1. A livestock owner is free to kill a dog that is killing, wounding, chasing, worrying, harassing, or attacking livestock. (This is discussed in more detail in Chapter 9, If a Dog Is Killed or Injured.)

2. A dog's owner or keeper is financially liable for any livestock damage the dog causes.

Several states have funds to reimburse farmers or ranchers who lose livestock to dogs. The animal owner must file a claim with the state, following procedures set out in the statute. To seek reimbursement from the Illinois Animal Control Fund, for example, an owner must:

- Be an Illinois resident;
- Report the loss to the state within 24 hours;
- Appear before the County Board and make a sworn statement setting out how many animals were killed, their value, and the owner of the dog, if known.[39]

The Board investigates and files a written report with the county treasurer, who makes payments once a year. Unless the county sets the amount to be paid at the reasonable market value, maximum amounts per injured or killed animal are set by state law. They range from $1 for a chicken to $300 for a cow, but can be increased 50% if the animal was a registered purebred. Exotic animals may not be covered at all; an Ohio man's claim was recently turned down by county officials who refused to reimburse him when dogs killed two of his ostriches.[40]

The livestock owner may still sue the owner of the dog responsible for the damage. An amount equal to what the livestock owner has received from the Animal Control Fund is simply deducted from what is awarded in court, if anything, and paid back to the fund.

Liability Insurance

It should by now be crystal clear that if a dog hurts someone or damages property, its owner can be on the hook for a very large bill. In many cases, however, insurance may take some of the sting out of paying.

Homeowner's Insurance

Both those who own dogs and those who are bitten by them will be glad to know that if the owner has homeowner's or renter's insurance, it usually covers damage from dog bites. A standard homeowner's policy covers any legal liability the owner incurs as a result of negligence. Usually, a homeowner's policy provides $100,000 to $300,000 worth of liability coverage; the larger amount is becoming common.

That's the good news. The bad news is that insurance companies typically have their own "one-bite rule." That is, a company will pay for the first occurrence, but will also either cancel the insurance or add a "canine exclusion." The next time the dog bites, the owner must pick up the tab. It follows that if an insurance company knows a homeowner has a vicious dog—something that may be rudely discovered during a routine pre-insurance inspection of the home—it may refuse to issue a policy in the first place.

The 'Business Pursuit' Exclusion. All insurance policies contain exclusions, clauses that say specific kinds of incidents aren't covered. Because homeowner's insurance is supposed to insure homes, not businesses, many homeowner's policies have a "business pursuits" exclusion. Such policies don't cover claims that arise from a homeowner's business activities. The exclusion may apply when an accident happens in the home even if the business conducted there is only a part-time activity.

Example: An Oklahoma man found his homeowner's insurance didn't cover him when a potential buyer was bitten while looking at his litter of St. Bernard puppies, which he kept at his home. The business pursuits exclusion applied, a court ruled, even though the man's primary occupation was as a salesman. The business activities in this case went beyond the infrequent sale of a litter of pups: the man had renovated his barn to use it as a kennel, and advertised dogs for sale in the newspaper and on a large sign.[41]

Incidents Off the Property. Homeowner's policies don't usually restrict coverage to incidents that take place on the policyholder's property. If a homeowner's policy insures against any legal liabilities the policyholder incurs, as many do, it doesn't matter that the dog bit someone while the owner was walking it in the park. For example, a homeowner's policy covered the owners of a dog that bit a child on a farm. The dog's owners owned the farm, but didn't live there; the policy insured their residence.[42]

Some policies, however, do not cover injuries connected with vehicles. So, although the policyholder might be covered if the dog bites someone in the park, the homeowner's policy might not provide coverage if the dog leans out of the car window and bites someone on the way there. Car insurance, however, might provide some coverage. For example, a Florida family's dog bit a passenger in their car. Their homeowner's insurance policy excluded claims arising from use of cars away from the premises, but their automobile insurance policy covered the incident.[43]

If Circumstances Change. Your policy probably requires you to notify the insurance company of significant changes in your circumstances. That means that if your dog bites someone, or is declared vicious under a local law, and you don't tell the company, the policy may not cover subsequent incidents of damage or injury caused by the dog. Of course, if you do notify the company that your dog has bitten someone, it may well cancel your policy or exclude coverage for the dog.

If you're not sure what your homeowner's or renter's insurance policy covers, take a deep breath and read the liability section. Then read it again. If it still doesn't make sense (this is a distinct possibility, and it's not your fault), call your insurance broker. Ask if you're covered for damage your dog causes, and how cooperative the company is about coughing up money in such cases.

Separate Liability Insurance for a Dog

If you really need liability insurance for your dog, but your homeowner's or renter's policy doesn't cover you, you may be in for a tough time. The reason is that if you feel a pressing need for insurance, you're probably in one of these predicaments:

- The dog has bitten someone;
- The dog has been declared "vicious" by a judge or animal control department, meaning you have to furnish proof of liability coverage; or
- Local law classifies your dog as a pit bull and requires you to have insurance.

Any of those circumstances is a red flag to an insurance company, which is in the business of taking as few risks as possible. You'll probably have to go to a specialty insurance company, which will charge you $1,000 to $1,500 a year for a policy that will provide $100,000 of liability coverage.

The Insurance Company's Duty to Pay

It's notoriously hard for a policyholder who has a claim to squeeze money out of some insurance companies. But when you're talking about liability insurance, and the company unreasonably refuses to settle with an injured person suing the policyholder, the company may have to pay the whole amount for which the policyholder is eventually found liable.

Example: A California man whose dog caused a serious traffic accident was sued by men permanently injured in the accident. He had $100,000 of liability insurance from his homeowner's policy, but the insurance company refused to settle the lawsuit for that amount. Instead, the lawsuit went to trial, and in 1987 the dog owner lost big—he was found liable for $2.6 million. But the policy owner charged that the insurance company had not acted in good faith when it refused to pay the policy limit, and the insurance company ended up paying the whole amount.

Multiple and Punitive Damages

Many insurance policies say the company must pay all sums that a policyholder becomes legally obligated to pay because of bodily injury or property damage. Whether or not that includes extra damages, which are imposed to punish the homeowner for some misconduct, depends on what state you're in. Courts don't agree.

Multiple Damages. A few statutes provide that in certain circumstances, the amount of damages awarded by a court or jury in a dog bite case is doubled or tripled. The goal is to punish the owners for their conduct. Wisconsin law, for example, triples an award if the dog has bitten someone before, and its owner knew about the previous incident. After one couple whose dog bit a child for the second time was sued, the tripled damages came to more than $30,000. The company that insured them tried to argue that it was liable only for the basic award, not the tripled amount. The Wisconsin Supreme Court ruled that "all sums" means "all sums," and the company did have to pay.[44]

Punitive Damages. Punitive damages are also intended to punish, but they differ from the extra damages mandated by statutes in several ways. First, whether or not to give them, and how much, is left up to the jury. The jury's decision is disturbed only if a judge thinks the jury is being completely outrageous. It's also proper for the jury to take into account the wealth of the person who has to pay the punitive damages, because an amount that might be a severe hardship on one person might barely be noticed by a richer person.

State courts are split over whether or not insurance policies cover punitive damages, but a slight majority seems to say that standard insurance policies do cover punitive damages. There are good arguments that insurance shouldn't cover punitive damages: after all, it's the wrongdoer, not the insurance company, who is supposed to be punished. On the other hand, if the person who bought the policy quite reasonably thinks it covers all such damages, it's not fair to change the rules in the middle of the game. And, obviously, an insurance company is free to put unambiguous language in its policies so that there would be no doubt about what's covered.

---

[1]*Jannuzzelli v. Wilkens*, 158 N.J. Super. 36, 385 A.2d 322 (1978).

[2]*Murdock v. Balle*, 144 Ariz. 136, 696 P.2d 230 (1981).

[3]1988 Cal. Stat. Ch. 297.

[4]Robinson and Corbett, *The Dreamer's Dictionary* (Taplinger Pub. Co., 1974).

[5]Thanks to Ralph Warner, author of *Everybody's Guide to Small Claims Court*, for this example, which was inspired by a near-miss with a big dog on a Berkeley running trail.

[6]*Make Your Own Contract* contains more information about releases, and release forms appropriate for other types of situations.

[7]Georgia has a dog-bite statute, but instead of imposing strict liability (liability without fault) as other statutes do, it merely puts in a statute the common law rule.

[8]See, for example, *Slack v. Villari*, 59 Md. App. 462, 476 A.2d 227 (1984).

[9]See, for example, *Fontecchio v. Esposito*, 108 A.D.2d 780, 485 N.Y.S.2d 113 (1985).

[10]See, for example, *Henkel v. Jordan*, 644 P.2d 1348, 7 Kan. App. 2d 561 (1982). The owners were held liable for injuries caused by their dog, who ran loose, bothering neighbors but not biting anyone. The dog ran after some bicyclists, who fell and were injured. The owners, who knew of the dog's habits, were held liable for the injury.

[11]*Nava v. McMillan*, 176 Cal. Rptr. 473, 123 Cal. App. 3d 262 (1981).

[12]As one court put it, the "question was the dog's propensity to attack a human. The canine code duello is something else. That involves the question of what constitutes a just cause for battle in the dog world, or what justifies a resort to arms, or rather to teeth, for redress." *Fowler v. Helck*, 278 Ky. 361 (1939).

[13]*Alfano v. Stutsman*, 471 N.E.2d 1143 (Ind. App. 1984).

[14]Los Angeles Daily Journal, Jan. 26, 1987.

[15]See, for example, *Toney v. Bouthillier,* 129 Ariz. 402, 631 P.2d 557 (1981).

[16]*Benton v. Aquarium, Inc.,* 62 Md. App. 373, 489 A.2d 549 (1985).

[17]*Pulley v. Malek,* 25 Ohio 3d 95, 495 N.E.2d 402 (1986).

[18]*Vanderlei v. Heideman,* 83 Ill. App. 3d 158, 38 Ill. Dec. 525, 403 N.E.2d 756 (1980).

[19]*Kenney v. Barna,* 215 Neb. 863, 341 N.W.2d 901 (1983).

[20]*Jones v. Manhart,* 120 Ariz. 338, 585 P.2d 1250 (1978).

[21]Restatement (Second) of Torts § 514 (1977).

[22]*Mech v. Hearst Corp.,* 64 Md. App. 422, 496 A.2d 1099 (1985).

[23]*DeRobertis v. Randazzo,* 94 N.J. 144, 462 A.2d 1260 (1983).

[24]*Mitchell v. Chase,* 87 Me. 172, 32 A. 867 (1895).

[25]*Verrett v. Silver,* 244 N.W.2d 147 (Minn. 1976).

[26]*Verrett v. Silver,* 244 N.W.2d 147 (Minn. 1976).

[27]*Zwinge v. Love,* 37 A.D.2d 874, 325 N.Y.S.2d 107 (1971).

[28]*Gilbert v. Christiansen,* 259 N.W.2d 896 (Minn. 1977).

[29]*Kirchgessner v. County of Tazewell,* 162 Ill. App. 3d 510, 114 Ill. Dec. 224, 516 N.E.2d 379 (1987).

[30]*Hagenau v. Millard,* 195 N.W. 718 (Wis. 1923).

[31]*Beeler v. Hickman,* 50 Wash. App. 746, 750 P.2d 1282 (1988).

[32]Ill. Stat. Ch. 8 §§ 352.16, 366.

[33]*Hampton ex rel. Hampton v. Hammons,* 743 P.2d 1053 (Okla. 1987).

[34]Cal. Civ. Code § 1714.1.

[35]*Graham ex rel. Graham v. Murphy,* 525 N.Y.S.2d 414 (App. Div. 1988).

[36]*Fontecchio v. Esposito,* 108 A.D.2d 780, 485 N.Y.S.2d 113 (1985).

[37]Strict liability statutes (which make an owner liable just because he owns a dog, not because he is at fault in any way) are relatively new when it comes to personal injury caused by dogs, but for years, dog owners have been strictly liable for damage to livestock. Many states that still don't impose strict liability for injury to persons do impose strict liability if the dog injures livestock.

[38]Minn. Stat. § 347.01(b).

[39]Ill. Stat. Ch. 8, § 369.

[40]Michael Erwin, of Morrow, Ohio. (Nat'l L.J. April 25, 1988).

[41]*Wiley v. Travelers Ins. Co.,* 534 P.2d 1293 (Okla. 1974).

[42]*Lititz Mutual Ins. Co. v. Branch,* 561 S.W.2d 371 (Mo. App. 1977).

[43]*National Indemnity Co. v. Corbo,* 248 So. 2d 238 (Fla. App. 1971).

[44]*Cieslewicz v. Mutual Service Casualty Ins. Co.,* 84 Wis. 2d 91, 267 N.W.2d 595 (1978).

12

VICIOUS DOGS AND PIT BULLS

vicious dog laws / pit bull bans / criminal penalties for owners

Most dogs, even those that bite someone, aren't career criminals: they bite from fear or nervousness or over-protectiveness. They may bite just once in their lives. But once a dog has bitten, or displayed dangerous tendencies, it makes sense to require its owner to take precautions to prevent further injury. Many cities, and an increasing number of states, are adopting "vicious dog" laws to identify dangerous dogs and make their owners take specific measures, such as confining the dogs securely, muzzling them when in public, or acquiring liability insurance to cover any injuries the dog causes. Owners who have deliberately created vicious dogs—by teaching them to attack or fight, or mistreating them—may be subject to criminal fines and even jail sentences.

Some cities have taken a different approach and equated "pit bulls," dogs thought to be inherently dangerous, with vicious dogs, and banned them from the city or imposed strict regulations on their owners.

Vicious Dog Laws

"Vicious dog" laws impose special restrictions on dogs that are officially labeled dangerous or potentially dangerous. These laws, which emphasize prevention, have much to commend them. By focusing on dogs that really do pose a danger, they protect the public, crack down on irresponsible dog owners, and lessen the temptation to over-regulate (as in the case of "pit bull" bans, discussed below).

Generally, a vicious dog law is set in motion by a formal complaint from an animal control officer or someone who has been threatened or injured by a dog. A hearing follows, at which a judge or public health official hears evidence and determines whether or not the accused dog is actually "vicious" under the terms of the law. If a dog is found to be vicious, the judge may order the owner to take specific precautions to prevent the dog from injuring anyone. At the least, the owner will have to keep the dog securely confined. Violating the order—in essence, the terms of the dog's "probation"—can result in fines for the owner and impoundment and even death for the dog.

Most vicious dog laws are local, but some states have also passed such laws. The state laws follow the same general pattern, but differ significantly from state to state.

STATES WITH VICIOUS DOG LAWS

Arizona	Massachusetts	Pennsylvania
Georgia	Michigan	Rhode Island
Hawaii	New Hampshire	Texas
Kentucky	New York	Vermont
Maine	North Carolina	Washington
Maryland	North Dakota	West Virginia

Some other states regulate vicious dogs, but don't provide a procedure for having a judge determine what dogs are vicious. In South Dakota, for example, it is illegal to keep a vicious dog, which is defined as a dog that attacks people unprovoked.[1] And in South Carolina and Minnesota, dangerous dogs must be muzzled and chained when off their owners' premises.

The Complaint

If a dog has attacked someone, the injured person may file a formal complaint with the agency or court in charge of implementing the law. Often a local court receives complaints, but sometimes they are handled by the local health or animal control department.

Who may make such a complaint depends on the law. Most laws allow anyone to complain, but some require the complaining person to have been attacked by the dog. And in Vermont, it takes three residents of a town to file a written complaint with the town legislature (selectmen, aldermen, or trustees), and they may do so only if they know that a dog has bitten someone while off the premises of its owner or keeper.[2] Under most laws, law enforcement and animal control officers may also file a complaint.

After a complaint is made, a dog that has seriously hurt someone may be seized and impounded until the hearing is held. New York law, for example, allows a judge to order a dog put in the pound before the hearing if there is "probable cause" to believe the dog is dangerous.[3] Similar rules apply most places. As a practical matter, by the time a hearing has been scheduled to determine the viciousness of a dog, the dog will probably have been impounded. An animal control officer can almost always seize a dog that has been caught in the act of attacking someone.

The Hearing

Under most vicious dog laws, after a dog owner has been notified of a complaint, a hearing is held to determine if the dog is vicious under the law. The owner, and sometimes members of the public, can attend and present evidence about the dog's behavior or disposition. Most often, these hearings are held before judges in local courts. Local health authorities, however, may sometimes hold hearings and make "vicious dog" determinations.

In some states, including Massachusetts and Georgia, there is an important difference: a hearing is held only if the dog owner requests one. After a complaint is made, an animal control officer investigates and decides whether or not the dog is vicious. The owner is mailed a notice of the decision. The owner gets a chance to argue only by requesting a hearing.

Rhode Island officials have a detailed definition of vicious dogs to help them make their decisions. All unlicensed dogs are automatically considered vicious—another very good argument for conscientiously licensing your dog. The law does provide, however, that the vicious dog label for unlicensed dogs is removed when the owner licenses the dog and pays the fine. According to the statute, a vicious dog is:

> (1) Any dog which when unprovoked, in a vicious or terrorizing manner approaches any person in apparent attitude of attack upon the streets, sidewalks, or any public grounds or places; or
>
> (2) Any dog with a known propensity, tendency or disposition to attack unprovoked, to cause injury or to otherwise endanger the safety of human beings or domestic animals; or
>
> (3) Any dog which bites, inflicts injury, assaults or otherwise attacks a human being or domestic animal without provocation on public or private property; or
>
> (4) Any dog owned or harbored primarily or in part for the purpose of dog fighting or any dog trained for dog fighting; or
>
> (5) Any dog not licensed according to state, city or town law.
>
> Notwithstanding the definition of a vicious dog above, no dog may be declared vicious if an injury or damage is sustained by a person who, at the the time such injury or damage was sustained, was committing a willful trespass or other tort upon premises occupied by the owner or keeper of the dog, or was teasing, tormenting, abusing or assaulting the dog or was committing or attempting to commit a crime.
>
> No dog may be declared vicious if an injury or damage was sustained by a domestic animal which at the time such injury or damage was

> sustained was teasing, tormenting, abusing or
> assaulting the dog. No dog may be declared
> vicious if the dog was protecting or defending
> a human being within the immediate vicinity of
> the dog from an unjustified attack or assault.

This statute is quite detailed. It doesn't apply, for example, if the person attacked was teasing the dog or trying to commit a crime. Although most vicious dog statutes aren't as detailed as the Rhode Island one, most of the factors it sets out would probably be considered by any judge faced with determining whether or not a dog is vicious.

Under this statute, a dog owner who wants to challenge a vicious dog determination has five days to petition the district court for a new hearing. The court then conducts its own hearing and decides for itself if the dog is vicious according to the law's definition.

Restrictions on Vicious Dogs

Usually, a judge who pronounces a dog vicious has fairly free rein to impose penalties or restrictions on the dog's owner. At a minimum, laws require that the vicious dog be kept enclosed on the owner's property at all times unless it's leashed and, in some places, muzzled as well. Again, Rhode Island spells out in great detail the conditions under which a vicious dog is allowed off its owner's property. There, it is unlawful for an owner to let a vicious dog outside the owner's dwelling or a locked enclosure:

> unless it is necessary . . . to obtain
> veterinary care . . . or to sell or give away
> the vicious dog or to comply with commands or
> directions of the dog officer . . . . In such
> event, the vicious dog shall be securely
> muzzled and restrained with a chain having a
> minimum tensile strength of three hundred (300)
> pounds and not exceeding three feet (3') in
> length, and shall be under the direct control
> and supervision of the owner or keeper of the
> vicious dog.

Depending on the specific city or state law and the dangerousness of the dog, its owner may also be required to:

- Post "Beware of Dog" signs prominently.
- Keep the dog in a locked enclosure, or one that meets certain specifications for height, strength, and other features.
- Buy liability insurance that covers damage or injury caused by the dog ($15,000 to $100,000 of coverage may be required).
- Post a bond with the city or county to cover any damage or injury caused by the dog.
- Obtain a special "vicious dog" license (more expensive than the standard license) from the city or county.
- Have the dog's license number tattooed on the dog.
- Notify animal control officials if the dog is sold or given away, and notify the new owner in writing that the dog has injured someone.

A judge who decides that a dog poses a great risk of serious harm may order that the dog be seized and humanely killed by animal control authorities. This penalty, of course, is reserved for dogs considered incorrigible: dogs that have repeatedly bitten people, severely injured or killed someone, or have been trained and used for fighting.

Violating Restrictions

Once a dog has been declared legally vicious but allowed to live, it's unlikely to get a second chance if its owner doesn't follow the judge's restrictions scrupulously. The laws of Kentucky and

Pennsylvania, for example, authorize peace officers to kill any dog that has been found to be vicious if it is running at large.[4]

At the least, a dog officially labeled vicious will be impounded if it later injures someone. Owners may also have to pay double or triple damages to the injured person. In Maine, for example, an owner who doesn't comply with a judge's order to confine or muzzle a dog is liable for three times the amount of damage the dog causes.[5]

The owner of a vicious dog who doesn't comply with the law's conditions on keeping the dog securely confined and away from people may be guilty of a crime. Some laws also impose criminal fines (usually $50 to $500) if a vicious dog injures someone. And a California court sentenced a dog owner to 90 days in jail and fined him $500 for failing to keep his dog on a leash, as ordered by the county after the dog attacked two people.[6] In Rhode Island, if a vicious dog injures someone, the owner must pay a fine to the government and triple damages to the injured person.

Criminal Penalties for Owners of Vicious Dogs

Dog owners whose dogs injure someone are rarely charged with serious criminal offenses. But if a dog mauls or kills someone, even if it hasn't yet been officially labeled a "vicious dog," its owner may be charged with manslaughter or even murder.[7] The best-known examples involve people who use dogs as weapons—people who train their dogs to fight, or drug dealers who keep vicious guard dogs.

Not all those prosecuted, however, are professional criminals. In 1987, a Georgia man was convicted of involuntary manslaughter after his three pit bulls, which he had allowed to run loose, attacked and killed a four-year-old boy. He was sentenced to five years in prison and five years of probation. One of the conditions of the probation is that he not own any dogs.

Special Restrictions on 'Pit Bulls'

Cities all across the country have passed ordinances specifically prohibiting "pit bulls." The sentiment behind these ordinances will probably subside with time, as it has against other kinds of dogs thought to be inherently vicious (German shepherds and Doberman pinschers are good examples). There are indications, in fact, that the trend is slowing; several local governments have recently declined to ban pit bulls.[8]

What Is a Pit Bull?

There is no one pit bull breed—which creates an obvious problem with ordinances that try to ban them. The name comes from "pit bulldog," a dog bred long ago from bulldog and terrier stock to fight in a pit. The name is used here because the laws usually use it, too.

PIT BULL PARANOIA THROUGH THE AGES

The prejudice against pit bulls is not entirely a modern phenomenon, as indicated by a statement made by a long-winded California court in 1907:

"It is, we think, safe to say that those writers who have written such glowing tributes to the dog in the abstract have never had any actual experience with a monstrous canine of the bull family, to which they were strangers. There is neither poetry nor sentiment in the dog, as a rule, especially when one meets him upon what he conceives to be his own preserves, for such an occasion is generally conceded to be an appropriate time to cast song and sentiment to the winds and to get busy by moving with all possible haste a comfortable distance beyond the danger line."[9]

The American Kennel Club does not recognize the pit bull as a breed. Generally, three breeds are considered within the pit bull category: the American Staffordshire terrier, the bull terrier, and the Staffordshire bull terrier. And most ordinances complicate things even further by including dogs that are a mixture of any of these breeds. The Cincinnati, Ohio ordinance banning pit bulls, for example, defines them this way:

"Any Staffordshire Bull Terrier or American Staffordshire Terrier breed of dog, or any mixed breed of dog which contains as an element of its breeding the breed of Staffordshire Bull Terrier or American Staffordshire Terrier as to be identifiable as partially of the breed of Staffordshire Bull Terrier or American Staffordshire Terrier by a qualified veterinarian duly licensed as such by the state of Ohio."

Veterinarians, understandably, protest that they aren't qualified or willing to be the arbiters of "pit bull" status for particular dogs.

Legal Challenges to Pit Bull Laws

A key weakness in these ordinances is the vagueness of the definition of pit bull. Simply put, if a law isn't specific enough to give dog owners fair warning about what kinds of dogs are illegal, it's unconstitutional. Ordinances in Lynn, Massachusetts; Broward County, Florida; Maumelle, Arkansas and other places have all been thrown out by judges who followed that reasoning.

WAS THE BARK WORSE THAN THE BITE?

Some dogs will do anything to please. At the command of his 19-year-old master, one pit bull attacked 13 trees in downtown Lancaster, Pennsylvania. Damage to the trees was estimated at about $1,200. The man, who his lawyer says was showing off for friends, was sentenced to 40 hours of community service. [10]

Another attack on these ordinances is that it is arbitrary to ban one kind of dog, so the laws violate the owners' constitutional due process rights. After all, pit bulls aren't the only dogs that injure people. A 1982 study of fatal dog attacks reported fatalities caused by, among other breeds, such small and apparently mild-mannered creatures as Yorkshire terriers and dachshunds. [11] More cases are pending, and more are likely to be filed.

Should Pit Bulls Be Banned?

One thing is certain in this controversy: pit bulls have seriously injured and sometimes even killed people. Why not ban them? What could outweigh our interest in preventing such serious harm?

· The fact is that the question is not that simple. Some injuries are inevitable when people live closely with any kind of animal. When it comes to dogs, our society has accepted this risk for centuries. Still, vicious dogs of any breed are a problem. What's different about pit bulls?

Pit bulls, however defined, are distinctive. Renowned for their strength, they are deep-chested, muscular, and have powerful jaws— a mail carrier reported that one punctured a tire on his truck in 1988. They are also famous for "gameness," a hard-to-define trait that is shorthand for courage and perseverance. These traits, by themselves, are no threat to humans; they become dangerous only when a dog's disposition is bad. When a dog is mean or excessively aggressive or protective, they can be deadly.

Behaviorists can argue, but most people who are familiar with dogs and who pay attention to how they interact with animals and people are convinced that virtually all mean dogs are made, not born. Pit bulls, more than dogs of other breeds, have been trained and tormented because people wanted them mean. The strength and gameness of the pit bull are its virtues and its misfortune; humans who derive pleasure from watching animals fight and die chose, unsurprisingly, a powerful and tenacious breed for their attention. The pit bull figures prominently in the ugly history of dog-fighting. And as much as we'd like to think dog fighting is an historical footnote, the sad truth is that it's flourishing today. Dogs are trained on indoor treadmills, encouraged to kill small animals, and taken to illegal fights.

The current publicity about pit bulls has made them only more popular with others who want to be identified with a tough, "macho" symbol. Big city drug dealers, as well as small town weekend dog fighters, like to be seen with pit bulls.

Unfortunately, as responsible pet owners shy away from pit bulls, the irresponsible ones make up a bigger percentage of owners. Every publicized attack, or rumor of an impending legal ban, sends fearful owners to the pound with their dogs. After a California pit bull (which had been trained to fight by its owner) killed a toddler in 1987, 19 pit bulls were turned in to the local pound for destruction over the next ten days. Most, according to a Humane Society spokeswoman, were family pets; their owners were afraid the dogs would develop vicious tendencies. In Los Angeles, owners sent approximately 300 dogs to the pound.

Other Solutions

Most pit bulls, like most dogs of other breeds, are no threat to people. But some pit bull owners are. Lawmakers and law enforcement officers should respond in two ways.

First, laws should address the problem of vicious dogs—not the problem of pit bulls. Laws like the ones discussed earlier in this chapter must make owners responsible for injuries caused by vicious dogs.

Second, laws against dog fighting should be beefed up and enforced. Even apart from the animals involved, dog fighting is not a victimless crime: it encourages the proliferation of vicious dogs and the inevitable harm that results. Because of the special attraction pit bulls hold for dog fight enthusiasts, public animal shelters that give dogs out for adoption need to keep close tabs on people who take pit bulls. The San Francisco SPCA, for example, has a special program for people who adopt pit bulls. The SPCA checks the background of the new owners, who must submit fingerprints and mug shots.

---

[1]S.D. Codified Laws Ann. § 40-34-14.

[2]Vt. Stat. Ann. tit. 20, § 3546(a).

[3]N.Y. Agric. & Mkts. Law § 121.

[4]Ken. Rev. Stat. § 258.235(6); Pa. Cons. Stat. § 459-501(d).

[5]Me. Rev. Stat. Ann. tit. 7, § 3605.

[6]San Francisco Chronicle, June 16, 1988, p. 11.

[7]The only person reported to have been charged with murder is a Morgan Hill, California man whose chained pit bull mauled to death a two-year-old boy. He was charged with second degree murder. When this book went to press, his trial had not yet begun.

[8]The Los Angeles County Board of Supervisors rejected a pit bull ban (which would have affected unincorporated areas of the county) in January, 1988.

[9]*In re Ackerman*, 6 Cal. App. 5, 91 P. 429 (1907).

[10]National Law Journal, May 16, 1988, p. 47.

[11]Pickney & Kennedy, "Traumatic Deaths from Dog Attacks in the United States," 69 Pediatrics (Feb. 1982), cited in "The New Breed of Municipal Dog Control Laws: Are They Constitutional?" 53 U. Cincinnati L. Rev. 1067 (1984).

13

CRUELTY

cruelty and neglect / animal experimentation / dog fighting

More than one philosopher has concluded that an accurate measure of a society's morals is the way it treats animals. America's official position toward animals is admirable: cruelty is forbidden and, at least on paper, severely punished. Then there is the real world, where cruelty is an undeniable reality.

In general, the law is even more reluctant to interfere with an owner-animal relationship than it is to get involved in parent-child relations. Or, as the late animal trainer Barbara Woodhouse lamented, "there is no law that permits dogs to be taken away from stupid owners."[1]

Criminal penalties are invoked only for what society considers the most serious forms of misconduct involving animals: cruelty and neglect, fighting, and theft. Experimenting on animals for scientific research is usually not considered cruelty punishable by law, and neither is injuring an animal to defend people or valuable property.

What to Do If You Suspect Mistreatment

Almost all of us have seen neglected animals—hungry, mistreated, left in filthy conditions without enough food or water. We want to help. But often, we can see animals' pain without being able to reach them.

Before you complain to the owner, a humane society, animal control authorities or any of the other officials we suggest below, take a careful look at both the circumstances and local standards for treatment of animals. Ideas about what is cruel vary with time and from community to community. These community standards, more than the language of the anti-cruelty laws, ultimately determine who is convicted or even who is prosecuted in the first place.

Community Standards of Animal Treatment

Before examining what the laws say about cruelty to animals, it's helpful to look at how the average person or community defines "cruelty." The customary, or tolerated, treatment of animals varies from place to place, and customs differ about when official intervention is expected and desired. Animals in rural areas, for example, usually lead less pampered lives than many city dogs do, and no one can say which is happier. Whether or not conduct constitutes cruelty depends both on the circumstances and on community standards. Consider a few scenarios:

- **A dog is almost always left tied in a yard, no matter what the weather.**
  Is the weather warm, and the dog given food, water and exercise? If it's cold outside, is the dog accustomed and well-suited to cold weather? Is it a rural area, where most dogs live outside?
- **An owner beats a dog for disobedience during training.**
  Does the trainer habitually beat the dog, or is the dog being taught not to run into the street, a lesson that might save its life later?

- **An owner goes away for three days, leaving a dog outside without food.**
  Does the dog have shelter, water and a chance for exercise? Does it refuse to eat, as some dogs do, while its owner is away?

Where to Complain

Authorities in many states rely on humane societies, which are private agencies, to monitor treatment of animals and to investigate complaints, especially in commercial operations such as pet shops or horse-drawn cabs. Sometimes a city and humane society have a contract under which the humane society enforces the city's animal control regulations. In other instances, humane society employees work with law enforcement personnel or carry out their own investigations of cruelty complaints and notify authorities.

No matter how enforcement efforts are organized, the humane societies and police responsible for investigating and prosecuting cruelty rely on complaints from members of the public. If you know or have good reason to suspect that an animal is being mistreated—abused, neglected, trained for fighting, or in any other way cared for improperly—talk to local humane society officials. They will have a good sense of what kinds of conduct the local police or prosecutor's office will act on. And even if the behavior isn't against the law, the humane society may step in to correct it, eliminating the need for recourse to the criminal justice system.

If a humane society isn't available or helpful, talk to:

- the owner, if you think explaining your concern might have a good effect;
- a local dog owners' organization;
- animal control authorities;
- city police or the county sheriff;
- the local prosecutor (often called the district attorney or state's attorney);
- your representatives in the state legislature or Congress, if the problem should be addressed by legislation (for example, the problem of "puppy mills"); or
- the FBI, if dogs are being taken across state lines for fighting.

If you make a written complaint to law enforcement officials, send a copy to a local or national humane society and keep a copy yourself.

What Happens to Rescued Animals

Neglected or mistreated animals are usually seized by animal control authorities when their owner is charged with cruelty. Except in an emergency, however, the owner of the animals has a constitutional right to notice and a hearing before the animals can be taken away.

If the animals are taken without first notifying the owner, the owner is entitled to a hearing, usually before a judge, as soon as possible.[2] In most places, the owner is responsible for reimbursing the government for the costs of impoundment, and can't get the animals back until the bill is paid.

(For more on what can happen to impounded animals, see Chapter 2, State and Local Regulation.)

A GOOD IDEA FROM ENGLAND

A troublesome problem with anti-cruelty laws is that there's nothing in them to keep someone who's convicted of cruelty from going right out and getting another dog. The English have found a simple way around the problem. Under English law, anyone convicted of cruelty to a dog may be forbidden to keep another dog for as long as the court thinks fit. Anyone who violates such an order may be fined and jailed for up to three months.[3] In the U.S., all a judge can do is forbid a convicted criminal from having a dog while on probation.

Cruelty and Neglect

Even a dog knows the difference between being tripped over and being kicked.

—Oliver Wendell Holmes

Cruelty to animals is against the law everywhere in this country, but it wasn't always so. If you were to pick up a famous old treatise called *Chitty's Criminal Law*, blow the dust from its leather-bound pages, and look inside, you would search in vain for mention of a crime called cruelty to animals. It simply didn't exist in 1819, when Chitty was expounding. At most, someone who beat an animal could be accused of being a public nuisance. Most states didn't pass anti-cruelty laws for another century.

And when anti-cruelty statutes were written, they were often vague. A statute may, for example, forbid "deliberate cruelty," inadvertent "neglect," or everything in between. People prosecuted for cruelty under these statutes sometimes complain that the language is too vague to warn them of what conduct is prohibited, but this argument virtually never works. Courts say that people are perfectly capable of knowing what kinds of conduct toward animals won't be tolerated.[4]

CRIMINAL LAW TERMS

Infraction: a minor offense, such as a driving over the speed limit, usually punishable by a small fine. Infractions aren't considered actual crimes, and they don't give you a "criminal record."

Misdemeanor: a crime that is punishable in most states by up to a year's imprisonment in a county jail, a fine, or both. Violating anti-cruelty statutes is often a misdemeanor.

Felony: a serious crime. Conviction can mean a state prison sentence of a year or more, a fine, or both. Entering a dog in an organized dog fight is a felony in many states. Some states have different "classes" of misdemeanors and felonies; for example, Class A crimes may be the least serious, Class C crimes the most serious.

What Is Cruelty?

Anti-cruelty laws usually punish several different kinds of conduct— ranging from abandoning a dog to neglecting it to intentionally harming it. Some states have only one or two broadly-worded statutes that simply prohibit any kind of "inhumane" or "needlessly cruel" treatment. Others have several statutes: both a catch-all ban on cruel treatment and specific prohibitions on acts that are considered cruel—abandonment, or ear-cropping without anesthesia, for example.

It's important to remember that a broadly-worded statute prohibits many kinds of cruelty, even though it doesn't list them specifically. Some states, for example, have specific laws against leaving a dog in a car without proper ventilation. But even if your state doesn't have such a law, locking a dog in a car that overheats could be illegal under a catch-all statute that forbids cruelty to animals.

Here's the Texas anti-cruelty statute, which combines the broad and the specific to cover nearly every kind of misconduct toward animals (except dog fighting, for which there is a more specific and detailed statute):

A person commits an offense [in Texas, a misdemeanor] if he intentionally or knowingly:

(1)   tortures or seriously overworks an animal;

(2)   fails unreasonably to provide necessary food, care, or shelter for an animal in his custody;

(3)   abandons unreasonably an animal in his custody;

(4)   transports or confines an animal in a cruel manner;

(5)   kills, injures, or administers poison to an animal, other than cattle, horses, sheep, swine, or goats, belonging to another without legal authority or the owner's effective consent;

(6)   causes one animal to fight with another; or

(7)   uses a live animal as a lure in dog race training or in dog coursing on a racetrack.[5]

When investigating the law of your state, you may have to dig to make sure you've found all the statutes that cover mistreatment of animals. Dog fighting statutes (discussed in the next section) are almost always separate from general anti-cruelty laws, with their own stiff penalties. (For help on looking up statutes, see Appendix 1, Legal Research.)

Let's look at the general kinds of conduct that are typically prohibited by state criminal law.

Neglect

A righteous man regardeth the life of his beast.
—Proverbs 12:10

Failing to provide an animal with the necessities of life is always cruelty. The Colorado statute, for example, makes it a crime not to furnish "food, water, protection from the elements, opportunity for exercise, or other care normal, usual and proper for an animal's health and well-being."[6] In California, it is illegal for anyone having "charge or custody of any animal, either as owner or otherwise, [to] . . . fail to provide the animal with proper food, drink, or shelter or protection from the weather."[7] A separate statute requires that confined animals be given an adequate exercise area.[8]

Whether or not a person accused of neglecting an animal will be convicted by a judge or jury depends, of course, on the circumstances and the evidence. But to convict someone of a crime, the state must prove guilt "beyond a reasonable doubt"—a tough standard to meet. For example, in 1970 a District of Columbia man was arrested for failing to give his dog adequate shelter and protection from the weather. A physician had seen the dog, a German shepherd, tied by a three-foot chain on an open concrete back porch, on a January day when the temperature never got above 28 degrees. The owner was convicted, but an appeal court overturned the conviction because no one "experienced in the care of a dog of this type" had testified that the dog had been made to suffer. After all, said the court, it's common knowledge that some breeds of dogs can stay out in bitter cold with no ill effects.[9] The moral: Don't take anything for granted when you're thinking about proving a case of criminal neglect. Every part of a crime must be proved beyond a reasonable doubt.

Unless a statute requires that the neglect be malicious, it doesn't matter that someone accused of neglecting animals didn't intend to be cruel. Under most statutes, it is enough that someone knowingly neglected animals. For example, an Ohio farmer who left cattle to die because the market price of cattle dropped was convicted under a neglect statute.[10] Presumably, he didn't stop feeding them because he wanted them to suffer, but he did intentionally stop feeding them, and as a result, they suffered.

Another example: Two New York men were convicted in 1975 of neglecting a horse by allowing it to pull a hansom cab even though they knew the horse was limping. Whether or not they had acted maliciously was irrelevant, the court said: "The question is whether they wilfully caused certain things to be done."[11]

Some neglect statutes don't even require the conduct to be knowing; it is enough that it was "reckless"—that the person showed a "reckless indifference" to the consequences of his actions. If, for example, a pet owner goes on vacation without bothering to make arrangements for the pet, that behavior might be considered reckless enough to warrant a neglect conviction.

A few statutes don't consider what's going on in the mind of the person charged with a crime. Under those statutes, if an animal is neglected because of someone's actions, that person is guilty, period. Such laws (called "strict liability" statutes) are fairly unusual. Colorado, for example, has a statute that makes anyone who, having custody of an animal, "unnecessarily fails to provide it with proper food, drink, or protection from the weather or cruelly abandons it," guilty of a misdemeanor, punishable by a fine up to $750, six months in jail, or both.[12]

Example: Simone lives in a state with a strict liability animal neglect statute. She goes on vacation and makes arrangements with her friend John to care for her dog, but John forgets to feed the dog. He could be prosecuted for neglect. What he intended or didn't intend doesn't matter; he had charge of the dog and neglected it.

Malicious Cruelty

Malicious (intentionally mean) cruelty, of course, is punished more severely than any other cruelty to animals. California law, for example, punishes malicious cruelty to an animal with a state prison sentence, a fine of up to $20,000, or both.[13]

The most obvious and widespread kind of malicious cruelty is organized dog fighting; someone responsible for putting two animals in a ring and having them tear at each other is certainly someone who "maliciously and intentionally maims, mutilates, tortures, or wounds a living animal," in the words of the California law. Dog fighting, however, is usually prosecuted under separate, specific state and federal statutes, not generic anti-cruelty laws. (See the section on "Dog Fighting," below.)

Conduct may be malicious even if it isn't particularly harmful. Take, for example, the case of the North Carolina man who grew so annoyed at his neighbor's cat (it threatened bluebirds and walked over his wife's car) that he set a live trap for it. He also put red paint in the trap, so that when the cat was caught it was covered with paint from neck to tail. The paint was to identify the cat, he said. He was convicted of animal cruelty and fined $40.[14] The cat was fine after a couple of shampoos.

CRUELTY TO YOUR OWN DOG

One interesting loophole in some old animal cruelty laws is that they punished only cruelty to an animal that belonged to another person. This reflected the legal idea of the dog as property, which an owner could treat according to personal whim. Most of these laws have been changed to make cruelty a crime no matter who owns the animal.[15] It's a step toward the recognition of animal rights—rights that aren't incidental to an owner's rights, but exist separately— although it's doubtful lawmakers think of it in those terms.

Abandonment

Anyone who lives in the country, or even on the edge of town, knows that dog owners who have tired of their pets sometimes dump the unfortunate animals on deserted roads. In most places, that's illegal. New York law makes it a misdemeanor, with a penalty of up to one year's imprisonment, a $1,000 fine, or both.[16] Enforcing this law, however, is extremely difficult. Just about all witnesses can do is report license plate numbers, to police and try to get them to follow up.

Confining a Dog in an Unventilated Car

Some states and cities specifically forbid confining a dog in a car without adequate ventilation. A Texas man was convicted of violating such a statute in 1986 after he left his dog in a car, parked in the sun on a hot day, while he and his wife went to a movie. The car windows were open about an inch and a half; the sun shone directly into the the car through a tinted glass roof.[17] Remember that even without a specific statute, this could constitute cruelty under a general anti-cruelty law.

Leaving a Dog Hit By Your Car

Pennsylvania law specifically provides that a driver who hits a dog and knowingly doesn't stop to help it is guilty of a crime.[18] Again, this might be a crime under more general laws.

Cosmetic cruelty: cropping ears and tails

It is still the fashion, among those who breed and show certain kinds of dogs, to cut off part of the ears and tails of puppies. Massachusetts is the only state that makes it illegal to exhibit a dog with cropped ears, unless a veterinarian has certified that the cropping was reasonably necessary.[19] A violation can be punished by a fine up to $250.

Some states (Connecticut, Michigan, Pennsylvania and New York, for example) at least attempt to make the process less painful for the pups. They require ear-cropping to be done by a veterinarian, while the dog is under anesthesia.[20] In New York, owners must state, when they apply for a dog license, whether their dog's ears have been cropped.

Penalties range from stiff in New York to trivial across the river in Connecticut. In New York, those convicted of violating the statute are punished by a fine of $1,000, imprisoned for a year, or both. In Connecticut, the fine is $50 for the first offense; for subsequent convictions, it's another $50, 30 days in jail, or both.

It's doubtful that these laws are enforced vigorously. If you're accused of violating them, you will have to prove that your dog's ears were cropped by a veterinarian, in conformance with the law. You should have a certificate from the vet, showing the date of the operation, a description of the dog, and your name.

PIPPI LONGSTOCKING COMES OUT AGAINST HURTING PUPPIES

It is now against the law in Sweden to trim a dog's tail for cosmetic reasons. Astrid Lindgren, the creator of the Pippi Longstocking children's stories, was 80 years old when she campaigned for the law, which became effective in 1988. The law is informally known as "Lex Astrid" (Astrid's law).

Inhumane Conditions in Pet Shops and 'Puppy Mills'

Some states have special anti-cruelty laws for pet shops, where animals are sometimes treated as just more merchandise. California, for example, requires pet shops to provide animals with sanitary conditions, adequate space, heating, ventilation, and humane care. Violators can be punished by a fine of up to $1,000, 90 days in jail, or both.[21]

The same problems are often found in "puppy mills"—large-scale private dog breeding operations "in which the health of the dogs is disregarded in order to maintain a low overhead and maximize profits," as one court succinctly put it.[22] Humane societies frequently investigate them, whether or not state laws are directed specifically at these commercial operations.

Exceptions to Anti-Cruelty Laws

Even if an anti-cruelty law doesn't say so explicitly, it may not apply if the cruelty to the animal was inflicted for what, under the law, is considered a good reason. The two most common justifications are the defense of a person or property, and scientific research.

Defense of Person or Property

Many anti-cruelty laws excuse anyone who injures or kills a dog that is attacking a person or livestock. The Kansas statute, for example, doesn't apply to:

"the killing of any animal by any person [off the property of its owner] which is found injuring or posing a threat to any person, farm animal or property . . . ."[23]

It's not always clear when this exception applies. Take the Kansas statute: does it protect a farmer who shoots one of three dogs that have just destroyed his children's Easter baskets, which were in the cab of his pickup truck, parked on his land? The Kansas Supreme Court said yes, ruling in 1981 that "property" wasn't limited to "farm property."[24] Eight years earlier, a New York court also acquitted a man who shot a dog that frightened his children and attacked his own dog during a family picnic.[25]

A comparable Oklahoma statute did not, however, protect a man convicted in 1963 of cruelty for shooting three hunting dogs as they chased a deer. He had left the dogs, wounded but still alive, on someone else's land. The law justified killing a dog that was chasing livestock, but not one chasing wildlife, the court ruled. The defendant "knew that he had hit the dogs and he was willing to let them drag themselves off and suffer and die," said the court. "The trial court felt that this was cruelty to animals, and we can but agree."[26]

Note on civil liability: Someone who injures or kills a dog while defending another person or livestock may not be liable in a civil lawsuit, if the owner sues to recover the value of the dog. (Those rules are discussed in Chapter 9, If a Dog Is Injured or Killed.)

Scientific Research

One controversial question about anti-cruelty laws is whether or not they apply to scientific experiments on animals. Only a few states (Texas, for example) actually exempt scientific research specifically. The New York law exempts experiments in labs that have been approved by the state health commissioner; Vermont exempts research by competent researchers "in a humane manner" with a minimum of suffering. In most states, however, scientists are not prosecuted because statutes prohibit only "needless pain or suffering," and pain inflicted in the name of science is not considered "needless."

One scientist who was prosecuted and convicted for cruelty to animals was Dr. Edward Taub, who in 1981 was in charge of animal research at the Institute for Behavioral Research in Silver Spring, Maryland. His experiments involved severing nerves in monkeys' arms and legs and then trying to teach the animals to use the limbs again. His federally-funded laboratory was regularly inspected by the U.S. Department of Agriculture, which has responsibility for laboratory animals' welfare; the USDA found no violations.[27]

An employee, however, complained about conditions, and county police took 11 monkeys from the lab and arrested Taub. Taub appealed his conviction to the Maryland Supreme Court, which reversed it. The court ruled that it didn't think the state legislature had intended the anti-cruelty statute to apply to federal research programs.[28] Apparently, the court was wrong: the legislature immediately amended the law to say quite clearly that it had meant to include research.[29]

By amending its statute, Maryland became the first state to explicitly say that scientific research is subject to an anti-cruelty law. Most statutes are silent on the issue, leaving local officials free to prosecute researchers for cruelty if they wish. They never do.

The emotional issue of whether or not scientific research should be exempt from anti-cruelty laws is being debated all over the country. Those who want to protect researchers emphasize the importance of animal research in discovering cures or treatment for human illnesses:

cancer, AIDS, and all the other killers. Those who want to protect animals stress the thoughtless overuse of animals, the indifference to suffering that could often be avoided, and the existence of alternative research methods.

There certainly seems no good reason for giving science a blanket exemption from anti-cruelty laws. It encourages callous disregard for animals and closes off legitimate debate on what, as a society, we want to allow in the name of science. Merely labeling an activity "science" should not put it beyond scrutiny.

But even under existing laws, it seems obvious that much of the cruelty inflicted on animals in the name of research or education is "needless"—and thus illegal. Much of the experimentation done on animals for scientific "education" is especially egregious. Students perform experiments that countless others before them have done, learning little except, perhaps, disregard for animal life.

If this kind of waste and cruelty were prosecuted under anti-cruelty laws, the people or institutions charged would, at least, have to justify their actions to a jury. As in any criminal trial, the outcome would hinge on the jury's decision as to whether the particular use violated the state statute. In many cases, this would mean deciding whether or not the cruelty was necessary for some greater good.

Making scientists justify their actions or face prosecution under anti-cruelty statutes might mean some abuses would be stopped. But criminal prosecutions are hit-and-miss. They depend on local politics, citizen involvement, government budgets and a host of other unpredictable factors.

A much better approach would be a comprehensive system of federal government regulation and approval. It would provide both much more consistent protection of animals and needed guidelines for researchers and educators. Current federal law (the Laboratory Animal Welfare Act) doesn't address actual research methods; it covers only laboratory conditions such as food and housing, and enforcement of even those minimal standards is spotty. A comprehensive program would prohibit certain methods of research and would require evaluation and approval of research programs involving animals before they begin. The analysis should be based on such factors as importance of the research, number of animals, availability of alternatives, and the methods to be used.

Organized Dog Fighting

Organized dog fighting, much in the news lately because of the public fervor over "pit bulls," is now a felony in most states. Federal law also punishes dog fighting, if the dog was moved across state lines to fight, with a year in prison and fines up to $5,000.[30] Despite the stiffening of these laws, the problem of dog fighting is escalating, in cities as well as rural areas. There is a dog fight "on any weekend in any of the 50 states," according to Eric Sakach of the West Coast Regional office of the Humane Society.[31] One inevitable consequence of the increasing popularity of organized dog fighting is that more and more people are getting hurt by these dangerous dogs.

Putting a dog in the ring to fight is not the only conduct these laws punish. Most dog fighting laws make it illegal to watch, bet on or train dogs for dog fights. In New York, it's a felony, punishable by up to four years in prison, a fine of up to $25,000, or both, to:

- cause an animal to fight;
- train an animal, under circumstances showing an intent to have the dog fight;
- let an animal fight, or be trained to fight, on premises under one's control; or
- own or keep an animal trained to fight on premises used for fighting.

It's a misdemeanor, punishable by a year's imprisonment and fine of up to $15,000, to own or keep a dog under circumstances showing an intent to have the dog fight. Paying an admission fee or making a bet at a dog fight is another misdemeanor, with a penalty of up to a year in jail, a fine of up to $1,000, or both.[32]

Convictions for dog fighting offenses are still infrequent. But arrests are made: 40 people at a backwoods site in Louisiana, nine at a dog fight in upper Manhattan, and so on. The organizer of the Louisiana dog fight was sentenced to the state's maximum penalty of one year in prison and a $1,000 fine, despite his lack of a criminal record.[33]

Law enforcement officials depend on citizens to help them find and break up illicit dog fights. Veterinarians are also being pressed into service. Laws in Arizona and California, for example, require vets to tell local law enforcement about any dog injuries or deaths they think were inflicted in a dog fight.[34]

---

[1]Woodhouse, *No Bad Dogs* (Summit Books 1982).

[2]See, for example, *Carrera v. Bertaini*, 63 Cal. App. 3d 721, 134 Cal. Rptr. 14 (1976).

[3]Protection of Animals (Cruelty to Dogs) Act, 1933, 23 & 24 Geo. 5, ch. 17, § 1.

[4]For example, *People v. Allen*, 657 P.2d 447 (Colo. 1983); *McCall v. State*, 540 S.W.2d 717 (Tex. Crim. App. 1976); *State v. Hafle*, 52 Ohio App. 2d 9, 367 N.W.2d 1226 (1977).

[5]Tex. Penal Code Ann. § 42.11.

[6]Colo. Rev. Stat. § 18-9-202.

[7]Cal. Penal Code § 597(b).

[8]Cal. Penal Code § 597t.

[9]*Jordan v. United States*, 269 A.2d 848 (D.C. App. 1970).

[10]*State v. Hafle*, 52 Ohio App. 2d 9, 367 N.W.2d 1226 (1977).

[11]*People v. O'Rourke*, 369 N.Y.S.2d 335 (Crim. Ct. 1975).

[12]Colo. Rev. Stat. § 35-42-112.

[13]Cal. Penal Code § 597(a).

[14]National Law Journal, Aug. 15, 1988.

[15]For example, Cal. Penal Code § 597 (amended 1987).

[16]N.Y. Agric. & Mkts. Law § 355.

[17]*Lopez v. State*, 720 S.W.2d 201 (Tex. App. 1986).

[18]See, for example, *Commonwealth v. Fabian*, 14 Pa. D. & C. 3d 551 (1980).

[19]Mass. Gen. Laws Ann. ch. 272, § 80B.

[20]N.Y. Agric. & Mkts. Law § 365; Conn. Gen. Stat. § 22-366.; Mich. Comp. Laws § 752.21; Pa. Stat. Ann. tit. 18, § 5511.

[21]Cal. Penal Code § 597L.

[22]*Avenson v. Zegart,* 577 F. Supp. 958 (Minn. 1984).

[23]Kan. Stat. Ann. § 21-4310.

[24]*State v. Jones,* 229 Kan. 528, 625 P.2d 503 (1981).

[25]*People v. Wicker,* 78 Misc. 2d 811, 357 N.Y.S.2d 587 (Town Ct. 1974).

[26]*Laner v. State,* 381 P.2d 905 (Okla. 1963).

[27]*"Taub v. State:* Are State Anti-Cruelty Statutes Sleeping Giants?" 2 Pace Envt'l L. Rev. 255 (1985).

[28]*Taub v. State,* 296 Md. 439, 463 A.2d 819 (1983).

[29]Md. Code Ann. art. 27 § 59.

[30]7 U.S.C. § 2156.

[31]Quoted in the excellent "The Pit Bull: Friend and Killer," by E.M. Swift, Sports Illustrated, July 27, 1987.

[32]N.Y. Agric. & Mkts. Law § 351.

[33]*State v. Digilormo,* 505 So. 2d 1154 (La. App. 1987).

[34]Ariz. Rev. Stat. Ann. § 32-2239; Cal. Bus. & Prof. Code § 4830.5.

APPENDIX 1
LEGAL RESEARCH

References to statutes and court decisions are sprinkled throughout this book. If you want to read a statute or case decision for yourself, here are a few tips on how to find them.

These brief instructions aren't intended to tell you how to do real legal research—that is, to take a problem and find out what law applies to it. For that, Nolo publishes a whole book: *Legal Research: How to Find and Understand the Law*, by Stephen Elias. It's an excellent resource.

Back to basics.

SOURCES OF LAW

The U.S. constitution: the basic document which guarantees all citizens certain rights.

Federal statutes: laws passed by Congress.

Federal case law: cases decided by federal court judges.

State constitutions: each state has a constitution, too, which guarantees certain rights.

State law: laws passed by state legislatures.

State case law: cases decided by state court judges.

Local ordinances: laws passed by city council and county boards.

Finding a Library That Has Law Books

Contrary to what you may expect, law libraries aren't the only places to find law books. If you're looking for a statute (state law) or ordinance (city or county law), you can probably find it in your local public library.

If you're looking for a written decision of a court, you will probably need a law library. The courthouse in your county will have one, and it should be open to the public (after all, county law libraries are commonly financed by the filing fees from lawsuits). You can also check out the libraries in law schools.

BEYOND *DOG LAW*

If you get tired of reading law books, check out some of these tomes, which are all real titles we found in the public library:

Horoscopes for Dogs

Pet Aerobics

How to Live with a Neurotic Dog

Your Neurotic Dog

When Good Dogs Do Bad Things

Finding a Statute or Ordinance

Many of the laws that affect dog owners are written in a state's or city's code of laws. Both state laws (statutes) and city or county ones (ordinances) should be easy to find, especially if you have a citation—a reference that tells you where to look.

If you have a citation

When you get your hands on a statute book, you'll see that all the statutes are numbered. If the numbering system seems confusing, ask a librarian for help.

Let's say you want to look up two laws that have to do with the rights of disabled people who have assistance dogs. You have the citations to the statutes from the footnotes in Chapter 8.

First, you want to look up the New York law that guarantees access to public places for persons with signal dogs.

The citation is **N.Y. Civ. Rights Law § 47**. New York's laws, like those of several states, are organized by topic. This statute is in the Civil Rights Law. There is also a Highway Law, Insurance Law and many others. To find this statute, find the volume of statutes that contains the Civil Rights Law, and look up Section 47.

The next statute you want to look up is the Arizona law that allows elderly or handicapped people to keep pets in public housing. Its citation is **Ariz. Rev. Stat. Ann. § 36-1409.01**. Arizona laws are simply numbered sequentially, not divided by subject into codes (the abbreviation stands for "Arizona Revised Statutes Annotated"). To find this statute, just get the volume numbered 36 and look up section 1409.01.

Dog-bite statutes. A complete list of dog-bite statutes is contained in Appendix 2. Chapter 11, Personal Injury and Property Damage, contains a special section on how to read a dog-bite statute.

If you don't have a citation

What if you want to see if your state has a statute like the California one that allows elderly public housing tenants to keep a pet? Statutes are indexed; just look there, under Dogs, Animals, Landlord-Tenant, Public Housing, and as many other likely headings you can think of until you find what you're looking for. Be prepared to look under several topic headings.

Annotations

If you can, find an "annotated" collection of statutes. You will find, following each statute, short summaries of court decisions that discuss or interpret the statute. They are often valuable help in understanding the statute, by showing you how courts have applied it in particular situations. If you find an case that sounds similar to your own situation, you will want to read the entire court decision it's based on. (See "Finding a Case," below.)

Finding a Case

Cases are the written decisions of appeals courts. They can be a big help if you want to know how a statute is applied to a real situation, or if your legal question involves a "common law" doctrine—one that is shaped by the courts, not the legislature.

If you have a citation

Let's say you're reading along about a landlord's liability for damage caused by a tenant's dog, and find an example that seems closely related to your situation. What's more, the actual court case from which we took the example was decided by a court in your state, Illinois. You want to read the case yourself, so you check the footnote and find this reference: Steinberg v. Petta, 139 Ill. App.3d 503, 94 Ill. Dec. 187, 487 N.E.2d 1064 (1985).

What are you supposed to do with those hieroglyphics? Don't panic; it's just a relatively simple code, and we can help you break it in no time.

Steinberg v. Petta: Last names of the people involved in the case (who sued whom).

139 Ill. App.3d 503: This tells you what book the decision of the court is printed in. This means volume 139 of the Illinois Appellate Reports, 3d series, page 503.

94 Ill. Dec. 187: An identical report of this case is also contained in volume 94 of the Illinois Decisions, at page 187.

487 N.E.2d 1064: This case is also contained in volume 487 of the Northeastern Reporter, second series, at page 1064.

(1985): The year the case was decided.

Here's another one:

Knowles Animal Hospital, Inc. v. Wills: Who sued whom.

360 So. 2d 37: volume 360 of the Southern Reporter, second series, page 37.

(Fla. App. 1978): This tells you that the case was decided in the Florida appellate court (called the Court of Appeals) in 1978.

If you don't have a citation

If you're looking for cases that have circumstances similar to yours, the first place to look is an annotated statute book (discussed above). But if there's no relevant statute, you'll have to look for cases in a book called a "digest." Digests are arranged by topic and contain short summaries (like the annotations in a statute book) of cases.

There is a digest for every state. So if you want to look up dog cases for Florida, you would go to the Florida Digest and look under "Animals," "Landlord-Tenant," or whatever topics look promising. Under each topic, you'll find a list of cases decided by Florida courts.

Background Research

Statutes and cases aren't much help if you read them in a legal vacuum—you need context to really understand them. You can get some of this background by consulting a legal encyclopedia for your state. Some examples are California Jurisprudence (commonly called Cal Jur), Michigan Law and Practice, and the Pennsylvania Law Encyclopedia. They contain discussions of the law and citations to cases and statutes.

APPENDIX 2

DOG-BITE STATUTES

State	Citation
Alabama	4 Ala. Code 3-6-1
Arizona	Ariz. Rev. Stat. 24-378, 24-521
California	Cal. Civ. Code § 3342
Connecticut	Conn. Gen. Stat. Ann. 22-357
Delaware	Dela. Code. Ann. 7 § 1711
District of Columbia	D.C. Code § 6-1012
Florida	Fla. Stat. Ann. §§ 767.01, 767.04
Georgia	Ga. Code. Ann. § 105-110
Hawaii	Hawaii Rev. Stat. § 663-9
Illinois	Ill. Ann. Stat. Ch. 8 § 366
Indiana	Ann. Ind. Code. 15-5-12-1
Iowa	Ia. Code. Ann. 351.2
Kentucky	Kan. Rev. Stat. 258.275
Louisiana	La. Civ. Code art. 2321
Maine	7 Me. Rev. Stat. Ann. 3651
Massachusetts	Mass. Gen. Laws. Ann. Ch. 140 §155
Michigan	Mich. Comp. Laws. Ann. § 287.351
Minnesota	Minn. Stat. Ann. § 347.22
Montana	Mont. Code Ann. § 27-1-715
Nebraska	Rev. Stat. Neb. § 54-601
New Hampshire	N. H. Rev. Stat. Ann. § 466.19
New Jersey	N.J. Stat. Ann. § 4:19-16
Ohio	Ohio Rev. Code. Ann. § 955.28
Oklahoma	Okla. Stat. Ann. 4 § 42.1
Pennsylvania	3 Pa. Cons. Stat. § 459-502(b)
Rhode Island	R.I. Gen. Laws § 4-3-16
South Carolina	Comp. Laws. S. C. 47-3-110
Utah	Utah Code Ann. § 18-1-1
Washington	Rev. Code Wash. Ann. § 16.08.040
West Virginia	W.Va Code § 19-20-13
Wisconsin	Wis. Stat. Ann. § 174.02

ABOUT THE AUTHOR

Mary Randolph is a lawyer and editor for Nolo Press. She received her law degree from the University of California-Berkeley (Boalt Hall). Her other Nolo books include *The Deeds Book: How to Transfer Real Estate in California* and, with co-author Frank Zagone, *How to Adopt Your Stepchild*. She lives in the Bay Area with her dog, Flash.

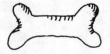

INDEX

SOFTWARE

willmaker
Nolo Press/Legisoft
Recent statistics say chances are better than 2 to 1 that you haven't written a will, even though you know you should. WillMaker makes the job easy, leading you step by step in a fill-in-the-blank format. Once you've gone through the program, you print out the will and sign it in front of witnesses. Because writing a will is only one step in the estate planning process, WillMaker comes with a 200-page manual providing an overview of probate avoidance and tax planning techniques.
National 3rd Ed.

Apple, IBM, Macintosh	$59.95
Commodore	$39.95

california incorporator
Attorney Mancuso and Legisoft, Inc.
About half of the small California corporations formed today are done without the services of a lawyer. This easy-to-use software program lets you do the paperwork with minimum effort. Just answer the questions on the screen, and California Incorporator will print out the 35-40 pages of documents you need to make your California corporation legal.

California Edition (IBM)	$129.00

the california nonprofit corporation handbook—computer edition with disk
Attorney Anthony Mancuso
This is the standard work on how to form a nonprofit corporation in California. Included on the disk are the forms for the Articles, Bylaws and Minutes you will need, as well as regular and special director and member minute forms. Also included are line-by-line instructions explaining how to apply for and obtain federal tax exempt status—this critical step applies to incorporating in all 50 states.
California 1st Ed.

IBM PC 5 1/4 & 3 1/2	$69.00
Macintosh	$69.00

how to form your own texas corporation—computer edition with disk
Attorney Anthony Mancuso

how to form your own new york corporation—computer edition with disk
Attorney Anthony Mancuso
More and more business people are incorporating to qualify for tax benefits, limited liability status, the benefit of employee status and financial flexibility. These software packages contain all the instructions, tax information and forms you need to incorporate a small business. All organizational forms are on disk.
1st Ed.

IBM PC 5 1/4 & 3 1/2	$69.00
Macintosh	$69.00

for the record
By attorney Warner & Pladsen. A book/software package that helps to keep track of personal and financial records; create documents to give to family members in case of emergency; leave an accurate record for heirs, and allows easy access to all important records with the ability to print out any section
National Edition

Macintosh	$49.95
IBM	$49.95

ESTATE PLANNING & PROBATE

nolo's simple will book & nolo's simple willbook with tape
Attorney Denis Clifford
We feel it's important to remind people that if they don't make arrangements before they die, the state will give their property to certain close family members. If you want a particular person to receive a particular object, you need a will. It's easy to write a legally valid will using this book.

National 1st Ed.	$14.95
wi/30-min audio cassette	$19.95

plan your estate: wills, probate avoidance, trusts & taxes
Attorney Denis Clifford
A will is only one part of an estate plan. The first concern is avoiding probate so that your heirs won't receive a greatly diminished inheritance years later. This book shows you how to create a "living trust" and gives you the information you need to make sure whatever you have saved goes to your heirs, not to lawyers and the government.

National 1st Ed.	$17.95

the power of attorney book
Attorney Denis Clifford
The Power of Attorney Book concerns something you've heard about but probably would rather ignore: Who will take care of your affairs, make your financial and medical decisions, if you can't? With this book you can appoint someone you trust to carry out your wishes.

National 2nd Ed.	$17.95

how to probate an estate
Julia Nissley
When a close relative dies, amidst the grieving there are financial and legal details to be dealt with. The natural response is to rely on an attorney, but that response can be costly. With How to Probate an Estate, you can have the satisfaction of doing the work yourself and saving those fees.

California 3rd Ed.	$24.95

the california nonprofit corporation handbook

Attorney Anthony Mancuso

Used by arts groups, educators, social service agencies, medical programs, environmentalists and many others, this book explains all the legal formalities involved in forming and operating a nonprofit corporation. Included are all the forms for the Articles, Bylaws and Minutes you will need. Also included are complete instructions for obtaining federal 501(c)(3) exemptions and benefits. The tax information in this section applies wherever your corporation is formed.

California 5th Ed. $29.95

how to form your own corporation

Attorney Anthony Mancuso

More and more business people are incorporating to qualify for tax benefits, limited liability status, the benefit of employee status and the financial flexibility. These books contain the forms, instructions and tax information you need to incorporate a small business.

California 7th Ed. $29.95
Texas 4th Ed. $24.95
New York 2nd. Ed. $24.95
Florida 1st Ed. $19.95

1988 calcorp update package

Attorney Anthony Mancuso

This update package contains all the forms and instructions you need to modify your corporation's Articles of Incorporation so you can take advantage of new California laws. $25.00

california professional corporation handbook

Attorney Anthony Mancuso

Health care professionals, marriage, family and child counsellors, lawyers, accountants and members of certain other professions must fulfill special requirements when forming a corporation in California. This edition contains up-to-date tax information plus all the forms and instructions necessary to form a California professional corporation. An appendix explains the special rules that apply to each profession.

California 3rd Ed. $29.95

marketing without advertising

Michael Phillips & Salli Rasberry

Every small business person knows that the best marketing plan encourages customer loyalty and personal recommendation. Phillips and Rasberry outline practical steps for building and expanding a small business without spending a lot of money.

National 1st Ed. $14.00

the partnership book

Attorneys Clifford & Warner

Lots of people dream of going into business with a friend. The best way to keep that dream from turning into a nightmare is to have a solid partnership agreement. This book shows how to write an agreement that covers evaluation of partner assets, disputes, buy-outs and the death of a partner.

National 3rd Ed. $18.95

nolo's small business start-up

Mike McKeever

Should you start a business? Should you raise money to expand your already running business? If the answers are yes, this book will show you how to write an effective business plan and loan package.

National 3rd Ed. $17.95

the independent paralegal's handbook: how to provide legal services without going to jail

Attorney Ralph Warner

A large percentage of routine legal work in this country is performed by typists, secretaries, researchers and various other law office helpers generally labeled paralegals. For those who would like to take these services out of the law office and offer them at a reasonable fee in an independent business, attorney Ralph Warner provides both legal and business guidelines.

National 1st Ed. $12.95

getting started as an independent paralegal (two audio tapes)

Attorney Ralph Warner

This set of tapes is a carefully edited version of Nolo Press founder Ralph Warner's Saturday Morning Law School class. It is designed for people who wish to go into business helping consumers prepare their own paperwork in uncontested actions such as bankruptcy, divorce, small business incorporations, landlord-tenant actions, probate, etc. Also covered are how to set up, run, and market your business, as well as a detailed discussion of Unauthorized Practice of Law.

National 1st Ed. $24.95

JUST FOR FUN

29 reasons not to go to law school

Ralph Warner & Toni Ihara

Lawyers, law students, their spouses and consorts will love this little book with its zingy comments and Thuberesque cartoons, humorously zapping the life of the law.—Peninsula Times Tribune Filled with humor and piercing observations, this book can save you three years, $70,000 and your sanity.

3rd Ed. $9.95

murder on the air

Ralph Warner & Toni Ihara

Here is a sure winner for any friend who's spent more than a week in the city of Berkeley...a catchy little mystery situated in the environs and the cultural mores of the People's Republic.—The Bay Guardian

Flat out fun...—San Francisco Chronicle $5.95

poetic justice

Ed. by Jonathan & Andrew Roth

A unique compilation of humorous quotes about lawyers and the legal system, from Socrates to Woody Allen. $8.95

collect your court judgment

Scott, Elias & Goldoftas

After you win a judgment in small claims, municipal or superior court, you still have to collect your money. Here are step-by-step instructions on hwo to collect your judgment from the debtor's bank accounts, wages, business receipts, real estate or other assets.
California 1st Ed. $24.95

chapter 13: the federal plan to repay your debts

Attorney Janice Kosel

For those who want to repay their debts and think they can, but are hounded by creditors, Chapter 13 may be the answer. Under the protection of the court you may work out a personal budget and take up to three years to repay a percentage of your debt and have the rest wiped clean.
National 3rd Ed. $17.95

make your own contract

Attorney Stephen Elias

Here are clearly written legal form contracts to: buy and sell property, borrow and lend money, store and lend personal property, make deposits on goods for later purchase, release others from personal liability, or pay a contractor to do home repairs.
National 1st Ed. $12.95

social security, medicare & pensions: a sourcebook for older americans

Attorney Joseph L. Matthews & Dorothy Matthews Berman

Social security, medicare and medicaid programs follow a host of complicated rules. Those over 55, or those caring for someone over 55, will find this comprehensive guidebook invaluable for understanding and utilizing their rightful benefits. A special chapter deals with age discrimination in employment and what to do about it.
National 4th Ed. $15.95

everybody's guide to small claims court

Attorney Ralph Warner

So, the dry cleaner ruined your good flannel suit. Your roof leaks every time it rains, and the contractor who supposedly fixed it won't call you back. The bicycle shop hasn't paid for the tire pumps you sold it six months ago. This book will help you decide if you have a case, show you how to file and serve papers, tell you what to bring to court, and how to collect a judgment.
California 7th Ed. $14.95
National 3rd Ed. $14.95

billpayers' rights

Attorneys Warner & Elias

Lots of people find themselves overwhelmed by debt. The law, however, offers a number of legal protections for consumers and Billpayers' Rights shows people how to use them.
Areas covered include: how to handle bill collectors, deal with student loans, check your credit rating and decide if you should file for bankruptcy.
California 8th Ed. $14.95

for sale by owner

George Devine

In 1986 about 600,000 homes were sold in California at a median price of $130,000. Most sellers worked with a broker and paid the 6% commission. For the median home that meant $7,800. Obviously, that's money that could be saved if you sell your own house. This book provides the background information and legal technicalities you will need to do the job yourself and with confidence.
California 1st Ed. $24.95

homestead your house

Attorneys Warner, Sherman & Ihara

Under California homestead laws, up to $60,000 of the equity in your home may be safe from creditors. But to get the maximum legal protection you should file a Declaration of Homestead before a judgment lien is recorded against you. This book includes complete instructions and tear-out forms.
California 6th Ed. $8.95

the landlord's law book: vol. 1, rights & responsibilities

Attorneys Brown & Warner

Every landlord should know the basics of landlord-tenant law. In short, the era when a landlord could substitute common sense for a detailed knowledge of the law is gone forever. This volume covers: deposits, leases and rental agreements, inspections (tenants' privacy rights), habitability (rent withholding), ending a tenancy, liability, and rent control.
California 2nd Ed. $24.95

the landlord's law book: vol. 2, evictions

Attorney David Brown

Even the most scrupulous landlord may sometimes need to evict a tenant. In the past it has been necessary to hire a lawyer and pay a high fee. Using this book you can handle most evictions yourself safely and economically.
California 1st Ed. $24.95

tenants' rights

Attorneys Moskowitz & Warner

Your "security building" doesn't have a working lock on the front door. Is your landlord liable? How can you get him to fix it? Under what circumstances can you withhold rent? When is an apartment not "habitable?" This book explains the best way to handle your relationship with your landlord and your legal rights when you find yourself in disagreement.
California 10th Ed. $15.95

the deeds book: how to transfer title to california real estate

Attorney Mary Randolph

If you own real estate, you'll almost surely need to sign a new deed at one time or another. The Deeds Book shows you how to choose the right kind of deed, how to complete the tear-out forms, and how to record them in the county recorder's public records.
California 1st Ed. $15.95

dog law
Attorney Mary Randolph

There are 50 million dogs in the United States—and, it seems, at least that many rules and regulations for their owners to abide by. *Dog Law* covers topics that everyone who owns a dog, or lives near one, needs to know about dispute about a dog injury or nuisance.

National 1st Ed. $12.95

the criminal records book
Attorney Warren Siegel

We've all done something illegal. If you were one of those who got caught, your juvenile or criminal court record can complicate your life years later. The good news is that in many cases your record can either be completely expunged or lessened in severity.

The Criminal Records Book takes you step by step through the procedures to: seal criminal records, dismiss convictions, destroy marijuana records, reduce felony convictions.

California 2nd Ed. $14.95

draft, registration and the law
Attorney R. Charles Johnson

This clearly written guidebook explains the present draft law and how registration (required of all male citizens within thirty days of their eighteenth birthday) works. Every available option is presented along with a description of how a draft would work if there were a call tomorrow.

National 2nd Ed. $9.95

fight your ticket
Attorney David Brown

At a trade show in San Francisco recently, a traffic court judge (who must remain nameless) told our associate publisher that he keeps this book by his bench for easy reference.

If you think that ticket was unfair, here's the book showing you what to do to fight it.

California 3rd Ed. $16.95

how to become a united states citizen
Sally Abel Schreuder

This bilingual (English/Spanish) book presents the forms, applications and instructions for naturalization. This step-by-step guide will provide information and answers for legally admitted aliens who wish to become citizens.

National 3rd Ed. $12.95

how to change your name
Attorneys Loeb & Brown

Wish that you had gone back to your maiden name after the divorce? Tired of spelling over the phone V-e-n-k-a-t-a-r-a-m-a-n S-u-b-r-a-m-a-n-i-a-m?

This book explains how to change your name legally and provides all the necessary court forms with detailed instructions on how to fill them out.

California 4th Ed. $14.95

legal research: how to find and understand the law
Attorney Stephen Elias

Legal Research could also be called Volume-Two-for-all-Nolo-Press-Self-Help-Law-Books. A valuable tool for paralegals, law students and legal secretaries, this book provides access to legal information—he legal self-helper can find and research a case, read statutes, and make Freedom of Information Act requests.

National 2nd Ed. $14.95

family law dictionary
Attorneys Leonard and Elias

Written in plain English (as opposed to legalese), the Family Law Dictionary has been compiled to help the lay person doing research in the area of family law (i.e., marriage, divorce, adoption, etc.). Using cross referencs and examples as well as definitions, this book is unique as a reference tool.

National 1st Edition $13.95

intellectual property law dictionary
Attorney Stephen Elias

This book uses simple language free of legal jargon to define and explain the intricacies of items associated with trade secrets, copyrights, trademarks and unfair competition, patents and patent procedures, and contracts and warranties.—IEEE Spectrum

If you're dealing with any multi-media product, a new business product or trade secret, you need this book.

National 1st Ed. $17.95

the people's law review:
an access catalog to law without lawyers
Edited by Attorney Ralph Warner

Articles, interviews and a resource list introduce the entire range of do-it-yourself law from estate planning to tenants' rights. The People's Law Review also provides a wealth of background information on the history of law, some considerations on its future, and alternative ways of solving legal problems.

National 1st Ed. $8.95

the living together kit

Attorneys Ihara & Warner
Few unmarried couples understand the laws that may affect them. Here are useful tips on living together agreements, paternity agreements, estate planning, and buying real estate.
National 5th Ed. $17.95

how to do your own divorce

Attorney Charles E. Sherman
This is the book that launched Nolo Press and advanced the self-help law movement. During the past 17 years, over 400,000 copies have been sold, saving consumers at least $50 million in legal fees (assuming 100,000 have each saved $500—certainly a conservative estimate).
California 14th Ed. $14.95
Texas 2nd Ed. (Sherman & Simons) $12.95

california marriage & divorce law

Attorneys Warner, Ihara & Elias
For a generation, this practical handbook has been the best resource for the Californian who wants to understand marriage and divorce laws. Even if you hire a lawyer to help you with a divorce, it's essential that you learn your basic legal rights and responsibilities.
California 9th Ed. $15.95

practical divorce solutions

Attorney Charles Ed Sherman
Written by the author of How to Do Your Own Divorce (with over 500,000 copies in print), this book provides a valuable guide both to the emotional process involved in divorce as well as the legal and financial decisions that have to be made.
California 1st Ed. $12.95

how to modify and collect child support in california

Attorneys Matthews, Siegel & Willis
California has established landmark new standards in setting and collecting child support. Payments must now be based on both objective need standards and the parents' combined income. Using this book, custodial parents can determine if they are entitled to higher child support payments and can implement the procedures to obtain that support.
California 2nd Ed. $17.95

your family records

Carol Pladsen & Attorney Denis Clifford
Most American families keep terrible records. Typically, the checkbook is on a shelf in the kitchen, insurance policies are nowhere to be found, and jewelry and cash are hidden in a coffee can in the garage. Your Family Records is a sensible, straightforward guide that will help you organize your records before you face a crisis.
National 2nd Ed. $14.95

a legal guide for lesbian and gay couples

Attorneys Curry & Clifford
A Legal Guide contains crucial information on the special problems facing lesbians and gay men with children, civil rights legislation, and medical/legal issues.
National 4th Ed. $17.95

how to adopt your stepchild in california

Frank Zagone & Mary Randolph
For many families that include stepchildren, adoption is a satisfying way to guarantee the family a solid legal footing. This book provides sample forms and complete step-by-step instructions for completing a simple uncontested adoption by a stepparent.
California 3rd Ed. $19.95

how to copyright software

Attorney M.J. Salone
Copyrighting is the best protection for any software. This book explains how to get a copyright and what a copyright can protect.
National 2nd Ed. $24.95

the inventor's notebook

Fred Grissom & Attorney David Pressman
The best protection for your patent is adequate records. The Inventor's Notebook provides forms, instructions, references to relevant areas of patent law, a bibliography of legal and non-legal aids, and more. It helps you document the activities that are normally part of successful independent inventing.
National 1st Ed. $19.95

legal care for your software

Attorneys Daniel Remer & Stephen Elias
If you write programs you intend to sell, or work for a software house that pays you for programming, you should buy this book. If you are a freelance programmer doing software development, you should buy this book.—Interface
This step-by-step guide for computer software writers covers copyright laws, trade secret protection, contracts, license agreements, trademarks, patents and more.
National 3rd Ed. $29.95

patent it yourself

Attorney David Pressman
You've invented something, or you're working on it, or you're planning to start...Patent It Yourself offers help in evaluating patentability, marketability and the protective documentation you should have. If you file your own patent application using this book, you can save from $1500 to $3500.
National 2nd Ed. $29.95

SELF-HELP LAW BOOKS & SOFTWARE

ORDER FORM

Quantity	Title	Unit Price	Total

Sales Tax (CA residents only):

7%   Alameda, Contra Costa, San Diego, San Mateo & Santa Clara counties

6 1/2% Fresno, Inyo, LA, Sacramento, San Benito, San Francisco & Santa Cruz counties

6%   All others

Subtotal _____

Sales Tax _____

TOTAL_____

Method of Payment:

☐ Check enclosed

☐ VISA   ☐ Mastercard

Acct # _____ Exp. _____

Signature _____

Phone ( ) _____

Ship to:

Name_____

Address _____

_____

Mail to:

**NOLO PRESS
950 Parker Street
Berkeley CA 94710**

For faster service, use your credit card and our toll-free numbers:

Monday-Friday 8-5 Pacific Time

US		1-800-992-6656
CA	(outside 415 area)	1-800-445-6656
	(inside 415 area)	1-415-549-1976
General Information		**1-415-549-1976**

Prices subject to change

Please allow 1-2 weeks for delivery

Delivery is by UPS; no P.O. boxes, please

ORDER DIRECT AND WE PAY POSTAGE & HANDLING!

NOLO PRESS
Dog Law Registration Card

We would like to hear from you. Please let us know if the book met your needs. Fill out and return this card for a FREE one-year subscription to the *Nolo News*, our "Access to Law" quarterly newspaper. It contains an update section which will keep you abreast of any changes in the law relevant to *Dog Law*. You'll find interesting articles on a number of legal topics, book reviews, and our ever popular lawyer joke column. In addition, we'll notify you when we publish a new edition of *Dog Law*. (This offer is good in the U.S.only.)

Name _____

Address _____

City _____ State _____ Zip _____

Your occupation _____

Briefly, for what purpose did you use this book? _____

_____

Did you find the information in the book helpful?

(extremely helpful)   1   2   3   4   5   (not at all)

Where did you hear about the book? _____

Have you used other Nolo books? _____ Yes, _____ No

Where did you buy the book? _____

Comments: (e.g., are there any local practices that would be of interest to us?) _____

_____

_____

_____

_____

_____

NOLO PRESS
950 Parker St.
Berkeley, CA 94710

Affix
25¢
Stamp